MUHAMMAD THE PROPHET

MUHAMMAD THE PROPHET

by

MAULĀNĀ MUḤAMMAD ‘ALĪ

THE AHMADIYYA ANJUMAN ISHA‘AT ISLAM
LAHORE -U.S.A.

1315 Kingsgate Road
Columbus Ohio USA 43221

FIRST EDITION 1924
SECOND EDITION 1933
THIRD EDITION 1951
FOURTH EDITION (Revised) . . 1972
FIFTH EDITION 1977
SIXTH EDITION 1984
SEVENTH EDITION 1993

Library of Congress card catalog number: 89-85991
ISBN: 0-913321-07-9

Typesetting U & I Type
Vancouver, B.C .
Canada

Printers Payette and Simms
300 Arran St.
St. Lambert, PQ
Canada

SOME OTHER BOOKS BY THE AUTHOR

English

Translation of the Holy Qur'ān (with commentary and Arabic text).
The Religion of Islām.
Muḥammad and Christ.
Early Caliphate.
Introduction to the Study of the Ḥadith.
Selections from the Holy Qur'ān.
Collection and Arrangement of the Holy Qur'ān.
The Muslim Prayer Book.
Prayers of the Holy Qur'ān.
Antichrist, Gog and Magog.
History of the Prophets.
The New World Order.
A Manual of Ḥadith.
Living Thoughts of the Prophet Muḥammad.

Urdu

Bayān al-Qur'ān, translation and commentary of the Holy Qur'ān, in three volumes.
Hamā'il Sharif, translation of the Holy Qur'ān with abridged commentary.
Faḍl al-Bāri, commentary of Ṣaḥiḥ al-Bukhāri, in 2 volumes.
Al-Nubuwwat fil Islām, proof of the finality of prophethood.
Sirat Khair al-Bashar, biography of the Holy Prophet.
Tārikh Khilāfat Rāshidah, history of the first four Caliphs.
Maqām-i-Ḥadith, the place of Tradition in Islām.
Zinda Nabī ki Zinda Ta'līm, the living thoughts of the Prophet Muhammad.
Jama' al-Qur'ān, Collection and arrangement of the Qur'ān.

Ahmadiyya Anjuman Is<u>h</u>ā'at Islām Lahore Inc. (U.S.A.)
1315 Kingsgate Road, Columbus, Ohio 43221 U.S.A.

The Ahmadiyya Anjuman Is<u>h</u>ā'at Islām (*Ahmadiyya Society for the propagation of Islām*), based in Lahore, Pakistan, is an international Muslim body devoted to the presentation of Islam through literary and missionary work. Since its inception in 1914, it has produced a range of highly acclaimed, standard books on all aspects of Islām, and has run Muslim missions in many parts of the world, establishing the first ever Islāmic centres in England (at Woking) and Germany (Berlin). The literature produced by the Anjuman, largely written by Maulana Muhammad Ali, is deep research work of the highest quality, based purely on the original sources of Islām. It has corrected many wrong notions about the religion of Islām, and has received world wide acclaim for its authenticity, scholarship and service of the faith.

Continuing the mission of *Ḥadrat* Mirza <u>Gh</u>ulām Aḥmad, the mujaddid of the 14th century Hijra and promised messiah, the Ahmadiyya Anjuman seeks to revive the original liberal, tolerant and rational spirit of Islām. It presents Islām as a great spiritual force for bringing about the moral reform of mankind, and shows that this religion has never advocated coercion, the use of physical force or the pursuit of political power in its support.

Information, books and free literature on Islam may be obtained by contacting *The Ahmadiyya Anjuman Is<u>h</u>ā'at Islām Lahore* (or A.A.I.I.L.) at 1315 Kingsgate Road, Columbus, Ohio 43221 U.S.A.

PREFACE

The idea of writing an exhaustive life history of the Holy Founder of Islām has ever been present in my mind since I took up the work of translating the Holy Qur'ān into English about fifteen years ago but, owing to various other engagements, I was not able to give it a practical shape. The short sketch that is now being presented is by no means a fulfilment of that idea. It is but a very brief and hurried account of a life which is full of the noblest lessons for humanity, a mere bird's-eye view of the greatest transformation which has been wrought in the history of man. I do not know if I shall live long enough to attempt the more laborious work of presenting that ennobling story in all its details; for the present I offer this humble tribute to the memory of him who devoted his whole life to the service of humanity.

I believe, as every Muslim does, that every nation had its superman, the luminary who gave it light, the reformer who inspired it with noble ideas, the Prophet who raised it morally. But Muḥammad, may peace and the blessings of God be upon him, is *par excellence* THE PROPHET, because he is the Prophet not of one nation but of all the nations of the world, because it was he who declared belief in all the prophets of the world as an essential of the faith he preached and thus laid down the basis of a lasting peace among different nations, because "he is the greatest of all reformers," having brought about a transformation unparalleled either before or after him and, lastly, because "he is the most successful of all the prophets and religious personalities."*[1] Every man ought to be judged by what he does, and the Holy Prophet Muḥammad accomplished within twenty years what centuries of the labours of Jewish and Christian reformers could not accomplish, notwithstanding the temporal power at their back. He swept away centuries-old idolatry, superstition, credulity, ignorance, prostitution, gambling, drinking, oppression of the weak, internecine war and a hundred other evils from a whole

[1] Bosworth Smith

country. History cannot show any other reformer who wrought so wonderful and complete a transformation on so large a scale within so short a time. "Never was reform more hopeless than at the advent of the Prophet," as Muir has remarked, "and never was it more complete than when he departed." In the words of Carlyle, "it was a birth from darkness into light." A life so great cannot be devoid of potentialities as great for the future; it cannot but inspire into any heart the noblest ideas of the service of humanity. If there is any one trait of his character which is more marked than another, it is his care of the orphan and the widow, his support of the weak and the helpless, his love of labour and work for the distressed. It is the life of a man who lived for God and who died for God. "If ever man on this earth found God, if ever man devoted his life to God's service with a good and great motive, it is certain that the Prophet of Arabia was that man." (Leonard).

The original work was written by me in Urdu, and the English rendering now being presented to the public is the result of the labour of love of Maulvī Muḥammad Ya'qūb Khān, Imām of the Mosque at Woking who did this work in addition to his duties as a Muslim preacher at Woking. My sincerest thanks are due to him, as well as to Khwājah Kamāl al-Dīn, head of the Woking Muslim Mission, who afforded every facility to M. Muḥammad Ya'qūb Khān for completing his task. And I place the manuscript in the hands of Maulana Sadr-ud-Din, who is now propagating Islām in Germany, as I did in the case of the English Translation of the Holy Qur'ān for supervising the work through the press and for its revision and the correction of proofs.

Ahmadiyyah Buildings,
Lahore
August 25, 1923

Muḥammad 'Alī

Every man ought to be judged by what he does, and Muḥammad (peace and blessings of Allah be upon him) accomplished within twenty years what centuries of the labours of other reformers could not accomplish, notwithstanding the temporal power at their back. He swept away centuries-old idolatry, superstition, credulity, ignorance, prostitution, gambling, drinking, oppression of the weak, internecine war and a hundred other evils from a whole country. History cannot show any other reformer who wrought so wonderful and complete a transformation on so large a scale within so short a time. Never was reform more hopeless than at the advent of Muḥammad (peace and blessings of Allah be upon him) and never was it more complete than when he departed.

"If greatness of purpose, smallness of means, and astounding results are the three criteria of human genius - writes the distinguished French writer Alphonse de Lamartine in his *Histoire de la Turquo* (1854) - who could dare to compare any great man in modern history with Muḥammad?" The most famous men created arms, laws and empires only. They founded, if anything at all, no more than material powers which often crumbled away before their eyes. This man moved not only armies, legislations, empires, peoples and dynasties, but millions of men in one third of the then inhabited world, and more than that, he moved altars, gods, religions, ideas, beliefs and souls. On the basis of a Book, every letter of which has become law, he created a spiritual nationality which blended together peoples of every tongue and of every race. He has left us, as the indelible characteristic of this Muslim nationality, the hatred of false gods and the passion for the One and Immaterial God. This avenging patriotism against the profanation of Heaven formed the virtue of the followers of Muḥammad; the conquest of one-third of the earth to his dogma was his miracle; or rather it was not the miracle of a man but that of reason. The idea of the unity of God, proclaimed amidst the exhaustion of fabulous theogonies, was in itself such a miracle that upon its utterance from his lips it destroyed all the ancient temples of idols and set on fire one-third of the world. His life, his meditations, his heroic revilings against the superstitions of his country, and his boldness in defying the furies of idolatry, his firmness in enduring them for fifteen years at Mecca, his acceptance of the role of public scorn and almost of being a victim of his fellow country-men: all these and, finally, his light, his incessant preaching, his wars against odds, his faith in his success and his superhuman serenity in misfortune, his forbearance in victory, his ambition, which was entirely devoted to one idea and in no manner striving for an empire; his endless prayers, his mystic conversations with God, his death and his triumph after death; all these attest not to an imposture but to a firm conviction which gave him the power to restore a dogma. This dogma was twofold, the unity of God and the immateriality of God; the former telling what God is, the latter telling what God is not; the one overthrowing false gods with the sword, the other starting an idea with the words.

"Philosopher, orator, apostle, legislator; warrior, conqueror of ideas, restorer of rational dogmas, of a cult without images; the founder of twenty terrestrial empires and of one spiritual empire, that is Muḥammad. As regards all standards by which human greatness may be measured, we may well ask: Is there any man greater than he?"

A life so great cannot be devoid of potentialities as great for the future. It is the life of a man who lived for God and died for God. It cannot but inspire into any heart the noblest ideas of the service of humanity.

In the present revised edition, besides some minor alteration, some chapters have been combined under one heading.

Mumtaz Ahmad Faruqui

CONTENTS

Bai'at al-Riḍwān - Terms of the Truce - Truce brings about triumph of Islām - Divine Promise fulfilled - Prophet's love of peace - Sad plight of Makkan converts - Message of Islām carried beyond Arabia - Caesar's attitude towards Islām - Chosroes orders Prophet's arrest - Negus accepts Islām - Prophet's deep-rooted conviction - The seal.

VIII - THE CONQUEST OF MAKKAH .. 131

Quraish contravened terms of Truce - Preparations for attack on Makkah - Ten thousand holy men - Abū Sufyān accepts Islām - General amnesty- Unparalleled magnanimity - Makkans embrace Islām - The Battle of Ḥunain - Retreat and rally of Muslim forces - Spread of Islām in Arabia - Deputations from Arab tribes - Expedition of Tabūk - Impending danger on the Syrian frontier - Muslim army at Tabūk - The hypocrites in Madīnah - Hypocrites' plans against Islām - The Prophet's love for enemies - End of the hypocrites - Year of deputations - The Najrān deputation - Whole of Arabia converted - Islāmic principles of war - Compulsion in religion interdicted - Fighting allowed conditionally - Peace to be preferred - Relations with non-Muslims - How apostates were dealt with.

IX - THE FAREWELL PILGRIMAGE .. 160

Prophet's last pilgrimage - Sermon at Minā - The Holy Prophet's last illness - Abū Bakr appointed Imām - The Holy Prophet's Demise - Abū Bakr's sermon.

X - THE PROPHET'S SUBLIME MORALS .. 167

The Prophet, an exemplar - No work was too low for him - Simplicity - Food - Dress - No attraction for comforts - Cleanliness - Love for friends - Generous to enemies - Equal justice for all - Humility - Sympathy for the poor and the distressed - Hospitality -

CHAPTER I

THE DARK AGE

"Certainly the first house appointed for men is the one at Makkah, blessed and a guidance for the nations" *- 3 : 96.*

The Arabian Peninsula

The land known as *Jazīrat al-'Arab,* or the Arabian Peninsula, occupies a central position in the hemisphere comprising the continents of Asia, Africa and Europe. It forms the heart, so to speak, of the Old World. This is the country that gave birth to Muḥammad (may peace and blessings of God be upon him), the last of the great religious reformers to found a religion. The Indian Ocean washes its coast on the south, the Mediterranean and the Red Sea on the west. To the east lie the Persian Gulf, the Tigris and the Euphrates, the latter two rivers traversing its northem part as well. According to ancient historians and geographers, it comprises within its boundaries the strip of land known as 'Irāq (Mesopotamia) as well as Arabian Syria. The map of the modern world, however, does not show these forming an integal part of Arabia. Leaving them aside, the country yet covers an area of twelve hundred thousand square miles. About a third of this is covered by sandy deserts, the largest being the one known as *al-Dahnā',* lying in the middle of the southern part. There are practically no rivers worthy of mention in the country. Small streams, however, are met with here and there. Some of these lose themselves in the desert sands, while others wind their way to the sea. From south to north runs a chain of mountains known as *Jabal al-Sārat,* the highest peak of which is eight thousand feet. Dates are the main produce. In ancient days, Arabia was famous for its gold, silver, precious stones and spices. Of the animals found here, the camel is the most valuable and useful, while the Arab horse has no match in the world for beauty, stamina and mettle.

'Irāq and Syria

As a matter of fact, 'Irāq and Arabian Syria form an integral part of Arabia, though modern political distribution shows them as distinct from the mainland. Of these, 'Irāq stretches adjacent to Iran. The towns of Basrah and Kufah, which long remained centres of Islamic learning, were founded here during the caliphate of 'Umar the Great. Arabian Syria lies to the north, extending right up to Aleppo. Arab geographers have, therefore, shown the Euphrates as the northern boundary of Arabia. In this part lies Mount Sinai, where Moses received Divine revelation. The Amalekites once had a mighty kingdom here.

Ḥijāz

Arabia Proper is subdivided into a number of parts. Of these Ḥijāz is the province in which the sacred land of *Ḥaram* is situated. The *Ḥaram* (sacred or forbidden territory) is so called because from time immemorial the place has been held in the highest veneration, and every kind of warfare is forbidden therein. It is within the precincts of the *Ḥaram* that the sacred house of Ka'bah stands. The Torah, sacred book of the Jews, speaks of Ḥijāz by the name of Parān. Its chief towns are Makkah, Madīnah and Ta'if. This province extends along the Red Sea in a rectangular strip. Jeddah and Yenbo are its two main sea-ports, where pilgrims for Makkah and Madīnah respectively land. On the east, Ḥijāz is bounded by the province of Najd and, on the south, by Asīr, part of Yaman.

Yaman

The second main province is Yaman, which lies in the south of the Peninsula. Ha<u>dz</u>ramaut and Aḥqāf form parts of this province. It is the most fertile tract in the country and has consequently been the most civilized. Even to-day relics of some most magnificent buildings are met with here. Huge embankments were once constructed here to control the springs of water from the mountains and utilize them for purposes of irrigation. The most famous of these was Ma'ārib, the destruction of which is mentioned in the Holy Qur'ān.[1] Yaman was, moreover, the centre of the trade in minerals, precious stones and spices for w_h_ich Arabia was once so famous. The mighty empire of 'Ād, of which the Qur'ān speaks[2], was established here. This particular area is known as Aḥqāf. Ha_dz_ramaut is that part of Yaman which lies in the extreme south, along the shore of the Indian Ocean. Ṣanā is the capital of the province and Aden its chief port. To the north of Ṣanā lies Najrān, where Christianity had spread before the advent of Islām. The well known Christian delegation, that waited upon the Holy Prophet and which was allowed to stay in the Prophet's Mosque, came from this place. To the north of Najrān lies 'Asīr.

Najd

The third great part of Arabia is Najd, which extends from *Jabal al-Sarāt* eastward across the interior of the country. It is a rich and fertile plateau, some three to four thousand feet above sea-level. Here lived the clan of _Gh_atafān, for whose chastisement the Holy Prophet had once to lead an expedition. The desert bounds it on three sides, while in its south lies Yamāmah. The Banū Ḥanīfah, of which tribe came Musailimah, the impostor, lived here.

'Umān

In the south-east of Arabia, and along the coast of the Gulf of 'Umān, stretches the tract of land known as 'Umān. Its capital is Masqat, where a nominally independent Sultan has now been established. To the north of 'Umān lies the port known as Bahrain also called al-Aḥsā, famous for its pearls. Close by is Hirāh, once a kingdom.

Ḥijr

Ḥijr, the home of the _Th_amūd, among whom Ṣāliḥ was raised as a prophet, is another place of note. It lies to the north

1 The Qur'ān, 34 : 16.; 2 Ibid., 7 : 65.

of Madīnah. On his march to Tabūk, the Holy Prophet happened to pass by this place. To the west of Ḥijr lies Madyan, the home of the prophet Shu'aib. To the north of Madīnah is Khaibar, once the strong-hold of the Jews.

Makkah and Ka'bah

The three chief towns of Ḥijāz, as previously mentioned, are Makkah, Madīnah and Ṭā'if. Ṭā'if owes its fame to the fact that, situated as it is at the foot of the mountains, it is cool and rich in verdure, with innumerable springs of water and abundance of fruit. It lies to the east of Makkah and is the general summer resort of the Ḥijāz nobility. But the most famous towns of Ḥijāz are Makkah and Madīnah. Makkah is also known as *Umm al-Qurā* (Mother of Towns). On all four sides it is enclosed by mountains. Its present population numbers fifty thousand. From days of hoary antiquity it has been the spiritual and religious capital of Arabia, for here stands the sacred House of God, known as Ka'bah, which has been the resort of pilgrims from every corner of Arabia from prehistoric days. Sir William Muir thus comments on the antiquity of the House in his *Life of Muḥammad:* "A very high antiquity must be assigned to the main features of the religion of Mecca ... Diodorus Siculus, writing about half a century before our era, says of that part of Arabia washed by the Red Sea, 'there is in this country a temple greatly revered by all the Arabs'. These words must refer to the holy house of Mecca, for we know of no other which ever commanded the universal homage of Arabia... Tradition represents the Ka'bah as from time immemorial the scene of pilgrimage from all quarters of Arabia: from Yaman, Hadzramaut, and the shores of the Persian Gulf, from the desert of Syria, and from the distant environs of Hirāh and Mesopotamia, men yearly flocked to Mecca. So extensive a homage must have had its beginning in an extremely remote age."

To establish the antiquity of the Ka'bah, Muir has drawn upon historical facts and oral traditions. The Qur'ān also points to the same. It speaks of the Ka'bah as "the first house appointed for men;"[1] in other words, the first house on the

1 The Qur'ān, 3 96.;

face of the earth assigned to the worship of God. The rays of Divine revelation emanated first of all from this place. And it is a remarkable coincidence that this same place enjoys the distinction of giving birth to the last of the prophets. Makkah owes its importance to this house. As early as 2,500 years B.C., it was a halting-station for caravans plying between Yaman and Syria. The Qur'ān also confirms that the sacred house was in existence before Abraham.[1] When leaving his son Ishmael there, the great patriarch prayed: "Our Lord, I have settled a part of my offspring in a valley unproductive of fruit near Thy Sacred House..."[2] These words show that the Ka'bah was there even at that remote date.

Madīnah

Madīnah was originally called Yathrib. Later, when it was adopted by the Holy Prophet as his residence, it came to be known as *Madīnat al-Nābi* (the Prophet's Town), which was gradually contracted into al-Madīnah. This, too, is an ancient town. Historical evidence suggests its foundation as early as 1600 B.C. It was originally inhabited by the Amalekites, after whom came the Jews, the Aus and the Khazraj. When the Holy Prophet came to settle here, these three peoples formed the population of the town. It was the latter two who, later, came to be known by the name *of Anṣār* (Helpers). In the fourteenth year of his mission, the Holy Prophet emigrated from Makkah to Madīnah where he spent the remaining days of his life. Here it was that he breathed his last, and here stands his tomb to this day. Madīnah lies 270 miles to the north of Makkah and, unlike the latter, is not barren. Besides rich cultivation, it has an abundance of fruit-bearing trees. In winter it is comparatively cooler than Makkah.

Arabian races

The 'Ād, Thamūd, Ṭasm and Jadīs are the most ancient races of Arabia, as far as can be traced, the first two having been spoken of in the Qur'ān. These aboriginal races are known as the *Bāidah* (ancient Arabs). The destruction of the tribe of Noah

1 The Qur'ān, 2 : 125.; 2 Ibid., 14 : 37.

the rise of 'Ād, whose settlements spread far nd the limits of Arabia. Historical evidence omination over Arabia, Egypt, and many other p… e fall of this race, the Thamūd rose to power.

The… ne the rise of the Banu Qaḥṭan, whose homeland was Yaman. In their days, they too attained to great power and ascendancy. The Aus and the Khazraj were the offshoots of this tribe. All these races are known as the 'Aribah (pure Arabs).

Ishmael and his progeny

Last of all came Ishmael, whose progeny goes by the name of *Musta'ribah* (naturalized Arabs). In obedience to a divine behest, he was left by his father, Abraham, along with his mother Hājirah, at the place, where stands the Ka'bah.[1] There is little truth in the belief that they were banished by Abraham at the instance of his second wife, Sārah. The idea is emphatically repudiated in a saying of the Holy Prophet which says that on Hājirah's question whether Abraham was leaving them there in obedience to a Divine behest, the Patriarch replied in the affirmative. The account given in the Qur'ān also leads to the same conclusion. Later, father and son reconstructed, at the Divine injunction, the Sacred House of Ka'bah which, it seems was in a dilapidated condition.[2] This done, together they addressed the Lord with a prayer which the Qur'ān reports in these words: "Our Lord, raise up in them a Messenger from among them ..."[3] This prayer found fulfilment in the person of the Holy Prophet Muḥammad. For this reason the Holy Prophet is reported as saying: "I am the prayer of my father Abraham." Ishmael's progeny multiplied and ramified into numerous tribes. One of these is known as the Quraish which is descended from Nadzr. This tribe was later subdivided into a number of clans, the Holy Prophet being a scion of one of these, known as the Banū Hāshim.

Time of ignorance

The period preceding the advent of the Holy Prophet has been designated as the Dark Age. The Qur'ān gives it the

1 The Qur'ān, 14 : 37; 2 : 125.; 2 Ibid., 2 : 127.; 3 Ibid., 2 : 129.

name "al-Jāhiliyyah," (Ignorance or the time of Ignorance).[1] The picture drawn in the verse "corruption has appeared in the land and sea ..."[2] portrays the fallen state of Arab idolaters, Jews, Christians and followers of other religions alike. It avers that corruption was rampant throughout the world. This does not, however, imply that the world had never witnessed a better state of things; but whatever civilization and moral awakening had ever sprung up anywhere through the various prophets sent from time to time among different peoples had by that time utterly disappeared in consequence of the lapse of long ages. Every nation of the world had at the time fallen into a state of decrepitude. These words found utterance through the mouth of one who was, no doubt, quite illiterate. He had had no opportunity of going round the world to study the condition of different countries; nor had he the benefit of the publicity systems of today that might have acquainted him with the state of the world at that time. Nevertheless, a reference to the pages of history corroborates the truth of the assertion in a striking manner. Barring the fact that Europe had a mighty Empire towards its south-east - the Christian Empire of Rome - it was sunk in barbarism. Asia, of all the continents of the world, had once been the nursery of civilization. But a study of the various countries of this cradle of philosophies and religions shows that here, as elsewhere, rank immorality was the order of the day. India, once the centre of ancient Eastern culture, presented the same horrid picture. Foul, base and heinous things were attributed even to those whom the people regarded as their gods. Evil had taken so great a hold on them, that even the virtuous were painted in dark colours. Persia and China, too, were in the same plight. This no doubt was due to the fact that centuries had elapsed since the advent of former teachers; and whatever reformation had been previously brought about had become gradually weak and finally extinct. The Qur'ān says that "time was prolonged for them, so their hearts hardened..."[3]

A modern writer, J.H. Denison, who has studied the different systems of religion and the civilizations that grew up therefrom has come to exactly the same conclusion in his *Emotion as the Basis of Civilization:* "In the fifth and the

1 The Qur'ān, 33 : 33, 48 : 26.; 2 Ibid., 30 : 41.; 3 Ibid., 57 : 16.

sixth centuries, the civilized world stood on the verge of chaos. The old emotional cultures that had made civilization possible ... had broken down and nothing had been found adequate to take their place ... It seemed then that the great civilization that it had taken four thousand years to construct was on the verge of disintegration and that mankind was likely to return to that condition of barbarism where every tribe and sect was against the next, and law and order were unknown... The new sanctions created by Christianity were working division and destruction instead of unity and order ... Civilization like a gigantic tree whose foliage had over-reached the world... stood tottering... rotted to the core... It was among these people that the man[1] was born who was to unite the whole known world of east and south."

Christianity in a decrepit state

Jesus was the prophet most proximate to the Holy Prophet Muḥammad in point of time. One would have naturally expected amongst Christians some relics of virtue and morality. But what was the state of Christianity at the time? Let us quote Christian writers themselves on the point. Drawing a picture of those days, a bishop says that the heavenly kingdom was utterly upset, and a state of veritable hell had been established on the earth, in consequence of inner corruption. Sir William Muir writes to the same effect: "Moreover, the Christianity of the seventh century was itself decrepit and corrupt. It was disabled by contending schisms, and had substituted the puerilities of superstition for the pure and expansive faith of the early ages."

This is a picture of Christianity concerning its general state. Belief in the Oneness of God had disappeared long since. The doctrine of Trinity had given rise to numerous complications. Diverse schisms and sects vied one another in the exercise of their ingenuities in the disentanglement of the riddle how man became God or how three made one and *vice versa*. This led to the production of a mass of polemical works, taking man far from the true purpose of religion. Gibbon, commenting on the event of the famous library at Alexandria having been set

1 The reference is to the Holy Prophet Muḥammad peace and blessings of Allah be upon him.

on fire by intolerant Christians, makes a significant observation in this connection: "But if the ponderous mass of Arian and Monophysite controversy was indeed consumed in the public baths, a philosopher may allow, with a smile, that it was ultimately devoted to the benefit of mankind." The general evils - drinking, gambling and adultery - were in full swing even in those days. Dozy quotes the Caliph 'Alī as speaking of the Taghlib, a Christian tribe, in the following significant words: "All they have borrowed from that Church is the practice of a wine-bibbing." In short Christianity - last of the revealed religions of the world - was practically defunct. It had lost, all driving force towards moral reformation.

Arab poetry

As to Arabia itself, it is true that Arab poetry was at its zenith, and pre-Islamic poetry displays a high degree of ability and skill. It is also true that the art of writing was not unknown to the Arabs; but they seldom turned it to useful purpose. Even their poetry was not preserved in writing. Poetical compositions of the Dark Age have all come down to us through oral tradition with the solitary exception of the pieces known as the *Mu'allaqāt* which were committed to writing and hung on the walls of the Ka'bah. As regards Arab development of the art of poetry, it is enough to say that mere poetry, as such, affords no sure criterion of a people's stage of civilization. Interest in poetry is observed in almost every stage of society, however crude and primitive. And the reason is not far to seek. Primitive people have very few interests, which multiply only with the growth of civilization, and hence their exclusive devotion to the only available form of fine art - poetry. But Arab poetry is devoid of the breadth of vision and loftiness of thought which come only with culture. Beauty of language is all it can boast of.

The Arab character

There were, no doubt, certain noble traits in the Arab character. Hospitality, love of freedom, daring, manliness, tribal fidelity and generosity were some of the qualities in which the

Arab had no equal. But a few virtues, by themselves, especially when overbalanced by the weight of barbarity and brutality can hardly be taken to constitute civilization. Side by side with the most hospitable treatment accorded to a guest, it was common practice to rob a wayfarer. The sentiment of tribal patriotism, though highly commendable in itself, had also been abused and carried to excess. Trifling disputes between individuals would lead to terrible conflagrations of war and blood-feuds extended from generation to generation.

The Arab idolatry

No doubt, the Arabs professed faith in the unity of God, but their belief was shallow. Their practical life belied their profession. They were given to idolatry, thinking that the Almighty had entrusted the discharge of the various functions of the universe to different gods, goddesses and idols. They therefore turned to these, invoking their blessings in all their undertakings. Thus their belief in the Unity of God was an empty dogma, finding no place in the system of their practical life. Besides, idols, they looked upon the air, the sun, the moon and the stars as the controllers of their destinies, and worshipped them as such. They had fallen as low as to worship pieces of stone, trees and sand-heaps. They prostrated before any fine piece of stone they might come across. Should they fail to find a piece of stone, they would worship a sand-hill, after having milked their she-camel thereon. They looked upon angels as the daughters of God! Even men of fame were worshipped, images being carved out in their names. It was not necessary to have the stones properly carved or shaped; even rough, unhewn ones served the purpose.

Going out on a joumey, they would carry four stones along with them, three to make a hearth, and the fourth to serve as an object of worship. Sometimes no separate one for purposes of worship would be carried. The cooking done, any of the three would be pulled out and worshipped. Besides the three hundred and sixty idols set up in the Ka‘bah, every tribe had an idol of its own. In fact, one was kept in each and every household. Idol-worship had, in short, become second nature with them and it influenced their everyday life in all its detail. The central idea of their faith was that God had made over the control and administration of the universe to others in whom He had vested all powers, such as healing the sick, granting children and removing famine and epidemic. Divine favour could not be obtained but through the intercession of these idols. They would prostrate before them, circumambulate them, offer sacrifices to them, and set apart some of the produce of their fields and their animals as offerings to them.

From such debasing idolatry, the Holy Prophet Muḥammad uplifted the whole of Arabia in the brief span of twenty years. Not only was idolatry extirpated root and branch from the soil of Arabia, but such enthusiasm for the Unity of God was kindled in the hearts of the self-same Arabs that it carried them far and wide over the length and breadth of the then known world to uphold the name of The One God. The weaning of a whole country extending over a vast area of twelve hundred thousand square miles from the curse of idol-worship, to which it was hopelessly wedded by long-established traditions and heredity, in no more time than a fifth of a century, so far as to win for it the title of iconoclast – is not this the mightiest miracle that the world has ever witnessed?

Religion a mockery

In addition to idol-worship, which was the order of the day, star-worship had taken as firm a root in the soil of Arabia. Human destiny was associated with the movements of various stars and the phenomena of nature affecting the fortunes of man for good or evil were attributed to their influence. Whereas on the one hand the worst form of idolatry had its hold on the Arab mind in general, there were also some who had no faith in the existence of God, the immortality of the human soul and the day of retribution. To them all religion was mockery. They held up to ridicule the very idols they professed to adore. It is said of the famous poet, Imra' al-Qais, that on the murder of his father he consulted an oracle in accordance with the traditional practice among the Arabs, to decide whether or not he should avenge the murder. The process consisted in marking two arrows, one with the word *na'am* (yes), the other with *lā* (no), to indicate respectively whether the undertaking should be entered upon or not. A blank one was also put in, which if drawn, advised the lot to be drawn afresh. Imra' al-Qais drew the arrows three times and each time the negative one came out. In a fit of rage he flung the arrow in the face of the idol, saying: "O Wretch! Had it been the murder of thy own father thou wouldst not have forbidden me to avenge it."

Social life

Such was the state of irreligion and idol worship in Arabia! Social life presented no better a picture. The Arabs were ignorant of the very rudiments of social virtues. Their manner of life made the evolution of any social virtue impossible. Tribal feuds engaged their whole attention. A settled and peaceful mode of life, indispensable to the cultivation of social qualities, was unknown to them. The prospect of hostilities with another clan that might break out at any time was ever present before their minds. They led a nomadic life, wandering with their cattle from place to place. They would set up their tents of camel-skins wherever they found water to drink and forage for their cattle. Only a small minority of them had settled in villages and still fewer in towns. How was it possible, under such circumstances, that the blessings of an ordered and settled society should accrue to them?

No law and order

There was no central govemment to enforce law and order in the country, which was rent into innumerable petty states, each clan forming a separate and independent political unit. They were too weak to enforce justice; to wrench one's rights from another, one had to depend upon one's strength of arm. Each tribe had a chief of its own, its leader in battle; but there was no law whatsoever binding the tribe to the nation. Each was independent, owing no allegiance to any central authority until Islām came with its unifying force. William Muir says that "The first peculiarity, then, which attracts our attention is the subdivision of the Arabs into innumerable bodies, governed by the same code of honour and morals, and exhibiting the same manners, speaking for the most part the same language, but each independent of the others; restless and often at war amongst themselves; and even where united by blood or by interest, ever ready on some insignificant cause to separate and give way to an implacable hostility. Thus at the era of Islām, the retrospect of Arabian history exhibits, as in the kaleidoscope, an ever-varying state of combination and repulsion, such as had hitherto rendered abortive any attempt at a general union ... The problem had yet to be solved, by what force these tribes could be subdued, or drawn to one common centre; and it was solved by Muḥammad."

The Qur'ān sums up succinctly this utter deterioration that embraced every phase of life in a single sentence: "You were on the brink of a pit of fire..."[1] Hostilities once breaking out continued for generations. Trifles, such as a word of contempt, or a slight mischief in a horse race, led to the slaughter of thousands and the eternal bondage of the vanquished. It was this fallen humanity whom the Holy Prophet raised to the highest level of moral rectitude. He welded these discordant elements into a brotherhood unique in the history of the world. A mighty transformation! A miracle, as a modern writer calls it in his *Ins and Outs of Mesopotamia:* "A more disunited people it would be hard to find, till, suddenly, the miracle took place. A man arose who, by his personality and by his claim to direct Divine guidance, actually brought about the impossible namely the union of all these warring factions."

Position of Woman

Woman occupied a very low position in Arab society. Despite love-songs in praise of the beloved, which were the outcome of carnal lust, woman was accorded no better treatment than the lower animals. Polyandry, which is a characteristic of the very primitive stages of human society, was also in vogue; yet neither was there a limit to the number of wives a man could take. Besides a plurality of wives, he could have illicit relations with any number of other women. Prostitution was a recognised profession. Captive women, kept as handmaids, were forced to make money for their masters in this debasing manner. Married women were allowed by their husbands to conjugate with others for the sake of offspring.[2]

1 The Qur'ān, 3 : 103.

2 This practice was called *Istibdẕā'* ; and was similar to the practice of Niyoga still prevalent among Hindus.

Moreover, woman was looked upon as a mere chattel. She was entitled to no share of the legacy of her deceased husband, father or other relations. On the contrary, she was herself inherited as part of the property of the deceased. The heir was at liberty to dispose of her as he would. He could even marry her himself, or give her in marriage to anybody he chose. On the death of his father, a son would even marry his step-mother, she being a part of the inheritance. The practice of divorce in vogue among them was no less barbarous. A thousand times could a man divorce his wife and take her back within a prescribed period (known as *'iddah).* Sometimes he would swear he would not go near her, sometimes he would announce that he would look upon her as his mother, thus leaving her in a state of suspension, being neither wife nor yet divorced. These methods were adopted simply to harass her. She had no way out of her sad plight.

The most obscene language was used in expressing sex-relations. Stories of love and illicit relationships were narrated proudly and with utter absence of shame in verses of the most indecent kind. Women of high families were openly addressed in love-songs. Considering the state of things obtaining among the Arabs with regard to the status of woman, it is not difficult to judge what a heavy debt of gratitude woman owes to Muḥammad, peace and blessings of Allah be upon him, who lifted her up from the depths of lowliness to a position of respect and dignity.[1]

Let us turn to the amelioration wrought in the condition of woman by Islām. The Quranic injunction, "Women shall have the same rights over men as men have over them,"[2] was the *Magna Carta,* so to speak, of women's franchise. In the same strain observed the Holy Prophet: "The best of you is he who treats his wife best." To implant veneration for woman in a soil where it was regarded as a mark of nobility to bury female offspring alive is surely no mean service to humanity. On hearing of the birth of a daughter, the father's face would

1 Even modern European civilization, which has a superficial respect for the gentle sex, fails to grant those rights to women which Islām has given them. Genuine respect for the female sex lies in having proper regard for its chastity and the equality of its rights with man, neither of which is, unfortunately, met with anywhere in Western society.

2 The Qur'ān, 2 : 228.

turn black with grief and rage. He had either to bury her alive or put up with social disgrace.[1] He would take his daughter to the desert, throw her into a pit dug there beforehand and bury alive the screaming child with his own hands underneath a heap of earth! The Prophet when informed of one such incident burst into tears of pity. Sometimes an explicit agreement was made at the nuptial ceremony that female offspring was to be killed, in which case it was the duty of the mother herself to commit the barbarous deed. She had to do it in the presence of all the female members of the family, especially invited to attend the grim function. All these cold-blooded brutalities were ended, at a single stroke, by the Quranic words: "And when the one buried alive is asked for what sin she was killed ..."[2] Never thereafter even in a single instance was the horrible cruelty repeated. In this respect, Muḥammad, peace and blessings of Allāh be upon him, stands unrivalled in the history of the world for his service to mankind.

Standing evils

Drinking was another vice to which the whole of Arabia was hopelessly wedded. Intoxicating liquors were served several times daily. There was not a household but had a number of wine pitchers in store. No sooner, however, was the Quranic prohibition proclaimed[3] than the very pots used for storing liquor were broken to pieces and thrown away; and, it is related, wine flowed like rain-water in the streets of Madīnah. The centuries-old habit of drinking was thus rooted out in no time, and utter abstinence became the order of the day.

Gambling was another curse which had a firm hold on the Arab society. It was indulged in as a common daily pastime. Those who abstained were looked down upon as miserly. The Holy Prophet Muḥammad's spiritual force made short the work of this as well, and relieved Arabia of another long-standing evil.

There was no education worthy of mention among the Arabs. Those able to decipher a script could be counted. Ignorance bred superstition, and they were given to all sorts

1 The Qur'ān, 16 : 58, 59.; 2 Ibid., 81 : 8, 9; 3 Ibid., 5 : 90.

of queer beliefs. They had faith in the existence of genii and evil spirits, whom they would conjure up in solitary places. To these they attributed certain diseases, to escape which they would make use of charms and incantations. In times of drought, they would fasten dry blades of grass and undergrowth to a cow's tail, set fire thereto and drive the animal to the mountains. They thought the flame of fire resembled a flash of lightning and would, by reason of similarity, attract rainfall. In case a calamity befell them, they would enter the house by the back door. From the flight of birds they took good or evil omens. If a bird crossed their way from left to right, it was regarded as a good omen; from right to left it was a bad omen. Those who believed in a life after death would tie a camel to a tomb and starve it to death, thinking the deceased would mount it on the day of resurrection. They held the human soul to be a tiny creature which entered a man's body at the time of his birth and went on growing. At his death it assumed the form of an owl and kept hovering over his tomb. In the event of violent death, the owl would keep droning "Give me water, Give me water," until the murder had been avenged. They believed in soothsayers and fortune tellers, and had implicit faith in whatever they told them. In short, these and a hundred and one other superstitions were believed in by the Arabs of the pre-Islāmic days. In the course of a few years, the Holy Prophet Muḥammad emancipated them from all these shackles of hereditary bondage and elevated them to the pinnacle of morality, learning and culture. History will vainly turn its pages to point to a parallel of the wholesale reformation and elevation of a fallen people such as the Arabs were. A mighty achievement indeed!

Earlier Prophets

Prophets appeared in various parts of Arabia before the dispensation of the patriarch Abraham as well as after. References to some of them have been made in the Qur'ān. Hūd was deputed for the reformation of the tribe of 'Ād that settled in a part of Yaman, known as Aḥqāf, and Ṣāliḥ was raised for the Th̲amūd, inhabiting the part called Hijr, to the north of Madīnah. Both these reformers preceded Abraham; while two others, Ishmael and Sh̲u'aib, who appeared in Yaman and

Madyan respectively, came after him. Traditions as well as inscriptions show that the 'Ādites were a very mighty people. They had founded a great empire which extended far beyond the confines of Arabia. It seems that prophets had been sent among them even before the advent of Hūd, who made his appearance at a time when the nation was sunk very low. They turned a deaf ear to this prophet and were severely punished. Their destruction was wrought by a dust-storm from the desert which lies to the north of Aḥqāf and goes by the name of the *Rub'Khālī (the* Barren Quarter). The Thamūdites, therefore, betook themselves to the mountains, where they carved homes for themselves out of the rocks.[1] But since the doom was sealed, strongholds could not save them. They perished in an earthquake. A look at the map of Arabia shows that, of these four, the mission of Hūd and Ishmael was confined to the south, and that of Ṣāliḥ and Shu'aib to the north of Arabia; the middle portion, known as Ḥij'āz, remained without a prophet. But Abraham's visiting Makkah and leaving Ishmael there, and afterwards his building the Ka'bah, have preserved to this day the association of Abraham's name with certain places there.

Jewish settlement

During the dispensation of the Israelite prophets, idol-worship had reached its highest pitch in Arabia. A queen of Yaman was converted to the doctrine of the Unity of God by Solomon. This was followed by another feeble ripple on the religious deep of Arabia. Jews migrated and settled there, probably about the 5th century B.C., when Nebuchadnezzar, drove them out of their homelands. Prophecies as to the appearance of the Last Prophet from the soil of Arabia were current among them. Therefore they took up their abode there, and Khaibar became a purely Jewish settlement. When they had gained a firm footing they began propagating their faith and about the 3rd century B.C., the King of Yaman, Dhū Nawās by name, embraced Judaism. This added fresh momentum to the Jewish movement of proselytism and in the course of time Judaism won considerable ascendancy in Arabia. But the Arab nation as a whole remained addicted to its ancestral

1 The Qur'ān, 26 : 149.

religion of idol-worship, and after a short-lived career the Jewish religious movement died a natural death, leaving the Arabs as a nation of idolaters.

Christians

A second wave of reformation followed. Christian missionaries began pouring into Arabia in the 3rd century A.D. and settled in Najrān. Their proselytizing activities were considerably supplemented by the political influence of the two Christian powers in the neighbourhood of Arabia, the Abyssinian to the west and the Roman Empire to the north. Consequently the entire province of Najrān, which lies between 'Asīr and San'ā, accepted Christianity. Barring just a bare sprinkling of converts here and there, little impress was made by Christianity on Arabia proper. Thus ended in utter failure the second attempt at the reformation of Arabia.

Unitarians

The third reformatory wave set in motion was internal. Just a little before the advent of Islām, there had sprung up a new school of thought known as Hanīf. It was a small band of earnest men who discarded idolatry but were not disposed towards Judaism or Christianity. They worshipped only one God, but did not trouble themselves at all about reformation in the social life of their country. Feeling aversion for idol-worship, some of them did no doubt join the fold of Christianity, such as Waraqah, Khadījah's cousin, and 'Abd Allāh ibn Jaḥsh, Ḥamzah's nephew, but their number was insignificant. The majority of them found no satisfaction in either Christianity or Judaism. Of these the noteworthy were Zaid ibn 'Amr ibn Nufail, 'Umar's uncle, and Umayyah, a renowned poet and the chief of Ṭā'if. These people had little zeal for promulgating their newly-conceived notions. Nevertheless they made no secret of their abhorrence of idolatry, and openly avowed Unitarianism as their faith, which they professed to be the religion taught by Abraham. Feeble though the movement was, it was undoubtedly there. But, like its predecessors, this internal movement also failed to go below the surface, leaving Arab society as unaffected as ever.

In fact, it was more feeble than either the Jewish or the Christian movement.

Failures

The Jews had family affinity with the Arabs. Both came of the same stock. Their language, their manners, their customs had much in common. Both held the great patriarch Abraham in high esteem. A king of Yaman, the most fertile province of Arabia, had accepted the Jewish religion. Thus to all human calculations, these various forces in favour of Judaism had a cumulative effect potent enough to secure the conversion of the whole of Arabia. But Arabia proved adamant to all these influences.

Then came Christianity with quite a new message. Its so-called Unitarianism resembled the Arab concept of Godhead. The idolatry obtaining among the Arabs was akin to Greek idol-worship under the influence of which the Christian doctrine of Trinity had taken birth. St. Paul, the real founder of the Church religion as we have it, had given such an idolatrous form to the monotheistic teaching of the Israelite prophets as to make it fascinating for the idolatrous peoples of his day. Consequently Christianity secured large numbers of converts from among the Arabs. It had another feature particularly attractive to them. It dispensed with the necessity of observing the law - a licence quite in keeping with the Arab mode of life. Having no religious or secular code of laws to regulate their conduct, these wild children of the desert had given themselves up to unbridled debauchery. Christianity allowed ample latitude for the gratification of their licentious propensities. It was therefore a creed offering the least line of resistance, and hence the easiest for them to adopt. In addition to these inherent attractions, Christianity had the advantage of temporal power to commend it to the Arabs. The great Roman Empire to the north, the Abyssinian kingdom to the west, the conversion of one of the provinces of Yaman and the hold acquired by Christianity over the states of Ḥīrah and Ghassān – these were the manifold influences in favour of Christianity. Under such circumstances the conversion of the peninsula seemed but a matter of days. Nevertheless, the Church failed to make any appreciable impression on Arab society.

The third movement, that of the Hanīfs was purely internal in origin and had little to do with the social reformation of Arabia, confining its aims to one single object - the supplanting of idolatry by Unitarianism. Notwithstanding such an unambitious progamme, it found the soil of Arabia far less congenial than had the preceding movements. It proved the weakest of all, perhaps, for the reason that it was backed by no worldly power.

It is remarkable that before the appearance of the Holy Prophet, three different movements were set afoot, all aiming at the reformation of Arabia. Keeping at work for centuries with all the advantages that worldly power can afford, all these movements vanish in smoke. But then arises an individual who achieves, single-handed and in a state of utter helplessness, what they had all failed to achieve. In the course of a few years, he brings about a transformation unparalleled in the history of the world. Not only is the debasing superstition of the country - idolatry - eradicated, but the entire social fabric is reclaimed and released from long-standing and deep-rooted corruption.

Arabia impervious to reform

In view of all this, a critical eye cannot fail to perceive that, behind the scenes, it was the mighty hand of the Lord that helped the Holy Prophet Muḥammad in working such a radical transformation in the religious, social and moral life of Arabia within the brief span of twenty years - a transformation that stands unique in the history of the world. William Muir, by no means a friendly critic of the Prophet, has to admit this miraculous regeneration of Arabia in the following words: "During the youth of Muḥammad, the aspect of the Peninsula was strongly conservative; perhaps reform never was at any period more hopeless. Causes are sometimes conjured up to account for the results produced by an agent apparently inadequate to effect them. Muḥammad arose, and forthwith the Arabs were aroused to a new and a spiritual faith. Hence the conclusion that Arabia was fermenting for the change, and prepared to adopt it. To us, calmly reviewing the past, pre-Islamite history belies the assumption. After five centuries of Christian evangelization, we can point to but a sprinkling here and there of Christian converts."

"In fine, viewed thus in a religious aspect, the surface of Arabia had been now and then gently rippled by the feeble efforts of Christianity; the sterner influence of Judaism had been occasionally visible in a deeper and more troubled current; but the tide of indigenous idolatry and of Ishmaelite superstition, setting strongly from every quarter towards the Ka'bah, gave ample evidence that the faith and worship of Mecca held the Arab mind in a rigorous and undisputed thraldom."

Further on, the same critic observes that "the prospects of Arabia before the rise of Muḥammad were as unfavourable to religious reform as to political union or national regeneration. The foundation of the Arab faith was a deep-rooted idolatry, which for centuries had stood proof, with no palpable symptom of decay, against every attempt at evangelization from Egypt and Syria."

Thus the Holy Prophet Muḥammad (peace and blessings of Allāh be upon him) was sent as a warner to a people who were proof against all warning. They had baffled all previous attempts at their regeneration. But phenomenal success attended his labours in bringing about the reformation of that self-same, incorrigible race. It is to this miraculous transformation of idolatrous Arabs, and through them of the followers of other religions, that the Qur'ān prophetically refers: "Those who disbelieve from among the People of the Book and the idolaters could not have been freed till clear evidence came to them - A Messenger from Allah, reciting pure pages, wherein are (all) right books."[1]

1 The Qur'ān, 98 : 1-3

CHAPTER II

THE PROMISED PROPHET

"Those who follow the Messenger-Prophet, the Ummī, whom they find mentioned in the Torah and the Gospel" 7: 157.

PROPHECIES about the advent of Prophet Muḥammad, peace and blessings of Allāh be upon him are met with in earlier sacred books and had great currency among the nations. In fact those very prophecies might have impelled Jews and Christians to settle down in Arabia; for the land of the Promised Prophet was specified by name in the Scriptures. We would touch upon a few of them.

The Qur'ān asserts that the appearance of the Holy Prophet was foretold by each and all of the foregoing prophets, through whom the covenant was also made with their respective peoples that they would accept him when he made his appearance.[1] The distinguishing feature of the Promised One, they were told, was that he would bear testimony to the truth of all the prophets of the world. It seems that Providence had deemed fit to depute a separate prophet for the reformation of each nation in the days of yore, when the various peoples inhabiting this planet lived in absolute isolation from one another and modern means of communication had not come into existence. To amalgamate the diverse religious systems into one all-comprehensive faith as well as to weld humanity into one universal brotherhood, was sent a prophet with a mission for the whole of mankind. Thus, while on the one hand the happy news of such a world-Prophet was given to each preceding prophet, the Promised one was, on the other, commissioned to testify to the truth of all the foregoing prophets wherever and whenever sent all the world over: "And

1 The Qur'ān, 3 : 81.

when Allāh made a covenant through the prophets: Certainly what I have given you of the Book and Wisdom - then a Messenger comes to you verifying that which is with you, you shall believe in him and you shall aid him ... "[1]

There is only one Messenger in the whole world and that is Muḥammad (peace and blessings of Allah be upon him) - who answers to this description. His description of the faithful runs thus: "And who believe in that which has been revealed to thee and that which was revealed before thee..."[2] It goes further still and asserts that a prophet was raised in every nation: "There is not a people but a warner has gone among them."[3] On another occasion it says that it makes mention of some of the prophets while there are others who have not been expressly spoken of.[4] So the Holy Prophet Muḥammad stands out unique from both these view-points: on the one hand, the predictions of all his predecessors find due fulfilment in his person; while, on the other, he alone out of all the prophets has made it a binding article of faith to believe in all the prophets of the world. Thus, he is the last of that noble band of prophets, as foretold by all his predecessors.

Abraham's prophecies

The Israelites and the Ishmaelites spring from a common progenitor - Abraham. Though the Divine Scripture revealed to Abraham has not come down to us, yet much light is thrown on God's promises to him concerning the future of his sons, Isaac and Ishmael, by the Old Testament in the book of Genesis. The Qur'ān also alludes to the same promises when it says: "And when his Lord tried Abraham with certain commands he fulfilled them. He said: Surely I will make thee a leader of men. (Abraham) said: And of my offspring? My covenant does not include the wrong-doers, said He."[5] And again in the joint prayer of Abraham and Ishmael: "Our Lord, and raise up in them a Messenger from among them who shall recite to them Thy messages and teach them the Book and the Wisdom, and purify them..."[6] The Old Testament records a Divine promise to the same effect, made to Abraham, even before the birth of Isaac and Ishamel: "And I will make of

1 The Qur'ān, 3 : 81; 2 Ibid., 2 : 4; 3 Ibid, 35 : 24; 4 Ibid., 4 : 164.; 5 Ibid., 2 : 124.; 6 Ibid., 2 : 129.

thee a great nation, and I will bless thee and make thy name great and thou shalt be a blessing: and I will bless them that bless thee, and curse him that curseth thee and in thee shall all families of the earth be blessed."[1]

Then reference is made to Ishmael by name, in the same book of Genesis: "And as for Ishmael, I have heard thee: Behold I have blessed him and will make him fruitful, and will multiply him exceedingly: twelve princes shall he beget, and I will make him a great nation."[2]

Moses' prophecies

The second prophecy announcing the advent of the Holy Prophet Muḥammad found utterance through Moses: "I will raise up a prophet from among their brethren like unto thee, and will put my words in his mouth."[3]

No one of the Israelite prophets that followed Moses in a long succession down to Jesus ever claimed to be the prophet promised in this prophecy. And for obvious reasons Moses' successors, who came only to fulfil his law, could not be like unto him. The prophecy was of common knowledge among the Jews who expected, generation after generation, a prophet like unto Moses. This is amply borne out by the conversation that passed between John the Baptist and those who came to ask him: "Who art thou?" And he confessed: "I am not the Christ." And they asked him, what then? Art thou Elias? And he saith, I am not. Art thou that Prophet? And he answered: No."[4] This shows positively that the Jews were in expectation of the appearance of three different prophets. Firstly, Elias, who, they thought, was to reappear in person; secondly, the Christ; and thirdly, a prophet of such universal fame that in his case, no further specification was thought necessary - *"that* Prophet" was enough to convey who was meant. Such was the household currency which Moses' prophecy concerning a prophet like unto him had gained among the Jews. It is thus evident that just before the appearance of Jesus, the Jews were in expectation of three prophets, as foretold in their scriptures.

Now two of these prophecies were fulfilled in the persons of Jesus and John, the one claiming to be the Christ and the

1 Genesis, 12 : 2,3.; 2 Ibid., 17 : 20.; 3 Deuteronomy, 18 : 18.;
4 John, I : 19-21.

other to have been sent in the spirit of Elias. But neither laid claim to be the Promised Prophet like unto Moses. Nor did any of those who accepted them identify them as such: With Jesus, the chain of prophethood among the Israelites came to an end. Thus the prophecy of Deuteronomy regarding a prophet like unto Moses remained unfulfilled so far as the Israelites were concerned. Turning to the history of the world, we find that no other prophet except Muḥammad (peace and blessings of Allāh be upon him) ever claimed to be the Prophet foretold by Moses, and no other sacred book but the Qur'ān ever pointed to anyone as fulfilling the prophecy. Facts also bear out the same conclusion. Moses was a law-giver and so was Muḥammad, peace be upon them. Among the Israelite prophets who succeeded Moses, no one brought a new law. The Holy Prophet Muḥammad, being the only law-giving Prophet, was thus the only Prophet like unto Moses. The Qur'ān says: "Surely We have sent to you a Messenger .. as We sent a Messenger to Pharaoh."[1] Again, it invites the attention of the Jews to the prophecy in Deuteronomy in these words: "A witness from among the Children of Israel has borne witness of one like him ..."[2] The words of the prophecy, "from among their brethren," throw further light on the fact that the Promised Prophet was to come, not from among the Israelites themselves but from among their brethren, the Ishmaelites.

A third prophecy in equally clear terms is met with in the same book - Deuteronomy. It says: "The Lord came from Sinai, and rose up from Seir to them; he shined forth from Mount Paran, and he came forth with ten thousands of saints; from his right hand went a fiery law for them."[3]

"Coming from Sinai" refers to the appearance of Moses, while "rising up from Seir" refers to the conquest of Seir by David. Now Paran is admittedly the ancient name for the land of Ḥijāz, where arose Muḥammad (peace and blessings of Allāh be upon him) from among the descendants of Ishmael. The words "he came forth with ten thousands of saints" point still more unmistakably to the identity of the person to whom they refer. The Holy Prophet Muḥammad of all the world-heroes, is the one solitary historical personage whose triumphal

1 The Qur'ān, 73 : 15.; 2 Ibid., 46 : 10.; 3 Deuteronomy, 33 : 2.

entry into Makkah with ten thousand saintly followers, is an event of common knowledge. The law he gave to the world is to this day known as *baiḍā'* (shining), for it throws full light on all matters pertaining to the religious, moral and social welfare of man. And it is to this that allusion is made in the words, "from his right hand went a fiery law for them."

Isaiah's prophecies

A fourth prophecy specifies Arabia as the land of the Promised Prophet: "The burden upon Arabia. In the forest in Arabia shall ye lodge, O ye travelling companions of Dedanites. Unto him that was thirsty they brought water, the inhabitants of the land of Tima did meet the fugitives with their bread. For they fled away from the swords, from the drawn sword and from the bent bow and from the grievousness of war."[1]

In the first place the word 'Arabia' is by itself significant enough. Then the mention of one who fled sheds still further light on the object of the prophecy. The history of the world records but one such flight that has won the importance of a red-letter event – the flight of the Holy Prophet Muḥammad from Makkah. It is from this point of time that the Muslim era commences; for it marked, in fact, the opening of a new chapter in the history of Islam - indeed in the civilization of the world. A yet clearer testimony, however, is contained in the words, "he fled from drawn swords." History confirms that the Holy Prophet Muḥammad fled from Makkah while his house was surrounded by blood-thirsty enemies with drawn swords ready to fall upon him in a body as soon as he came out. One will in vain turn the pages of history to find another instance of flight which resulted in issues so far-reaching and momentous, or another prophet who ran for his life through drawn swords. These two authoritative facts of history, supplemented by a direct mention of the land of Arabia as the birth-place of the Promised Prophet, furnished an indisputable clue that the prophecy refers to the Holy Prophet Muḥammad.

1 Isaiah, 21 : 13-15.

Jesus' prophecies

There are several other similar prophecies by Israelite prophets, such as David, Solomon, Habakkuk, Haggai, and others. But for the sake of brevity let us refer to one only, by the last of the Israelite prophets - Jesus - which runs thus: "If ye love me, keep my commandments. And I will pray to the Father and He shall give you another Comforter, that he may abide with you for ever, even the Spirit of Truth."[1]

Again: "But the Comforter, which is the Holy Ghost, whom the Father will send in my name, he shall teach you all things."[2]

And again: "Nevertheless I tell you the truth; it is expedient for you that I go away; for if I go not away, the Comforter will not come unto you, but if I depart, I will send him unto you."[3]

Yet again: "I have yet many things to say unto you, but ye cannot bear them now. Howbeit when he, the Spirit of Truth, is come, he will guide you into all truth."[4]

All these prophetic words predict in unequivocal terms the advent of another prophet after Jesus. The terms of the prophecy do not warrant the conclusion that they are applicable to the Holy Ghost. "If I go not away, the Comforter will not come unto you" are words too clear to need any comment. The New Testament says that John was filled with the Holy Ghost even before he was born. Then it speaks of Jesus himself as receiving the Holy Ghost in the shape of a dove. Thus the Holy Ghost used to visit men before the time of Jesus as well as in his own time. To what is then the reference made in the words, "If I go not away, the Comforter will not come unto you?" Surely not to the Holy Ghost; for it is almost sacrilegious to think that Jesus was without the Holy Ghost. Genuine reverence for Jesus requires that we should recognize even his disciples, purified as they were at the hands of their great Master, to have been pure enough to merit the company of the Holy Ghost. The Qur'ān, at least, credits the companions of the Holy Prophet Muḥammad with such company in clear terms: "These are they in whose hearts He has impressed faith and strengthened them with a Spirit from Himself."[5]

1 John, 14 : 15-17.; 2 Ibid., 14 : 26.; 3 Ibid., 16 : 7.; 4 Ibid., 16 : 12,13.
5 The Qur'ān, 58 : 22.

The words "Holy Ghost" which have also been used in the prophecy, if not an interpolation, are intended to be taken that the Promised one would have such an inseparable union with the Holy Ghost that his advent might be taken, metaphorically of course, as the coming of the Holy Ghost itself. There are other words in the prophecy which are applicable only to the Holy Prophet Muḥammad. The characteristic features set forth in the prophecy are found one and all in him. "That he may abide with you forever" indicates that there would be no prophet after the Promised one. This is exactly what the Qur'ān says of the Holy Prophet Muḥammad: "The seal of the Prophets."[1] Again, "He shall teach you all things," says the prophecy. The same is in the Qur'ān about the dispensation of the Holy Prophet Muḥammad: "This day have I perfected for you your religion.."[2] Then the Promised one is called the Spirit of Truth in the prophecy, which is also confirmed by the Qur'ān in the words: "The Truth has come and falsehood vanished."[3]

The Holy Prophet's genealogy

Ishmael was the eldest son of Abraham. He had twelve sons, as confirmed by the Old Testament, one of them named Kaidār, whose progeny spread over the Arabian province of Hijāz. That the Arabs are the descendants of Kaidār also goes without saying on the authority of the Old Testament. Again, it is admitted on every hand among the Arabs that 'Adnān, to whom the Holy Prophet Muḥammad's genealogy has been traced beyond all doubt, was also a scion of Ishmael in about the fortieth degree. There have never been two opinions as to the fact that the Holy Prophet Muḥammad was in direct descent from 'Adnān. Further down, in the ninth degree from the latter, there follows Naḍr ibn Kinānah, founder of the Quraish dynasty. Another descent in the genealogical scale and then comes in the ninth place, one Qusay by name, to whom was entrusted the guardianship of the Ka'bah - an office of the highest honour in Arabia. He was the grandfather of 'Abd al-Muṭṭalib, the Holy Prophet Muḥammad's grandfather. Thus in respect of nobility, the Holy Prophet's dynasty occupies the highest place.

1 The Qur'ān, 33 : 40.; 2 Ibid., 5 : 3.; 3 Ibid., 17 : 81.

'Abd al-Muṭṭalib's mother came of the Banū Najjār, which tribe thus stood in the relation of maternal ancestors to the Holy Prophet. 'Abd al-Muṭṭalib begot ten sons, noteworthy among them being Abū Lahab who was the arch-leader of the opposition to the Holy Prophet, Abū Ṭālib who brought him up, Ḥamzah who was among the earliest converts and fell at the battle of Uḥud, 'Abbās who though a long time outside the pale of Islām, yet remained very affectionate to the Holy Prophet and 'Abd Allāh, his father. The latter was married to Āminah, daughter of Wahb ibn 'Abd Manāf, of the Zuhrah family. The couple was pre-eminent not only in respect of the nobility of their families, but for what stood for greater distinction in that age of darkness and corruption, they both possessed pure and sublime characters.

A few days after the nuptials, 'Abd Allāh undertook a commercial journey to Syria. On his way back he fell ill and passed away at Madīnah. The Holy Prophet was thus a posthumous child. Monday, the 12th of Rabī' al-Awwal is his commonly accepted birth-date. According to another research it is the 9th of the same month as corresponding to the 20th of April 571 of the Christian era. Before his birth, his mother received the happy news in a vision. It transpires from certain sayings of the Holy Prophet that he was given the name Muḥammad by his grandfather and Aḥmad by his mother, each in accordance with a vision. He has been spoken of in the Qur'ān by both of these names.[1] He himself is reported on trustworthy authority to have said: "I am Muḥammad as well as Aḥmad." In poetical compositions too, he was addressed by both names.

Abrahah's attack on Makkah

This is hardly the place for dwelling at length on the extraordinary events that are related to have attended the Holy Prophet's birth. We content ourselves with referring to just one, by itself a mighty sign. The very year that the Holy Prophet was born, the Christian chief of Yaman erected a magnificent church in his capital Ṣan'ā with a view to make it a general centre for people, both commercial and religious, in

1 The Qur'ān, 61 : 6 ; 3 : 144 ; 33 : 40 ; 48 : 29.

place of the Ka'bah which he resolved to demolish. This was, in fact, a life and death struggle between Trinity and Unity. Abrahah, the chief, marched at the head of a large army against the Ka'bah to pull it down. He encamped at a distance of three stages from Makkah, and sent word to the Makkans, intimating his mission to them. In the meantime, some of 'Abd al-Muṭṭalib's camels were captured by Abrahah's soldiers. 'Abd al-Muṭṭalib came in person to the chief to demand the return of his camels. Much impressed by his imposing appearance, Abrahah asked him what had brought him thither, believing no doubt that he had come to implore him to spare the Sacred House. 'Abd al-Muṭṭalib told him that he was there to demand his camels. Astonished at this unexpected reply, Abrahah said: "You are so anxious about your camels, but you are not concerned about the Ka'bah which I have come all this way to demolish." "I worry myself about the camels," replied 'Abd al-Muṭṭalib, "for I am their master, as to the Ka'bah its Master will Himself look after it." The Quraish, finding themselves too weak to offer any resistance to Abrahah, evacuated Makkah, taking shelter in the neighbouring hills. While leaving the city, 'Abd al-Muṭṭalib took hold of a curtain of the Ka'bah and prayed: "O Allāh! this is Thy own house. We feel too feeble to defend it. Be pleased to take care of it Thyself." Historians say that a most virulent form of smallpox broke out in the camp of Abrahah, which wrought a terrible havoc, destroying the major part of his forces. The rest took to flight in utter confusion.[1] This miraculous event came to pass simultaneously with the Holy Prophet's birth. According to some reports, the day of Abrahah's discomfiture was the very day of the Holy Prophet's birth. According to others he was born forty days after this event.

Before the Call

It was a custom among the Arab gentry and nobility that the mothers did not nurse their children; they were sent out to be reared in the country. At his birth the infant Muḥammad, peace and blessings of Allāh be upon him, was nursed by his mother for a couple of days and for two or three days by

1 "Hast thou not seen how thy Lord dealt with the possessors of the elephant? Did He not cause their war to end in confusion?" (Qur'ān, 105:1,2)

Thuwaibiyah, a handmaid of Abū Lahab. After this he was entrusted to Ḥalīmah of the tribe of the Banū Sa'd. Two years later, Ḥalīmah, brought the child to his mother, Āminah, who sent him back with her, Makkah being at the time stricken with an epidemic. He remained in the charge of Ḥalīmah till the age of six, when he was returned to his mother. At this time, his mother, desiring to pay a visit to the tomb of her husband, undertook a journey to Madīnah where he was buried, taking the child along with her. On the way, however, the orphan child was deprived also of his mother, who passed away at a place called Abwā' where she was interred. The Holy Prophet Muḥammad was thus bereaved at the tender age of six of both his father and mother. It was not his lot to be brought up under the loving care of his parents, nor had he the opportunity to prove his filial devotion to them. Nevertheless, he gave the same affectionate treatment to his foster-mother and foster-sisters, in his later days as though they were his blood relations. Ḥalīmah once called upon him, after he had received the Divine Call. No sooner had she appeared, than the Holy Prophet stood up to greet her - a mark of deep respect - and spread his own mantle for her to sit upon. Likewise he showed special regard for his foster-sisters and foster-brothers, indeed for the whole tribe of the Banū Sa'd of which Ḥalīmah came.

On the death of his mother, charge of the child fell to his grandfather, 'Abd al-Muṭṭalib. Barely two years had elapsed, however, when this patronage was also snatched away by death. Thus he was eight years old when his guardianship passed to his uncle, Abū Ṭālib. From his very childhood he possessed the virtues which won him the deep affection of Abū Ṭālib. Whosoever came in contact with him, even at that early age, was impressed by his ways and manners. Abū Ṭālib kept him in his own company and took him out wherever he went. As reading and writing were almost unknown in Arabia, there being only rare exceptions, the Holy Prophet had no book-learning. When he was twelve years of age, Abū Ṭālib undertook a trading mission to Syria. The nephew was so attached to his uncle that he could not bear the idea of such a long separation and was consequently allowed to accompany him on that long journey. It was during this journey that he is said to have met a Christian anchorite called Baḥīrah. Beholding the boy, so goes the story, Baḥīrah could discern in his face marks of his future greatness and he advised Abū Ṭālib to take good care of him, for he would some day be the recipient of a Divine Call.

Alliance of protection of the weak

At the age of twenty, the Holy Prophet took part in the battle between the Quraish and the Qais which goes under the name of *Ḥarb al-Fijār,* lit., a war of transgression, so called because it was fought in the sacred months when warfare was forbidden. His part in it was, however, not that of actual fighting, but only of handing arrows to his uncles. After that he participated in the alliance known as the *Ḥilf al-Fuḍūl,* formed to vindicate the rights of the weak and the oppressed against tyranny. Each member of the alliance was bound in honour to defend the helpless against all oppression. The credit of taking the lead in the formation of this humanitarian organization was due to the Holy Prophet and his family, the Banū Hāshim. Thus his early inclinations to render help to the distressed go to show that human sympathy was implanted in his very nature.[1]

At this early age, the Holy Prophet's integrity had already won household fame in the town of Makkah. He was commonly known as *Al-Amīn* - the faithful. The epithet does not imply honesty in money matters alone but is all-comprehensive, denoting righteousness in every form. Whosoever happened to have any dealings with him at this period never ceased to praise him all his life. It was about this time that the necessity arose for the reconstruction of the sacred house of Ka'bah. The requisite material being provided, the Quraish jointly undertook the work. In the course of construction a serious dispute arose as to who should have the proud privilege of laying the Black Stone. This might have resulted in the outbreak of inter-tribal feuds and the consequent destruction of a number of families, had not a hoary-headed elder advised arbitration. Whoever, he suggested, should be the first to appear at the Ka'bah the following day should be accepted as

1 "I have lived among you a lifetime before it. Do you not understand" (Qur'ān, 10:16)

a judge to decide the point at issue. The proposal was unanimously agreed to. All were eagerly awaiting the next morning, when lo, to the satisfaction of all, none other than Muḥammad, peace and blessings of Allāh be upon him, was the first to appear. "Here is *al-Amīn*. Here is *al-Amīn!*" all shouted with one voice. And the general confidence in him was fully justified. Taking a sheet of cloth he placed the Black Stone thereon with his own hands. Then he invited principal men from every clan to hold the sheet by the four ends and thus equally share in the honour of lifting the stone into position. He thus averted what might have developed into a terrible conflagration of internecine warfare. He was then thirty-five years of age.

Marriage with Khadījah

A high-placed widow, Khadījah,[1] who had acquired in pre-Islamic days, by her virtue and righteousness, the title of *Tāhirah* (the virtuous), hearing of the righteousness of Muḥammad, peace and blessings of Allāh be upon him, entrusted to him the sole charge of her business. Before long much profit accrued to her through his honest dealings. These dealings gave evidence of his high morals and it was this circumstance which led Khadījah to make a proposal for marriage. Thus was he married, at the age of twenty-five, to a widow, fifteen years older than himself. Of Khadījah the Holy Prophet begot four daughters and two sons. The first-born was Qāsim, after whom the Holy Prophet was called Abu-l Qāsim, but he died at the age of two. His eldest daughter was Zainab who was married to Abu'l-'Āṣ. Next to her was Ruqayyah, married to 'Uthmān. She died on the day of the Muslims' victory at the battle of Badr. Next to her came Umm Kulthūm, who was also married to 'Uthmān on the death of her elder sister. The youngest of all the daughters was Fatimah, from whom sprang the progeny known as *Sayyids* in the history of Islām. She was wedded to 'Alī. The youngest offspring of

1 The life of the Holy Prophet Muḥammad may be divided into four periods so far as his domestic life is concerned. Up to twenty-five, he lead celibate life, from twenty-five years, he lived in a married state with one wife; from fifty-four to fifty-six he contracted several marriages and lastly from sixty till his death he did not contract any new marriage.

Khadījah was a male child who passed away while yet an infant. The Holy Prophet lost in his lifetime all his children except Fātimah, who survived him for only six months. He had only one son, Ibrāhīm, from another wife whom he married later at Madīnah, but the child died when only 18 months old.

The Holy Prophet was greaty attached to Khadījah and often remembered her in affectionate terms, even after her death. Once when he was speaking highly of her, 'Ā'ishah put him a pert question. Had not God given him, in herself, - she asked - a better substitute for Khadījah? "No," replied the Holy Prophet "she accepted me at a time when others rejected me." He was devoted heart and soul to Khadījah for her moral excellences. Although he freely spent of her wealth in the way of God, Khadījah never rejected his recommendation for spending her riches on charitable purposes. She purchased a slave for the Holy Prophet but was only too pleased when the latter set him free. Zaid, the well-known companion of the Holy Prophet who himself had once been a slave, was also liberated through Khadījah's generosity. When the Call came, the Holy Prophet was weighed down with the sense of onerous responsibility, and was diffident as to his ability to carry out the charge entrusted to him. Khadījah, at this moment, cheered up his distressed mind with the encouraging words: "God will never let thee see the humiliation of failure. Verily, thou showest due regard for blood-ties, carriest the burden of the infirm, practisest virtues that are extinct, entertainest guests and standest by what is righteous in the face of calamities." This shows how deeply Khadījah was impressed with the virtues and human sympathy of the Holy Prophet. This, in fact, was the cause of the deep love between husband and wife. Both were imbued with a profound sense of human sympathy. No one knows better the ways of a man than his own wife, who is in a position to have free access to the innermost recesses of his heart. The fact, therefore, that Khadījah had such implicit faith in the Holy Prophet furnishes indisputable testimony to the unimpeachable integrity of his character. The most hostile critic cannot in the face of this evidence dare throw suspicion on the Holy Prophet's sincerity. An imposter cannot possibly command the whole-hearted devotion of one so privy to his secrets.

Charming morals

Khadījah's testimony to the sublimity of the Holy Prophet's character carries, no doubt, the greatest weight. But others who came in contact with him were no less devoted. The father of Zaid, the liberated slave, hearing of the freeing of his son, came over to Makkah to take him away with him. The Holy Prophet, gentle as he was, could not possibly stand between father and son. He was only too glad to see a son restored to his father. Nevertheless, he could not separate Zaid from himself against the latter's own wishes. So on his father's request to allow Zaid to go with him, he left the matter to the free choice of Zaid himself. And what more could a father wish for? Little did he dream that his son's love for the Holy Prophet outdid his filial affection. Though set free from physical bondage, Zaid had already been enthralled by the charm of the Holy Prophet's personality. To the disappointment of the father, he preferred to stay with the Prophet. Similarly, Abū Bakr's steadfast attachment to him is a fact of common knowledge. Abū Ṭālib was no less impressed with the nobility of his character. Notwithstanding his adherence to his ancestral form of religion, he stood by the Holy Prophet through thick and thin, defending him, at grave risk to his own person, against the wrath of the united Quraishite tribes. Such was the deep impression the Holy Prophet's charm of character had made on his mind. He looked upon it as the height of cowardice to desert one of so sublime a character. He would run any risk for his sake, in opposing overwhelming odds. When asked by the Quraish to give up Muḥammad, peace and blessings of Allāh be upon him, he rebuked them in a beautiful couplet: "Woe unto you? no tribe has ever deserted its chief - a chief who carefully guards everything worth guarding. He is not overbearing, nor is he so weak as to entrust his affairs to others. He is generous of heart; through the intercession of his face, rain is prayed for. He shelters the orphan and the widow."

Magnetic personality

In a word, the Holy Prophet commanded the deepest attachment of all who came into contact with him. But what is still more significant, all who associated with him were men possessed of sterling moral qualities. Besides his fast friends, well-known in the history of Islām for the sublimity of their morals, there were others among his earlier friends equally distinguished for the nobility of their character, such as Ḥakīm ibn Hazām, a respectable Quraish chief who did not give his adherence to Islām until after the fall of Makkah, and Ḍamād ibn Tha'lbah. Both were his intimate friends and both were men of strong moral calibre. This leads to the conclusion that, like the golden touch in the story, whosoever came into contact with the magnetic personality of the Holy Prophet even at this early stage of his life, was enlivened by the sublimity and nobility of his morals.

One of the most precious gems in his character was his deep sympathy for the poor, the helpless, orphans and widows. He would exert his utmost to see to their needs. As regards this virtue, friend and foe were at one in admiring him. Khadījah's consolatory words to him bear testimony to this same trait of his character. Abū Tālib gave it as an argument why he must defend him against his enemies. His participation in the *Ḥilf al-Fuḍūl,* an alliance formed with the express object of championing the cause of the oppressed, testifies to his solicitude for the weak. Sympathy for the poor, the helpless, orphans and widows was, in short, ingrained in his very nature. The teachings of the Qur'ān clearly lay it down as the very essence of religion to look after the orphan and the helpless. Whoever discards the orphan or does not prompt others to feed the poor is spoken of as belying religion itself.[1] The loftiest summit of human dignity consists in tending the orphan and the poor.[2] Whosoever does not show respect to the orphan has been threatened with degradation. National decadence follows as a matter of course where neglect of the orphan and the poor prevails.[3]

We learn from the account of the Holy Prophet's early life that he was, from his very childhood, possessed of the highest order of modesty and gravity. He was not given to the boyish frivolities characteristic of his age. Abū Ṭālib, speaking of him to 'Abbās, bears testimony to this effect: "I have never seen him tell a lie, indulge in jests and vulgarity, or mix with street boys." Warfare was the favourite pastime in the Arabia of his

1 The Qur'ān, 107 : 1-3.; 2 Ibid., 90 : 11-16.; 3 Ibid., 89 : 17,18

days, but by his very nature he held it in aversion. At the battle of *Fijār* he did not go beyond supplying arrows and other fighting material to his uncles. Superstitions of all sorts, rampant in the country, were repugnant to his nature. He abhorred idol-worship from his very youth. On a certain occasion when conversation turned upon the chief Arab idols, the *Lāt* and the *'Uzzā,* he observed that he held nothing in greater detestation than idolatry. He would never participate in the observation of the polytheistic rites of his day. He refused to partake of the meal intended as an offering to an idol.

His heart ached within him at the fallen state of humanity. A burning desire to elevate degraded fellow beings and bring them round to the path of righteousness agitated his bosom. He would often retire to the cave of Ḥirā and fervently pray to God, shedding tears, for the regeneration of mankind.

CHAPTER III

THE DIVINE CALL

"Read in the name of thy Lord Who creates – Creates man from a clot, Read and thy Lord is Most Generous, Who taught by the *pen, Taught man what he knew not"* –
96: 1-5.

First revelation

Shortly before he reached the age of forty, Muḥammad, peace and blessings of Allah be upon him, began to immerse himself more frequently in solitary meditation. Retiring to the cave of Hirā, he would give himself up to Divine contemplation for days. In the meanwhile he received many visions, which came to fulfilment to the very letter.

While thus absorbed in Divine worship in the Ḥirā, the angel Gabriel appeared before him one night, in the month of Ramaḍān – it was the 609th year of the Christian era – and told him to read out. "I do not know how to read," was the Holy Prophet's reply. Then the angel hugged him close to his bosom and asked him again to read. Three times the angel repeated the request to read, as many times the Holy Prophet pleaded his inability to do so. Then the angel recited the verses quoted above. And so did the Holy Prophet. This was the first day when the heavy responsibility of prophethood was placed on his shoulders. The right path in the quest of which he had been so long engaged was at last revealed to him. The light for which he had been eagerly searching came to him. It was, however, made known to him at the same time that the stupendous charge of human reformation was to rest on his shoulders. Weak as man is by nature, he is apt to feel the weight even of an ordinary responsibility. Reformation of mankind is the heaviest task that can be placed on human shoulders. Moses was commissioned for the reformation of a single nation; yet he found it too much for him single-handed and cried for Divine help: "Give to me a helper"! The Holy Prophet Muḥammad was charged with the regeneration of the whole of mankind, sunk into the lowest depths of degradation. Yet his strong heart did not give way for a single moment to the slightest wavering, notwithstanding the almost crushing weight of the responsibility. He shouldered it all by himself, relying solely upon the help of God. He asked for no assistant. But Divine inspiration is an extraordinary phenomenon and beyond average human experience. It necessitates absolute detachment from one's environment. At the time of this experience the entire corporeal frame of the recipient is possessed with Divine Power. Even when the Holy Prophet grew used to the experience, his body would perspire profusely and become very weighty. One of his companions reports that on one such occasion, the Holy Prophet's thigh happened to be on his knee. It became so heavy that he feared that his knee would be crushed. The first experience of inspiration told all the more heavily on his body and caused him to tremble.

Shivering he went home; his hands and feet grew cold and he asked Khadījah to wrap him up. After a short while when the shaking, with its inevitable accompaniment of a feeling of fear, disappeared, he related the whole experience to his wife. On hearing his account, she encouraged him with the inspiring words that God would never desert him and that he would succeed in his mission. She spoke of his many virtues, his treatment of his kith and kin, his helping the poor, the helpless, the orphan and the widow, his hospitality and his vindication of right under the most trying circumstances. "How – she assured him – was it possible that one possessed of so many virtues should ever come to grief?"

Waraqah ibn Naufal was Khadījah's cousin. Wearying of idolatry he was on the look-out for a true religion and had at length embraced Christianity. Khadījah was well aware of her kinsman's mental anguish for lack of a religion that would carry conviction to a heart yearning after truth. Probably she had heard him talk of the appearance of the Promised Prophet, the Comforter whose advent had been foretold by Jesus. As soon as she found the Holy Prophet Muḥammad called to that office, she took him to her cousin out of sympathy for the latter, who had lost his eyesight and was unable to move, aged as he was. No sooner did Waraqah hear what inspiration the Holy Prophet had received and how, than he spontaneously exclaimed: "This is the very angel God sent down to Moses"! – referring obviously to the prophecy by Moses. Then he said: "Would that I might be alive when thou art exiled by thy people!" The Holy Prophet asked him in surprise if he would be thus treated by his kith and kin. "Yes," replied Waraqah. "This is the treatment meted out to every prophet." Soon, thereafter, Waraqah passed away. For this very confirmation on his part, of the truth of the Holy Prophet's mission he is regarded as one of the companions of the Prophet.

Temporary cessation of revelation

After the first revelation in the cave of Hirā, Gabriel did not visit the Holy Prophet for some time. This is known as the period of *fatrat al-waḥy* or the cessation of revelation. There is a great divergence of opinion as to the duration of this period. Some say it was two or three years long. But the version of Ibn 'Abbās, that it lasted but for a short time, is more reliable and is corroborated by historical evidence. The story that during this period the Prophet would go out to the tops of mountains with the intention of hurling himself headlong is sheer nonsense. According to the established criteria of the authenticity of reports this is not reliable, for Zuhrī from whom the report has come down, belonged to a later generation, and a report to be reliable must be traced right back to some of the Prophet's companions. Hence little weight can be attached to it. Moreover, the idea that the Prophet was thinking of committing suicide is utterly incompatible with the ideas which ruled uppermost in his heart. From his early age his heart had been glowing with the desire for human reformation. Now that the very mission was entrusted to him, is it conceivable that he should have thought of suicide? If the Prophet was observed doing anything unusual, it was only the bare fact that he would retire to the mountains oftener than before; but we must not jump to the preposterous conclusion, unwarranted by evidence, that he went there to commit suicide. He used to go to the mountains long before he received the revelation. Having a meditative turn of mind, he would seek the solitude of mountains, a retreat best suited for calm uninterrupted contemplation. But there is no reason whatever to suppose that he went to the mountains in order to commit suicide. If he roamed about in a state of greater perplexity than before, and this is the utmost that may be alleged, the reason is not far to seek. The Divine Light, which he had been so eagerly seeking, disappeared as soon as it had flashed upon his mind. This made him all the more restless. All the more did his heart long to hear once again the word of God. It was in search of what was so dear to his heart that he would go out to the mountains. It was done with no idea of suicide. Every incident of his subsequent as well as his previous life belies the conjecture. In the face of the most disappointing circumstances, his faith in Divine help never wavered for one moment, nor did he ever yield by a hair's breadth to the most overwhelming difficulties.

Second revelation

At length, there came an end to the period of cessation. To the Prophet the period looked unusually long; for it was a period of separation from One he loved with all his heart. It is in this sense that the period has been spoken of by some as having been prolonged. As a matter of fact, the cessation of revelation was based on Divine providence. The pressure attendant upon it had already told upon the Prophet's physique. His body might not stand a rapid repetition. The interval, therefore, was necessary for the sake of his physical health. Even after a lapse of time, which could in no case exceed six months, the revelation was accompanied with the same feeling, though not in the same intensity. Again he asked Khadījah, now less awe-stricken than before, to wrap him up. This was the first time he was required to set about his mission in right earnest: "O thou who wrappest thyself up! Arise and warn"[1] With this command began another stage in the life of the Prophet - that of announcing the word of God and delivering His message to all.

The early converts

The foremost to profess faith in the truth[2] of the Holy Prophet's mission was his wife Khadījah. Never for a moment

1 The Qur'ān, 74 : 1-2.
2 See Footnote #2 on following page

did she entertain the slightest doubt as to the truth of his claim to prophethood. In moments of depression, she proved a never-failing source of solace to him. Fifteen years before when she did not yet stand to him in the relation of a wife, she had discerned in him noble qualities which had deeply impressed her. And this early impression had grown deeper and deeper the more she came to know of him, through their greater intimacy as wife and husband. When the Holy Prophet received Divine inspiration for the first time and was in a state of perplexity as to how he should accomplish the mighty task of reformation set before him, this virtuous lady consoled him with the genuine testimony of her own heart. A man of the Holy Prophet's lofty character and broad sympathies, she observed, could not possibly come to grief. With intimate knowledge of his innermost thoughts, she felt convinced that he alone was the right person to have received the Divine summons for human reformation. Khadījah was thus the first as well as the most earnest believer in the mission of the Holy Prophet.

Next to Khadījah comes Waraqah on the list of early believers. He passed away during the cessation period, before the Prophet was called upon to preach his religion, and was thus deprived of the opportunity formally to declare his faith. Nevertheless, he had borne testimony, at the interview already referred to, arranged by Khadījah between him and the Holy Prophet, to the fact that the latter was undoubtedly the Promised Prophet. This is enough to entitle him to a place in the list of believers.

Then follows Abū Bakr, a Makkan notable. He was held in high esteem for his soundness of judgment and commanded great respect among his compatriots. Long before the Holy Prophet received the Call, Abū Bakr had been on intimate terms with him. His faith in the righteousness of the Holy Prophet was as implicit as that of Khadījah. Like her's, his faith never wavered for a minute. No sooner did he hear of the Holy Prophet Muḥammad's claim to prophethood, than he made an open profession that he was indeed a Prophet of God. He comes at the top of the list of male believers.

'Alī, the son of the Holy Prophet's uncle, Abū Ṭālib, was also one of the earliest believers. He knew the Holy Prophet

2 "And the foremost are the foremost - these are drawn nigh (to Allāh)" (Qur'ān, 56 : 10-11)

very intimately, for he had been brought up under his loving care. Knowing that the Holy Prophet's veracity was unquestionable, he did not hesitate for a moment to accept him.

Zaid ibn Hāri<u>th</u> was a liberated slave of the Holy Prophet. His deep attachment to his master has already been touched upon. He gave preference to the company of the Holy Prophet to that of his kith and kin, refusing to accompany his father back to his home. He was also one of the earliest believers.

These people were on most intimate terms with the Holy Prophet and had the greatest access to his private life, and they had also the most implicit belief in the sincerity of his claim to the prophetical office. Not one of them entertained the slightest doubt as to the genuineness of his mission. They had known him to be truthful, *Al-Amīn*, throughout his life so far. Never during the long period of forty years, before the Call came to him had they heard the Holy Prophet tell a lie. Thus it was inconceivable to them that he should have fabricated a lie in laying claim to prophethood. Surely they could not look upon him as an imposter. Being his associates from his early days, they had the opportunity for thorough insight into the innermost traits of his character. The more a person knew of the Holy Prophet, the more he was enamoured of him, and the more forward he was to accept his claim. This aspect of his character constrains even critics like Muir and Sprenger to admit that Muḥammad, peace and blessings of Allah be on him, was quite sincere in his claim. He had full confidence in the Divine character of his revelations. If there were even the shadow of hypocrisy in the claim, the first to suspect and reject him would have been those so intimately connected with him. Yet they were the foremost to accept him as a true Prophet.

Other important converts

As soon as Abū Bakr embraced Islām, he set about preaching the truth to others. So deep-rooted was his faith in the righteousness of the Holy Prophet's claim! At a very early period, men of eminent position such as 'U<u>th</u>mān, Zubair, 'Abd al-Raḥmān, Sa'd and Ṭalḥah, who subsequently figured prominently not only in the history of Islām but also in world history, accepted Islām through his earnest missionary zeal. Of those belonging to a humbler status, Bilāl, Yāsir, his wife

Sumayyah and his son ‘Ammār also joined the faithful at this early period. ‘Abd Allāh ibn Mas‘ūd and Khabbāb were also among the early converts and so was Arqam, whose house was made the centre of the Holy Prophet’s missionary activities, about the fourth year after the Call. Within the first three years as many as forty persons accepted the faith. This fact belies the conjecture that the Cessation period extended over three years. For if that conjecture were true, the commencement of the propagation of the faith would have to be relegated to the fourth year whereas the historical fact stands that Islām had won quite a considerable following by that time. It was this steady growth of Islām that alarmed the Makkans and aroused them to bitter opposition. For this reason the Holy Prophet had to betake himself to a quarter removed from the hostile atmosphere to carry on his mission more peacefully. Arqam’s house was selected for the purpose.

The number of Muslims continued to grow, and the conversion of some prominent men from among the Quraish added to the strength of the small brotherhood. Of these the most noteworthy was Ḥamzah, the Holy Prophet’s uncle and foster brother. He was a man of martial spirit and fond of sport. On account of his high morals he enjoyed great esteem and regard among his compatriots. He cherished special love for the Holy Prophet. His conversion came about in the following manner. One day, Abū Jahl was as usual persecuting the Holy Prophet when Ḥamzah’s handmaid appeared on the scene and was shocked to see the cruel treatment. Ḥamzah had been out on a hunting trip. On his return home the maid related the incident to him. He was already impressed with the character of his nephew. Now that he heard how pitilessly he was being subjected to all manner of ill-treatment, he was deeply moved. He thought it unchivalrous in the extreme not to stand by a righteous man such as the Holy Prophet was. So he made up his mind to throw in his lot on the side of Truth and defend it with might and main. Straightaway he made for the Ka‘bah where Abū Jahl and his partisans were holding a meeting to wage a campaign against Islām, and announced his acceptance of Islām.

The second great man to prove a tower of strength to Islām was ‘Umar. A man of fiery temper, he was bitter in his opposition to Islām. He made up his mind one day to put the Holy

Prophet, the root-cause of the new movement, to the sword and thus put an end to the whole trouble. With this intent he took up his sword and made for the Holy Prophet's house. As yet he did not know that his own sister, Fāṭimah, and her husband Sa'īd, had both joined the faith. On his way, a Muslim happened to meet him and, noticing that he was out for mischief, asked him where he was going. "To kill Muḥammad," replied 'Umar. The Muslim told him he had better set his own house in order first and then think of killing the Holy Prophet, for his sister and cousin had both embraced Islām. On hearing of the conversion of his own relations, he was much enraged. He took his way towards their house first to settle accounts with them. It so happened that Khabbāb was reciting a passage from the Qur'ān to them when 'Umar entered their house. Out of fear they concealed the sheets on which the passage was written. But 'Umar had ample proof of their conversion. He had overheard them recite the Qur'ān. No sooner did he step into the house than he shouted at them saying he had come to know of their apostasy and, taking hold of Sa'īd, began to belabour him. His sister, trying to save her husband from his wrath, interposed; but she too received injuries and was besmeared with blood. At length, she broke out in a defiant tone: "Do what you will. We have professed Islām." This bold front on the part of his sister in spite of maltreatment had an immensely pacifying effect on 'Umar. Forthwith he ceased beating them and asked for the sheets of the Qur'ān to be shown to him. His sister, fearing lest he should offer any insult to the Holy Book, felt reluctant; but on his assurance that he would no more hurt their religious susceptibilities, she handed over the sheets, which contained the chapter entitled *Ṭāhā*. This is how it opens: "O man! We have not revealed the Qur'ān to thee that thou mayest be unsuccessful. Nay, it is a reminder to him who fears. A revelation from Him Who created the earth and the high heavens." As he listened, he could no longer resist the force of the truth of the Qur'ān. It made him think of the foolishness of hostility and opposition to what was so beautiful and noble. Khabbāb who had out of fear kept concealed all this time, was not slow to seize upon the psychological moment. Coming out, he began preaching to him. The mighty 'Umar could not withstand the spiritual gravitation of Islam. Enquiring of Khabbāb as to the whereabouts of the Holy Prophet, he went straight off to Arqam's house which, sheltered, at that moment, the Holy Prophet with forty of his companions, male as well as female. 'Umar knocked at the door, from which one of the inmates peeped to see who it was. Seeing 'Umar with his sword hanging about his neck, he was filled with fear, suspecting he was there on a foul errand. The Holy Prophet, however, told him to open the door and let him in. On his appearance, the Holy Prophet had hardly addressed a word to him before he proclaimed: "O Messenger of Allāh! I declare faith in Allāh and His Prophet." This filled the whole of the Muslim congregation with intense joy, and all proclaimed aloud the glory of Allah till the surrounding hills resounded to their shouts of *Allāh-u-Akbar* (Allah is Great).

Religious humanities

'Umar's conversion proved a tower of strength to the young Muslim brotherhood, too tender yet to face the storm of opposition. It was in the sixth year of the Holy Prophet's mission that these two important additions, Ḥamzah and 'Umar were made. So far, the Muslims had not ventured to come out into the open. They had confined their religious activities to the four walls of Arqam's house. Now that 'Umar had declared his adherence to Islam, they felt strong enough to come out and say their prayers publicly in the sacred house of Ka'bah. In the meantime many from the humbler class had also joined. Those coming from higher families would sometimes manage to escape the persecutions of the opponents; but the poor slave converts were in a very helpless and miserable plight. They were ruthlessly put to all manner of tortures, with nobody to protect them from the wrath of their masters. One of the virtues that constitute the sublimity of Abū Bakr's character was that he freely spent his wealth in purchasing these persecuted slaves from their cruel masters and set them free. Bilāl, Āmir, Lubainah, Zunnīrah, Nahdiyah, and Umm 'Ubais were some of those who owed their freedom to Abū Bakr's generosity.

It is a striking feature of the early spread of Islām that it was limited mostly to the common hewer of wood and drawer of water. The aristocracy for the most part turned a deaf ear to the message. An incident narrated in the Qur'ān throws light on the Divine purpose why the upper classes were deprived of the blessings of Islām in the days of its infancy. The Holy Prophet was one day busy preaching to some of the Quraish nobility when a poor blind man, Ibn Umm Maktūm by name, made his appearance. Not knowing that the Holy Prophet was busy, he put him a few questions, expecting thereby to attract attention. The Holy Prophet, occupied as he was with important talk, naturally did not like interruption. He did not scold him nor did he utter a word of displeasure, but a shadow of disapproval passed over his forehead. But the Almighty God Who wanted him to attain to the highest pinnacle of morals as well as manners did not let this incident pass unnoticed. Forthwith came the warning through Divine revelation: "He frowned and turned away, because the blind man came to him."[1] It went on to say that it was just possible that that very blind man might benefit by his preaching; for the Qur'ān was a code of life whereby humble people could be raised to the greatest heights. The advancement of the cause of Islām was bound up with the poor and the weak who, in their struggle to uphold the cause of Islām, would themselves be glorified. And as a matter of fact this was the underlying Divine purpose why the light of Islām was hailed mostly by the weaker element of the inhabitants of Makkah. They were intended to serve as a concrete illustration of how ordinary people, supported by the Divine hand, can accomplish what is beyond the power of the most mighty. And we know it for certain, in the light of history, that not only did Islām enable the same class of the weak and the despised to wield the sceptre of royal authority, but at the same time raised them to the highest plane of morality and made them torch bearers of learning, art, science and philosophy at a time when the world was enshrouded in the darkness of ignorance. Can there be a greater testimony to the uplifting force of Islamic teachings?

Revelation was not a voice from within

The incident of the blind man, however insignificant, throws a flood of light on another problem of great moment. It furnishes data to determine the much-disputed nature of the Divine revelation of which the Holy Prophet was the recipient. Was it a voice from within his own heart, or was it a mes-

1 The Qur'ān, 80 : 1,2.

sage received from an external source? The revelation made in consequence of his inattention to the blind man bears testimony to the fact that it could not possibly be the outcome of the inner workings of the Holy Prophet's own mind. It consists of a Divine admonition reproaching him for his ignoring the blind man. Nobody can afford to have his faults brought to public notice if he can avoid it, however penitent he might feel within himself. The Holy Prophet, notwithstanding the magnanimity of his heart, could have no special need to give general publicity to an omission on his part, however immaterial. This shows that it was some external source from which the revelation came - the Divine Being Himself. Cheerful submission to the supreme will of God was the key-note of his life. In addition to establishing conclusively the external source of revelation, the incident speaks volumes for the Holy Prophet's entire self-effacement in submission to the will of God.

CHAPTER IV

THE STORMY OPPOSITION

"Do men think that they will be left alone on saying, We believe, and will not be tried?" - 29 : 2.

Whenever the Divine will inspires a band of righteous people to work as torch-bearers of Truth to a corrupt humanity, there never fails to appear at the same time a band of those who pitch themselves in deadly opposition to them, and inflict upon them all kinds of trouble and torture. And in truth the storm of opposition is absolutely indispensable. The persecutions to which they are subjected serve as a crucial test of the sincerity of their motives. They unhesitatingly put up with humiliations, endure hardships and cruelties, but never for a moment give up the truth for which they stand. In fact, they live if they can, for the Truth; and die, if they must, for the Truth. Besides, afflictions constitute the only training ground for fostering virtues of steadfastness and perseverance, without which man cannot attain to moral perfection. Unless one is hemmed in on all sides by overwhelming obstacles and visited with hardships and privations, one cannot cultivate these qualities. Adversities that befall such people are in fact blessings in disguise, which conduce to their moral advancement. Over and above these, there is a third object. The Almighty God wants to bring home to mankind that a plant tended by the Divine hand, however slender it may look survives the most furious blasts of hostile winds. Consequently, in accordance with this Divine law, the Holy Prophet and his companions had to suffer untold troubles at the hands of the opponents.

The Holy Prophet persecuted

In the beginning, Makkan opposition to the message of Islām took the form of sneering and jeering at the Holy

Prophet. They did not attach much importance to the movement, thinking that it would die out in due course. It was treated with contempt and indifference as being unworthy of serious attention. All that the believers received at the hands of the Makkans in those days was ridicule and disdain. Resort to violence was not yet thought necessary. When they passed by the believers, they would laugh and wink at them in derision.[1] Sometimes they would call the Holy Prophet an idle visionary, given to poetic fancies, destined to come to naught as a matter of course.[2] There was something wrong with his brain, they would say. But as men of light and position gradually gathered round him, the Makkans were awakened to a sense of danger. Now they did not content themselves with indifference and ridicule, but took to active violence. Once, when the Holy Prophet was saying his prayers in the Ka'bah, lying prostrate, Abū Jahl placed the dirty foetus of a she-camel on his neck. As he used to go out of his house for prayers at dawn, one way adopted to annoy him was that branches of prickly shrubs were strewn in his way, so that in the darkness he should become entangled in them. Sometimes dust was thrown at him; sometimes he was pelted with stones. One day, a number of men from among the Quraish nobility fell upon him. One, 'Uqbah ibn Abī Mu'ait threw his mantle around his neck and twisted it till he was on the point of strangulation. Abū Bakr, appearing at the scene intervened and rescued him, saying: "Do you mean to kill a man merely because he says that God is his Lord?"

Slave converts tortured

The brunt of the oppression had to be borne by those not coming of some family of note among the Quraish and especially by the slaves, male as well as female. These were subjected to the most cruel tortures. Islamic teachings, however, possessed a charm too strong for all these afflictions. They would part with life itself rather than give up Islām, which had taken deep root in their hearts. Bilāl, the Abyssinian, was tortured in a most heartless manner by his master to make him renounce Islām. His oppressor made him lie flat on the burn-

1 The Qur'ān, 83 : 30, 34; 2 Ibid., 52 : 30.

ing ground in the scorching heat of the Arabian midday sun. Heavy slabs of stone were then placed on his chest. Notwithstanding such extremely painful torments he would loudly repeat, almost in a state of senselessness *"Aḥad"* (One), *i.e.*, there is but one God. Ammār's father, Yāsir, and his mother, Sumayyah, were persecuted in a most barbarous way. Yāsir's legs were tied to two camels and the beasts were driven in opposite directions. He was brutally torn to pieces. Sumayyah was killed in a similarly brutal but far more disgraceful manner. Lubainah was the hand-maid of 'Umar. The latter in his pre-conversion days used to beat her till he was tired. Then he would say: "I leave thee now not because I pity thee but because I am tired of beating thee."

Even converts of high birth were not spared. They were persecuted by their own kinsmen. 'Uthmān came of a noble family and occupied a high social position. Yet his uncle tied him with a rope and gave him a severe beating. 'Umar's treatment of his cousin and sister has already been described. Zubair was wrapped up in a matting and made to inhale smoke. Abū Bakr was not immune. They were, one and all, subjected to one form of cruelty or another; but no amount of suffering could drive the love of Islām out of their hearts. The Makkans themselves were struck with wonder at such steadfast adherence. But their fortitude only added fuel to the fire of their persecutors' rage, and the latter resorted to still more bitter persecutions.

First emigration of Abyssinia

By the fifth year after the Call, the Holy Prophet had collected round him a band of over fifty devoted comrades. A common faith consolidated them into a brotherhood which was cemented all the more closely by Makkan persecutions. Besides, their numerical strength was growing day by day. The Holy Prophet was so tender-hearted that his heart would ache at the sight of pain, even of his foes. How could he then bear the sight of the tortures of his own friends? Doubtless, these friends were a source of great strength to himself, and of much good to his cause. He could ill afford to dispense with a single one of them. Nevertheless when he saw that the Makkans were daily growing in their bitterness and cruelty, he advised Muslims to betake themselves to a place of safety.[1] Single-handed would he brave the worst storms of the Makkans' opposition rather than see his companions subjected to such ruthless tortures. He had no anxiety or dread of his infuriated foe on his own account. He, therefore, advised his companions to seek shelter in Abyssinia, saying: "There is a land where no one is wronged - a land of justice. Stay there until it pleases Allāh to open for you a way out of these difficulties." The inhabitants of Abyssinia as well as their king, called the Negus, were Christians by faith. The first batch of emigrants, numbering eleven, was formed to sail for Abyssinia. Four of them were accompanied by their wives, 'Uthmān with his wife Ruqayyah, the Prophet's daughter, among them. In the month of Rajab in the fifth year of the Call, the party left Makkah, some mounted, others on foot. Arriving at the port they hurriedly embarked and left the shores of their homeland to seek safety elsewhere.

The Quraish, as soon as they heard of their departure, despatched men post-haste to bring them back. To their disappointment, however, the vessel had already left. But this was not the end of their wrath. They were anxious that Islām should not get a foothold anywhere. It was at last decided to send a delegation to the Negus to ask him not to give the Muslims shelter and to hand them over to the Makkans. 'Abd Allāh ibn Rabī' and 'Amr ibn 'Ās were chosen for the mission, and they went to Abyssinia with handsome presents. The first step they took on arrival was to enlist the sympathies of the priestly class. They told them that the Muslims had set up a religion which was antagonistic to Christianity, and supplemented this appeal to their religious prejudice by making them valuable presents. Thus they succeeded in prevailing upon clerics to exert their influence with the King on their behalf, and made their way to the court of the Negus. They put up a claim for the extradition of the Muslim immigrants who, they alleged, were guilty of an innovation in religion in opposition to their ancestral faith as well as to Christianity. The King thereupon summoned the Muslims to his court demanding of them to submit what defence they could, to the

1 "And those who flee for Allāh's sake after they are oppressed, We shall certainly give them a good abode in the world" (16 : 41).

charge of heresy brought against them. On this, one of them Ja'far ibn Abī Ṭālib, rose, and thus addressed the King:

> *"O King! we were an ignorant people, given to idolatry. We used to eat corpses even of dead animals, and to do all kinds of disgraceful things. We did not make good our obligations to our relations, and ill-treated our neighbours. The strong among us would thrive at the expense of the weak, till, at last, God sent a prophet for our reformation. His descent, his righteousness, his integrity and his piety are well-known to us. He called us to the worship of God, and exhorted us to give up idolatry and stone worship. He enjoined us to speak truth, to make good our trusts, to respect ties of kinship, and to do good to our neighbours. He taught us to shun everything foul and to avoid bloodshed. He forbade all manner of indecent things - telling lies, misappropriating orphans' belongings, and bringing false accusations against the chastity of women. So we believed in him, followed him, and acted upon his teachings. Thereupon our people began to wrong us, to subject us to tortures, thinking that we might thus abjure our faith and revert to idolatry. When, however, their cruelties exceeded all bounds, we came out to seek an asylum in your country, where we hope we shall come to no harm."*

After this Ja'far recited to him a passage from the Holy Qur'ān, which touched his heart. The Negus told the Quraish embassy that he would by no means hand over the refugees to them. Thus disappointed they hit upon another plan. Next day, they tried to incite the King by telling him that the heretics did not believe in the Divinity of Jesus. But in this too their hopes were frustrated. The Muslims confessed they did not look upon Jesus as God but as a prophet. The Negus, picking up a straw and pointing to it, said: "Jesus is in fact not even this much more than the Muslims have described him to be." The Quraish delegation was thus unsuccessful.

It is noteworthy that the Quraish felt much upset at the Muslims' emigration to Abyssinia. They pursued them first to the port to capture them, and, being disappointed, followed them to the court of the Negus. What, after all, made them so ill at ease? Was it the Muslims' anti-idolatrous propaganda that turned the Quraish so dead against them? But the emigrants were now too far off to offend their susceptibilities by speaking ill of their idols. Assuredly, the animosity aroused through religious differences had by now become personal. They could not tolerate that the Muslims, whom they had driven from their homes, should flourish anywhere. They were bent upon their destruction and therefore went all the way to the Negus to cause them trouble. For precisely the same reason they allowed the Holy Prophet and his companions no rest even at Madīnah, where they had subsequently emigrated. At Madīnah, there was no power to shield the Muslim refugees against their blood thirsty enemies, the Quraish, who, therefore, were emboldened to extirpate them with the sword. The instinct of self-preservation roused the Muslims to strike a blow in self-defence. This was the beginning of Islamic wars, entered upon as a purely defensive measure. The Quraish did not let them alone even when they had driven them from their hearth and home. The Muslims were therefore left with no alternative but to turn at bay and face their persecutors manfully. Nevertheless, there are critics who, blindfolding their eyes to solid historical facts, ascribe the initiatory steps in these battles to the Holy Prophet, and on that account stigmatize Islām as a religion of the sword. Nothing, however, can be farther from the truth. The events in connection with the Abyssinian Emigration, as set forth above, throw enough light on the fact, that, heresy or no heresy, the Quraish were bent upon the utter annihilation of the Muslim brotherhood at all costs.

The Second Emigration

When the Quraishite delegation returned unsuccessful from Abyssinia, their rage knew no bounds. They continued their persecutions with added fury. So far they had been viewing the Muslims' fortitude under such cruelties with great astonishment. But the Abyssinian emigration gave them conclusive proof that the Muslims were ready to run all risks and undergo every form of hardship in the cause of Islām. They would shrink from no danger in the path of Allāh. Moreover, when the Muslims remaining at Makkah came to know of the generous protection extended by the Negus to their brethren, a number of them left for Abyssinia the next year. This is known as the second Emigration to Abyssinia. The Quraish did their utmost to check this tide of emigration, but in vain. Besides children, as many as one hundred and one, both male and female, fled to Abyssinia. They settled there, all of them, with the exception of 'Uthmān and his wife, who soon returned to Makkah. It was not until seven years after the Holy Prophet's flight from Makkah that they rejoined their Muslim brethren at Madīnah. In accordance with the Truce of Ḥudaibiyah in the sixth year of Hijra there was to be a state of truce between Muslims and the Quraish for ten years. This provided a certain amount of security for the Muslims in the land of Arabia and made it possible for the Abyssinian Muslims to come back to their kith and kin. It also furnishes a clue to the fact that even in Madīnah, the Muslims were not in a state of safety until 7 A.H., when the Truce of Ḥudaibiyah brought them a brief respite.

The sympathetic treatment accorded to the Muslims by the Negus was gratefully reciprocated by the former. During their sojourn in the kingdom when hostilities broke out with a rival state, Muslims ungrudgingly placed their quota of service at his disposal. They also prayed to God for his victory. This shows how grateful a people they were. From that early period they had for their motto the Quranic verse: "Nothing but good must be the return for good."[1]

Alleged compromise with idolatry

An incident in connection with the First Emigration to Abyssinia is noteworthy. Some time later the chapter entitled *al-Najm*[2] was revealed to the Prophet, at the end of which comes the verse enjoining prostration before God. The Holy Prophet, while reciting this chapter, prostrated as soon as he came to the verse which says: "Then prostrate before God and adore (Him)".[3] According to an authentic report, the idolatrous Makkans present there also joined in the prostration, for they professed faith in God notwithstanding their worship of idols. A perverted version of this incident has been given by some. The Holy Prophet, they allege, thinking it expedient to make a compromise with the idolaters, allowed in this chapter a concession to idol-worshippers. And this is why the idolaters too bowed down in prostration. But the report on which this allegation is based is absolutely unwarranted. There is no trustworthy account of the incident except the one referred to above. The fact that some Abyssinian emigrants returned home does not show that a compromise had been effected.

1 The Qur'ān, 55 : 60.; 2 Ibid., Chap. 53.; 3 Ibid., 53 : 62.

The news of the disbelievers' prostration may, on the other hand, have created an impression that they had accepted Islām, and, the news having reached the Abyssinian Muslims, some of them may have come back to their motherland. But as a matter of fact, the few emigrants who returned to Makkah did so with a view to informing the rest of their brethren of the peace and liberty they enjoyed under the rule of the Negus, and thus persuading them to accompany them thither. This is what actually happened, and it resulted in the second Emigration to Abyssinia.

Public preaching

Attempts to suppress the propagation of Islām were not confined to the persecutions to which the Holy Prophet and his comrades were subjected.[1] Many and varied were the ways adopted to extinguish the Divine light. Preaching was in the beginning carried on in secret. But soon the Holy Prophet received Divine revelation to promulgate his commission publicly and to warn his near relations.[2] Thereupon he had openly to proclaim the Divine message. Climbing one day on Mt. Ṣafā, he called out to each one of the Quraishite tribes till they all assembled there. "Have you," enquired the Holy Prophet, "ever heard me tell a lie?" In one voice they replied that they had ever known him to be righteous and trustworthy. "If I tell you that hidden behind this mountain is a large army ready to attack you" enquired the Holy Prophet, "would you believe me?" "Certainly," was the unanimous reply "for we have never heard you tell a lie." Then he announced to them the word of God, exhorted them to give up idolatry, to eschew all forms of evil, to believe in the oneness of God, and to come to the path of virtue. At this they all became furious, Abū Lahab in particular behaving most rudely. By and by this man's enmity to the Holy Prophet became extremely bitter. He and his wife tormented and persecuted him in every way possible. In the days of pilgrimage when people from all parts of Arabia met together, the Holy Prophet used to move about

1 "And if We had not made thee firm, thou mightest have indeed inclined to them." (The Qur'ān, 17 : 74).
2 The Qur'ān, 15 : 94 ; 26 : 214.

among them communicating his message. Wherever he went, Abū Lahab followed close upon his heels, warning the people not to take him seriously, for, he said, he was insane.

First deputation to Abū Ṭālib

When the Quraish saw that neither oppression nor obstacles succeeded in suppressing the Islamic movement, that its adherents did not mind undergoing any amount of hardship, and that they would rather suffer exile than give up Islām, they secretly resolved to make away with the Holy Prophet. Consequently, every effort was made to put an end to his life in an underhand manner, failing which the Quraish made up their mind to make an open attempt on his life. But, according to the social code of Arabia, every tribe was in honour bound to protect each one of its members. An attempt to take the life of the Holy Prophet, it was apprehended, might lead to civil war. It was thus necessary to obtain the consent of Abū Ṭālib, the Prophet's uncle, before taking the proposed bloody step. Accordingly, a deputation of Quraish chiefs, including Abū Jahl, waited upon Abū Ṭālib in this connection. In order to win him over to their wicked plot, they addressed him thus: "Your nephew slights our gods, finds fault with our ancestral religion, calls us and our forefathers ignorant and misguided. You should deal with him yourself or permit us to settle accounts with him. You are as much duty-bound to vindicate the honour of our common faith as we are." Abū Ṭālib, however, put them off with evasive though polite words. Obviously the accusations brought against the Holy Prophet were highly exaggerated. He never abused their gods, for the Holy Qur'ān positively forbids doing so: "Abuse not those whom they call upon besides Allāh."[1] The Holy Qur'ān, intact as it is to-day, in all its original purity, may be consulted from one end to the other to see that it contains not a single word of abuse against the gods of the infidels. All it says concerning them is that they can do no good, nor can they avert any harm, and that polytheism and idolatry are evil courses.[2]

1 The Qur'ān, 6 : 108.; 2 The Qur'ān, 25 : 55.

Second deputation

The Holy Prophet, however, delivered his message, as usual, and as days rolled by, many a heart was deeply impressed with the truth of Islām. The Quraish, finding their previous warning to Abū Ṭālib utterly ignored, firmly resolved this time to press the point to a decisive issue. They reminded Abū Ṭālib of their first representation and told him they could no longer tolerate the state of things. He must either withdraw his protection from the Holy Prophet or make common cause with him, so that they might fight it out to a finish. This ultimatum precipitated a very critical situation. Abū Ṭālib found himself on the horns of a dilemma. The prospect of a war against his own kith and kin on the one hand, and the deep attachment he cherished for his nephew on the other, made it hard for him to decide which course to adopt. In this state of perplexity, he sent for the Holy Prophet and explained the entire situation to him. "Have pity on me" he said, "and do not charge me with a responsibility too heavy for me. I am not a match for the united opposition of the whole of the Quraish."

The Prophet's strong stand

A critical situation! The entire clan was thirsting for his blood and, but for the intervention of Abū Tālib, would have taken his life in broad daylight. But alas! Abū Ṭālib's door was also about to close against him. Now there was no earthly protection to shield him against the wrath of his enemies. His companions, who would have laid down their lives for his sake were far off on the continent of Africa. Could all this mean anything other than sure and imminent destruction? It would have been but human had the Holy Prophet's heart sank within him. It would have been but natural, had the instinct of self-preservation reconciled him to the expedience of coming to a compromise with his opponents and thus, having saved his life, betaken himself to some other place and there propagated his faith. Did any such inclination, perfectly excusable under circumstances so critical, creep into his heart? No, not a shadow of it. He had an unshakable conviction in Divine protection. He would not yield an inch of ground in regard to his mission which was in fact the be-all and end-all of his life. No sooner did the above words issue from Abū Ṭālib's lips than he declared without the least hesitation: "O uncle! should they place the sun in my right hand and the moon in my left in order to make me renounce this mission, it shall not be. I will never give it up until it pleases God to make it a triumph or I perish in the attempt." But, conscious of the disappointment his attitude must have caused to his uncle, who had so tenderly brought him up and had been protecting him at great risk, tears welled up in his eyes and he departed with a sad heart. Abū Ṭālib had not abjured his ancestral form of worship, but of the Holy Prophet's high character he was much enamoured. It was far easier for him to face death rather than leave the Holy Prophet alone. Forthwith he sent for the Holy Prophet again, and thus assured him: "Do whatever you will. Under no circumstances will I desert you."

Third deputation

The Quraish had little doubt about Abū Ṭālib's yielding to their united demand. They were much surprised when they heard of his determination to stand by the Holy Prophet. An internecine war among themselves, they thought, was fraught with grave danger. It might ruin the sovereign authority of their clan for good. This time, therefore, they made an attempt to prevail upon Abū Ṭālib by offering him a lure instead of forcing him with a threat. Taking 'Ammārah ibn Walīd a handsome youth, along with them, they asked Abū Ṭālib to adopt him as his son and hand over Muḥammad (peace and blessings of Allāh be upon him) to them for execution for his offence against their established ancestral religion. "What an amazing proposal!" replied Abū Ṭālib. "You want me to take charge of your boy to bring him up, while you have mine to be put to death. This can never be." The Quraish were thus once again disappointed. Apprehending lest they should resort to violent measures against his family, the Banū Hāshim, Abū Ṭālib summoned all members of the family, and warned them of the danger. It was unanimously agreed that the Holy Prophet would in no case be handed over to the Quraish, whatever measures they might adopt against the Banū Hāshim. With the solitary exception of Abū Lahab, who had joined hands with the enemy, the entire family was prepared to take up arms in defence of the Holy Prophet, so great was the regard in which he was held by the Banū Hāshim. They all loved him for his lofty morals.

Notwithstanding religious differences, they were ready to protect him at the risk of their own lives.

Quraish offer leadership and wealth

The Quraish, however, had not yet exhausted their resources for reaching a settlement without resort to bloodshed. They had yet another card to play. Persecution had proved futile, but it struck them that allurements, offered direct to the Holy Prophet, might yet succeed. A deputation was accordingly formed to come to an understanding with him on this basis. They called on the Holy Prophet and offered him the most tempting terms, which were:

> *"If your ambition is to possess wealth, we will amass for you as much of it as you wish; if you aspire to win honour and power, we are prepared to swear allegiance to you as our overlord and king; if you have a fancy for beauty, you shall have the hand of the finest maiden of your own choice."*

Irresistible temptations no doubt! From a destitute, helpless and persecuted man to a mighty potentate is a big lift. But the Holy Prophet's heart was free from the alloy of self-seeking. To the utter surprise and disappointment of the Quraish delegation he replied:

"I want neither pelf nor power. I have been commissioned by Allāh as a warner to mankind. I deliver His message to you. Should you accept it, you shall have felicity in this life as well as in the life to come; should you reject the word of Allāh, surely Allāh will decide between you and me."

This frustrated the last attempt of the Quraish at a compromise. Persuasion through temptation proved as fruitless as persecution. The persecution was unbearable, but the temptation was well-nigh irresistible. Were it not for Divine steadfastness infused into the Holy Prophet's bosom, the tortures inflicted on him and the temptations placed in his way would have shaken him from his position. But he stood firm as a rock, baffling all attempts to dissuade him from his mission. It is to this that the Holy Qur'ān alludes in the following verse: "And if We had not made thee firm, thou mightest have indeed inclined to them a little."[1]

1 The Qur'ān, 17 : 74.

Ban against the Hashimites

Disappointed on all sides, the Quraish decided to resort to the use of their last weapon. It was the seventh year since the Call, and the majority of Muslims had made good their escape to Abyssinia. Hamzah and 'Umar had embraced Islām. Abū Ṭālib had refused point-blank the Quraishite demand that he should withdraw his protecting hand from the Holy Prophet. Excepting Abū Lahab, the whole of the Banū Hāshim family had decided to stand by him and fight for him till the last man. Moreover, the light of Islām went on spreading from one clan to another. The Quraish therefore decided to place a social ban on the Banū Hāshim. Inter-marriage and commercial relations with them were strictly forbidden. An agreement to this effect was drawn up and the scroll hung up in the Ka'bah to give it a look of sanctity. On hearing of this the Banū Hāshim betook themselves to a secluded part of Makkah, known as the *Shi'b,* the prohibited quarter. But Abū Jahl spared no pains to keep a vigilant watch to ensure that the blockade was strictly observed. When Ḥakīm ibn Hazām, for instance, tried to supply provisions to Khadījah, who was nearly related to him, Abū Jahl offered obstruction. But never throughout these trying times did the Banū Hāshim waver in their resolution. They cheerfully suffered all this for the sake of the Holy Prophet, which they would never have done if they had not had a deep rooted respect for him. While the ban lasted the preaching of the Holy Prophet was confined to within the four walls of the *Shi'b.* In the days of pilgrimage, however, when Arabs looked upon bloodshed as an unpardonable sacrilege, he would come out and communicate his message to people assembled from far and near. Abū Lahab followed him like a shadow, warning the people against his teachings. He was a liar, he would say, and must not be believed. As a result, wherever the Holy Prophet went to deliver his message he met the taunting questions why was it that his own people discarded him if he was righteous in his claim. In short, this was a period of great hardship for the Banū Hāshim and of suspension of all propagating activities.

In the meantime, there arose a murmur against the hardship to which the Banū Hāshim were subjected. The gentle-hearted among the Quraish increasingly felt the injustice and severity of the ban till the day came when some openly condemned it.

Consequently five of their leading men decided among themselves that the ban should be removed and the agreement torn to pieces. The scroll, containing the agreement, suspended on the Ka'bah, had been eaten by ants. This was brought to the notice of the Quraishite chiefs by Abū Ṭālib as a mark of Divine disapproval. It was consequently agreed upon that the pledge should be declared null and void if on inspection it was found defaced. Accordingly they went to the Ka'bah to examine the agreement which turned out to be actually eaten away. The opportunity was eagerly seized upon by those who had already felt the injustice of the ban. Putting on their arms they went over in a body to the gate of the *Shi'b* and openly announced their opposition to the agreement of interdiction. They brought the Banū Hāshim out and sent them to their respective homes. Nobody had the courage to offer resistance. The ban had lasted three years.

Death of Abū Ṭālib and Khadījah

Immediately after coming out of the *Shi'b* Abū Ṭālib, the Holy Prophet's uncle, who had so far proved his mainstay, passed away. Though he had not accepted Islām, yet the Holy Prophet had a very deep attachment for him. The bereavement was, therefore, a great shock. But calamities, they say, seldom come single. Shortly afterwards, his faithful wife Khadījah, also died. She had all along served the Holy Prophet wholeheartedly and had been a never failing source of solace in moments of sadness and sorrow. In her death he suffered an irreparable loss. Both these losses were sustained in the tenth year after the Call, which is on that account known in Islamic history as *'Ām al-Huzn,* i.e., the Year of Grief. With the loss of two great comforters and helpers, such as Abū Ṭālib and Khadījah, the Prophet had to face even greater difficulties.

Journey to Ṭā'if

The Holy Prophet had now to face still greater difficulties in the propagation of his message. Whatever restraint Abū Ṭālib and Khadījah had exerted on the malice of the Quraish was now removed. Their hands were now free to deal with him to the full gratification of their malice.[1] In spite of the gloomy situation, however, the Holy Prophet's conviction in his ultimate triumph remained unshaken. When walking about one day, dust was thrown at him. He came home; his daughter washed his head and shed tears at the sad plight of her beloved father. "Do not weep, my child," said he consolingly, "Allāh will surely help your father." So deep-rooted was his faith in the ultimate success of his mission, in the face of this bitter opposition! He never entertained the idea of betaking himself, like the rest of his companions, to Abyssinia, where he would have found a safe asylum. He did not for one moment despair of the regeneration of the land of his birth. He felt confident that the peninsula must some day awaken to the truth of Islām. Surrounded as he was by a thick mist of disappointing circumstances, his eye could yet perceive a ray of hope. The conviction that his deadly enemies would one day be his devoted friends was deeply seated in his heart. The hard-heartedness of the Makkans, however, forced him to turn his attention to Ṭā'if, where he hoped people might listen to his word. Thither he went with Zaid and approached three brothers, who came of the noblest family of the place. But to his disappointment, all of them turned a deaf ear. For about ten days he stayed there delivering his message to several people, one after another, but all to no purpose. On every side he was met with the taunt that he must first convince his own people if he were true in his claim. At last, he was asked to go away; but as soon as he walked out of the town, the dregs of society, at the instigation of the elders of the town, followed him hooting. They lined the route on both sides for a great distance and, as he passed along between them, his legs were pelted with stones. When dripping with blood and unable to walk further he sank to the ground, a wretch would again raise him up by the hand. "Walk on," he would shout at him "this is no place for you to rest." This went on for three long miles. He was pelted with volleys of stones till his very shoes were filled with blood. At last, when his persecutors left him, he seated himself in an orchard, to take a little rest. The owner of this small garden, 'Utbah ibn Rabī'ah, non-believer though he

1 "And surely they proposed to unsettle thee from the land that they might expel thee from it, and then they will not tarry after thee but a little" (The Qur'ān, 17 : 76).

was, took pity on him and sent him a bunch of grapes by his Christian slave 'Addās. The Holy Prophet, as he stretched out his hand towards the grapes, uttered the words, "In the name of Allāh," – words which every Muslim is commanded to repeat when setting his hand to any piece of work. Surprised at this, the slave curiously asked him what the words were. On being informed of the message of Islām, he readily accepted its truth.

Rejected by man in every quarter, the Holy Prophet turned in this state of utter helplessness to Almighty God. His prayer is not an expression of despondency or plaintiveness; on the other hand, notwithstanding apparent helplessness, it is full of confidence in the future. It runs thus:

> *"O my Lord! to Thee do I complain of the feebleness of my strength, of lack of my resourcefulness and of my insignificance in the eyes of people. Thou art Most Merciful of all the merciful. Thou art the Lord of the weak. To whom art Thou to entrust me, to an unsympathetic foe, who would sullenly frown at me, or to a close friend, whom Thou hast given control over my affair. Not in the least do I care for anything except that I may have Thy protection for me. In the light of Thy face do I seek shelter – the light which illumines the heaven and dispels all sorts of darkness, and which controls all affairs in this world as well as in the Hereafter. May it never be that I should incur Thy wrath, or that Thou shouldst be angry with me. There is no strength, but through Thee."*

What human heart can appreciate the purity of the soul that gave utterance to sentiments so sublime under circumstances so trying? Is it imaginable that the heart of an imposter should be capable of emotions so noble, especially after suffering so much? With what marvellous calmness he underwent hardships that no son of man could bear. With what surprising fortitude he bore privations that might have driven others to self-destruction. With what firm faith in God, with what cheerful resignation to His supreme will, with what unalloyed spiritual happiness! All sufferings he says, are insignificant so long as he enjoys God's pleasure.

Pledges of 'Aqabah

A few days later he returned to Makkah, on the assurance of Muṭ'im ibn 'Adī to protect his life. He had been clearly told that he had to leave Makkah, but light had not yet shone upon him as to the place to which he should emigrate. The days of pilgrimage came and he called on each one of the clans that had flocked there from all parts of Arabia. But whichever gathering he addressed, explaining Islamic principles, Abū Lahab kept by him, telling the people not to believe him as he was a heretic and wanted to overthrow the spiritual sway of the Lāt and the 'Uzzā. Consequently, he could attract little attention. Some of the clans harshly rejected him. But he did not lose heart. One tribe expressed a liking for his teachings but pleaded their inability to renounce their ancestral religion all at once. Another put him a question whether, in the event of his triumph, they would have a share in the kingdom he might achieve, should they join hands with him. In reply, the Holy Prophet told them that it rested entirely with God to bestow kingdom on whomsoever He thought fit. The incident, though trivial, speaks volumes for the Holy Prophet's sincerity of purpose. If personal ascendancy were the object of his efforts, as so often alleged, what prevented him from winning over a whole clan by merely holding out a promise to them? But the fact is that the achievement of temporal power was never the goal of his endeavour. His heart was burning within him at the degenerate state of man. Man's elevation in the scale of humanity was the one purpose of his life. He was eagerly looking to Divine help which, he had no shadow of doubt, must be forthcoming, although he could not tell when.

While thus preaching Islām to the various tribes at the time of pilgrimage, the Holy Prophet happened to meet a few men of the Khazraj, a clan of Madīnah. After ascertaining who they were, he asked them if they were from among the associates of the Jews, to which they replied in the affirmative. Then he communicated the message of Islām to them. As Madīnah contained a considerable Jewish element in its population, they had already heard that the time of the appearance of the Promised Prophet, as prophesied in the Jewish scriptures, was at hand. Thus the claim of the Holy Prophet to be *that Prophet* was not altogether a surprise to them. What with the intrinsic beauty of the teachings of Islam which the Holy Prophet explained to them and their expectation of the advent of that Prophet, the conviction that he was indeed the Prophet went home to these visitors. Consequently all six accepted Islām. This came about in the eleventh year of the Call. On their return to Madīnah, much enthusiasm concerning the new faith prevailed there and the Holy Prophet's name became a household word. A considerable number joined the fold of Islām, and a dozen of them went over to Makkah next year to perform the pilgrimage. These swore allegiance to the Holy Prophet, at a place known as 'Aqabah in the following words: "We will not set up any associates with Allāh. We will not steal, nor commit fornication, nor kill our offspring, nor bring false accusations against others. We will not disobey the Holy Prophet in anything that is right." This goes by the name of the First Pledge of 'Aqabah and it took place in the twelfth year of the Call.

Mus'ab ibn 'Umair was deputed by the Holy Prophet to instruct them in the teachings of Islām. As a result of Mus'ab's efforts, Islām spread in Madīnah with rapid strides. Leading men from among the Aus and the Khazraj embraced the faith, so that on the occasion of the next pilgrimage season as many as seventy-three men and two women visited Makkah. The Holy Prophet met with them one night, again at 'Aqabah. 'Abbās his uncle, who bore him company, though yet a non-believer, thus opened the conversation:

> *"You are aware of the position Muḥammad occupies amongst us. So far we have been protecting him from his enemies. He is quite safe and respected here. But now you wish him to accompany you to your town and live with you there. If you believe you will fulfil the covenant on which you wish to take him there, and pledge to shield him in every way, you are at liberty to undertake the responsibility. If, however, you think you will not be able to protect him you had better give him up from this very moment. And mind you, you are welcome to take him along with you, provided you are prepared to withstand the united opposition of both the Arabs and the Gentiles."*

The Madinites, who came to be known as *Anṣār* (Helpers), in the history of Islām, replied that they were ready to swear allegiance to the Holy Prophet just as it might please the latter. Thereupon the Holy Prophet recited a passage from the Holy Qur'ān, delivered a brief sermon and then said: "I demand allegiance of you to the effect that you would defend me against my enemies, just as you defend your wives and children." On this, the chief, among them, Barā ibn Ma'rūr, placing his hand on the Holy Prophet's, said that they all swore allegiance to him on the point. This done, the Holy Prophet appointed twelve of them as their chiefs.

It is thus evident that the Holy Prophet went over to Madīnah at the invitation of the Madinites themselves. It was customary in Arabia that whenever a member of a particular clan joined another, they would pledge themselves to protect him; for as a rule a clan was responsible only for the protection of its own particular members. It also transpires from the event that he knew full well, as did ‘Abbās, that even in Madīnah, the Makkans would allow him no rest. It was therefore necessary to have the Anṣār's pledge to defend the Holy Prophet in the event of an attack by the enemy. The apprehension was justifiable; the Makkans had already given ample proof of their malice by going all the way to Abyssinia in pursuit of Muslim emigrants. The pledge taken on this occasion is known as the Second Pledge of ‘Aqabah and it took place in the thirteenth year of the Call.

The understanding arrived at and the allegiance sworn being strictly confidential, its knowledge was confined to the few Muslims including ‘Abbās. Even the non-Muslims of Madīnah did not know what exactly had happened. The Makkans, therefore, could get no information from them. But when the pilgrimage was over and people had departed from Makkah, the matter became known, for the Holy Prophet himself was not keen about its secrecy. The Makkans went out in pursuit of the Madinite caravan but could not overtake it. They seized two men, one of whom escaped, while the other, Sa‘d ibn ‘Ubadah, was dragged all the way back to Makkah. But the latter had once done a kindly office to some Makkans at Madīnah, and on their intercession he was set free. Thereafter the companions emigrated to Madīnah, in small parties, in complete secrecy from the Makkans.

At last the time came when the Holy Prophet was left at Makkah in the company of but two of his companions, Abū Bakr and ‘Alī, all the rest having reached Madīnah. The circumstances throw further light on the implicit faith which the Holy Prophet had in God. The bitterness of the Makkans' enmity was daily growing in intensity. The fact that Islām was taking root in Madīnah added fuel to the flame of their wrath. Practically alone in the midst of his deadly foes, the Holy Prophet was exposed to great danger. Nevertheless he was not so anxious for himself as for his companions, whom he sent off to a place of safety, himself staying behind in the midst of his blood-thirsty enemies.

CHAPTER V

THE FLIGHT TO MADĪNAH

"If you help him not, Allāh certainly helped him when those who disbelieved expelled him – he being the second of the two; when they were both in the cave, when he said to his companion: 'Grieve not, surely Allāh is with us'." -9 : 40.

Council of the Quraish

The fourteenth year of the Call set in, and the Holy Prophet, with Abū Bakr and 'Alī for his only companions, was left in Makkah surrounded by his enemies. All the rest of his comrades, bidding farewell to their homes, had taken shelter either in Abyssinia or Madīnah. But the moment of the Prophet's utter helplessness was yet to come. Abū Bakr would often ask him to emigrate to Madīnah; but God, he replied, had not yet commanded him to do so. In this too there was at work a Divine purpose which was made manifest by the final decision of the Quraish. Up till then, individual efforts to make away with him had been made, and all had failed. Bitter opposition had been offered and severe persecution inflicted. But the last drop was yet needed to fill the cup of the Makkan's crimes to the brim. At last the hour came. Finding the Holy Prophet almost alone, they held a big conference in the *Dār al-Nadwah* (House of Assembly), where national affairs were discussed and settled. The chiefs of the Quraish met there to deliberate on what might be done with the Holy Prophet. Some thought he should be fettered, thrown into a cellar, and starved to death. But this was open to the objection that his companions, gaining strength, might find an occasion to effect his release. Another proposed that he should be exiled. But it was apprehended that wherever he might be sent, he might win over the people there with his impressive teachings and might some day overcome the Quraish. Abū Jahl at length came forward with the proposal that strong and stout youths of noble lineage should be selected, one from each of the Quraishite clans and armed with sharp swords, they should fall upon the Holy Prophet in a body. Thus no particular clan would be held accountable for his murder. The Banū Hāshim would therefore have to content themselves with blood-money instead of vengeance. This was unanimously agreed upon.

In the cave of Thaur

While the Quraish were thus maturing their plans, Divine revelation informed the Holy Prophet of their foul intent, warning him not to remain in his bed that night. Sending for 'Alī, he informed him of the Divine command, and told him to sleep in his (the Holy Prophet's) bed; for he himself had charge of many a trust which 'Alī should duly make over to the respective owners the following morning, and then follow him to Madīnah. What a tribute to his integrity that, notwithstanding such strong opposition public trusts were still placed in his charge! And for this express purpose he commissioned 'Alī to stay behind, whereas Abū Bakr was told to make the necessary preparation for flight; for the Divine behest had been received. Abū Bakr eagerly enquired if he might accompany the Holy Prophet and, on being told that he should, he burst into tears of joy. Why such intense pleasure at the prospect of hardships and troubles? Only because he would be in the company of him for whom he was prepared to sacrifice his all. Abū Bakr had already arranged for two camels in anticipation of this hour. All other necessaries being forthwith provided, a meeting place was arranged between him and the Holy Prophet. Just after dusk, the body of armed men drawn from among the Quraishite tribes laid siege to the Holy Prophet's house, ready to fall upon him as soon as he ventured out. (It was against the Arab sense of chivalry to kill any one within the four walls of his house.) 'Alī, however, was lying in the Holy Prophet's bed and this gave the Quraish the impression that the Holy Prophet was there and fostered the belief that their intended victim was in their hands. Meanwhile, the Holy Prophet, trusting in the protecting hand of Allāh who had all these thirteen years preserved him in the midst of his enemies, waited for darkness and then calmly walked out through the midst of his would-be assassins and went to Abū Bakr's house as prearranged. Together they set out for Madīnah and reached a certain cave known as the Cave of Thaur, three miles from Makkah. Abū Bakr went in first, cleaned it and closed the holes that he could feel in the dark cave. Then the Holy Prophet followed.

The names of two caves figure prominently in the history of Islām. It was in the Cave of Ḥirā' that the Divine Call first came to the Holy Prophet. Now it was in the Cave of Thaur that Islām was taking a new birth. The Flight is a red-letter day in the annals of Islām, so much so that the Muslim calendar begins from that time.

Next morning, at daybreak, the Quraish were amazed to find 'Alī rising from the Holy Prophet's bed. Careful search was made on all sides and large rewards were offered. A tracking party, following the footprints of the fugitives, reached the mouth of the Cave. Hearing the sound of their footsteps, Abū Bakr grieved within himself, not on his own account but for one whose life was dearer to him than his own. It was indeed a critical moment. The sword of the blood-thirsty enemy was almost at their throats. A glance into the Cave and the inmates would be cut to pieces. In such a situation the bravest heart might sink, the calmest mind might be dismayed. Death was staring them in the face and there was no way to escape, nor any earthly protection. Yet, even in this extreme hour of uttermost helplessness the Holy Prophet's heart was at perfect peace and knew no fear. With supreme and matchless faith and perfect trust in the protecting arm of God, the All-Mighty, the All-Protecting, he quieted the anxiety and fears of his friend, with the words: "Be not grieved, for surely Allāh is with us." Surely this could not have been a voice from within. For the heart of a mortal human being, as the Holy Prophet was, could not have remained so imperturbed in circumstances so imminently perilous. It was not a voice from within, but the voice from above, from Allāh, the Lord of all, came to console and compose a heart afflicted for His sake. And who but the All-Knowing God could tell that, on the very point of succeeding in their foul designs, the enemy would be frustrated.

Leaving for Madīnah

For three whole days the Holy Prophet remained in the Cave. Abū Bakr's son brought them news of all that went on in the town and his daughter, Asmā', would bring them food. His servant, 'Amir ibn Fuhairah, while tending his goats, would drive them up to the mouth of the Cave and milk them for its inmates. At last, when the search was over, and all was clear, on the fourth day they emerged. They took one 'Abd Allāh ibn Uraiqiṭ, a non-Muslim, as their guide. 'Āmir mounted behind Abū Bakr. When on the way the heat grew scorching they halted to rest. Abū Bakr, cleaning the ground in the shade of a rock, spread his mantle for the Holy Prophet to lie upon, and himself went off in search of food. Coming across a Bedouin tending his goats, he cleaned the teats of a goat, milked her in a clean pot and then, covering it with a piece of cloth, brought it to the Holy Prophet. The Holy Prophet's companions knew how he loved cleanliness.

Pursued by Surāqah

The Quraish had announced that whosoever should apprehend the Holy Prophet should have a hundred camels as reward. Among those that were on the lookout for him, in order to win the reward, there was one Surāqah ibn Mālik by name. Hearing that three mounted persons had been seen on the way to Madīnah, Surāqah, a strongly built man, put on his armour, mounted a swift horse and went in pursuit of them. On the way the horse stumbled and he fell to the ground. On drawing lots to find out whether he should continue the chase or not, as the Arabs usually did in such circumstances, he found the omens unpropitious. Disregarding them, he resumed the chase but the same stumbling and the same forbidden omen recurred. Again he jumped into the saddle and galloped on till he came quite close to the Holy Prophet, and was about to shoot an arrow at him when the horse stumbled once more, its feet this time sinking into deep sand. "Then it transpired to me," as Surāqah is reported to have recounted the incident later, "that it was preordained that the Holy Prophet's cause should triumph." Abandoning the intention of murder, he came to the Holy Prophet with a penitent heart, begged his forgiveness, asking not to be punished for his offence when the Prophet came to power. The Holy Prophet gave him in writing the promise asked for.[1] He also gave Surāqah the happy news that the time would come when he would be wearing the gold bangles of the ruler of Persia. This was a wonderful vision of an event that was to come about sixteen years later – an event far beyond the imaginative faculty of man, especially of one fleeing for his very life. In this state of helplessness, with his life hanging in the balance, the Holy Prophet received the happy news that the kingdom of the Chosroes of Persia would come into his possession. The words then uttered found fulfilment during the caliphate of 'Umar when, at the fall of Madā'in, the capital of Persia, Surāqah was sent for and decorated with the bangles of the Chosroes.

Consoling revelation

The marvellous steadfastness of the Holy Prophet in the midst of overwhelming perils was due to Divine revelation that visited him at intervals and confirmed his faith. "He who has made the Qur'ān binding on thee will surely bring thee back to" the Place of Return.."[2] was another consolation which he received in the course of his flight to Madīnah. In fact, the emigration was to him nothing unexpected. He had been informed long before that he would have to leave Makkah and that the rise of Islām was to start from some other centre. The Holy Qur'ān abounds in prophecies to this effect. Just at the time when the storm of opposition was at its highest and the helplessness of the Holy Prophet at its uttermost, it was proclaimed that Islām must triumph in the long run, even though the opponents exerted themselves to the utmost. The accounts of previous prophets, the opposition they had met with, and their ultimate success, as narrated in the Holy Qur'ān were mostly revealed in this period of the Holy Prophet's career as consolation to sustain him in his troubles. A little before the flight, he had a vision that he had emigrated to a place, rich and fertile. It was no other than Madīnah, which is still famous for its gardens.

1 Pen and ink were always kept at hand in order to write down Divine revelation as soon as it was received.

2 The Qur'ān, 28 : 85

That the prosperity of Islām was bound up with *the Hijrah* or the Flight, was well-known to early Muslims. Thus they looked upon this event as the birth of Islām, and the Muslim calendar, as already observed, dates not from the first Call in the Cave of Ḥirā', but from the time of the Holy Prophet's flight. It was in the Hijrah that the climax of the Holy Prophet's helplessness was reached. Therefore the Holy Qur'ān refers to this event as a testimony to the fact that the helping hand of God was at the back of Islām and was a guarantee for its ultimate success. If the Makkans did not help him, the Holy Qur'ān says, Allāh did surely help him, in the hour of his extreme helplessness, when he had to flee from Makkah, with but one companion.[1] The two had to take refuge in a cave, it goes on to say, but even there they were not safe. Pursuers following close on their heels traced them up to the mouth of the Cave. His companion felt anxious that they had been overtaken. At so anxious a moment, he consoled his friend not to entertain any fear, for Allāh was surely with them. This implicit and deep-rooted faith in Divine help was in fact the very secret of his courage and hope under the most trying and discouraging circumstances. Never did a word of despair or complaint escape his lips. He knew no despondency, no despair, no dismay. Even in the most critical situations, his heart was aglow with hope. In this hour of dire helplessness when, humanly speaking, even the very last shelter in the Cave appeared to have been withdrawn, he exclaims with a heart full of hope and confidence: "Most surely Allāh is with us."

During the Makkan period, extending over thirteen years, the Holy Prophet had to work in the teeth of the most bitter opposition. His spiritual force produced three hundred giants of spirituality, who never for a single moment wavered in their faith in him, stood by him in spite of excruciating tortures and bade farewell to their homes and their property but did not desert him. The phenomenal transformation brought about by him in the brief space of thirteen years, notwithstanding the united resistance of the whole nation, has won unwilling appreciation, even from a critic like Muir, who thus draws a sketch of his companions:

1 The Qur'ān, 9 : 40

"In so short a period, Mecca had by this wonderful movement been rent into two factions which, unmindful of the old landmarks of tribe and family, had arrayed themselves in deadly opposition one against the other. The Believers bore persecution with a patient and tolerant spirit, and though it was their wisdom to do so, the credit of a magnanimous forbearance may be freely accorded. One hundred men and women, rather than abjure their previous faith, had abandoned home and sought refuge, till the storm should be overpast, in Abyssinian exile. And now again a large number, with the Holy Prophet himself, were emigrating from their fondly loved city with its sacred Temple, to them the holiest spot on the earth, and fleeing to Madīnah. There the same marvellous charm had within two or three years been preparing for them a brotherhood ready to defend the Prophet and his followers with their blood. Jewish truth had long sounded in the ears of the men of Madīnah; but it was not until they heard the spirit stirring strains of the Arabian Prophet that they too awoke from slumber, and sprang suddenly into a new and earnest life. The virtues of his people may be described in the words of Mahomet himself:

'The servants of the Merciful are they that walk upon the earth softly, and when the ignorant speak unto them, they reply, Peace.

'They that spend the night worshipping their Lord, prostrate and standing;

'And who say, O our Lord! turn away from us the torment of Hell; verily, from the torment thereof there is no release. Surely it is an evil abode and resting place.

'Those that when they spend are neither profuse nor niggardly, but take a middle course;

'Those that invoke not with God any other god; and slay not a soul that God has forbidden, otherwise than by right; and commit not fornication;....

'They who bear not witness to that which is false; and when they pass by vain sport, they pass it by with dignity.

'They who, when admonished by the revelations of the Lord, fall not down as if deaf and blind;

'Who say, O our Lord! Grant us of our wives and children such as shall be a comfort unto us, and make us examples unto the pious.' "

As a matter of fact, these as well as hundreds of other verses in the Holy Qur'ān, which depict the characteristics of the virtuous, do not draw an imaginary picture. They set forth a true description of the lives of the Holy Prophet's companions. It was the soul-force of a single personality that wrought this miraculous transformation. In a marvellously short time, hundreds of people, sunk in vice and superstition given to the most debased forms of idolatry and fettered in the shackles of the vilest and most cruel social customs, were uplifted and raised to the heights of morality. He breathed a new Life into them so that the principles of truth, of virtue, of doing good to fellow-men, once accepted were never lost despite terrible harassment. He infused into them a sense of human dignity and responsibility. Here indeed was the greatest benefactor of humanity.

The New Era

The Holy Prophet and his companions accomplished in eight days the journey to Madīnah which usually took eleven days and arrived there on the 12th of Rabī' I, in the 14th year of his mission corresponding to June 28, 622 A.D. News of his disappearance from Makkah had preceded him, but his three days' hiding in the Cave was known to no one. The city had been in eager expectation of his arrival. Every morning people would go out on the road to Makkah to await the appearance of their Master. The tedious hours of impatient expectancy were at last over, and the illustrious visitor appeared on the horizon. At a distance of three miles from Madīnah lies the habitation known as Qubā'. It is considered a suburb of Madīnah. Here dwelt several families from among the *Anṣār* or the Helpers, of which that of 'Amr ibn 'Auf was the most distinguished. Before entering the city, the Holy Prophet accepted his invitation and stopped at Qubā'. A number of Emigrants *(Muhājirīn)* were also putting up there.

Muslims from the city flocked to Qubā' in crowds to meet their revered leader. For fourteen days the Holy Prophet stayed here. 'Alī joined him at this place. A mosque was built there, the first mosque in the history of Islām, known as the mosque of Qubā'. It is of this mosque that the Holy Qur'ān speaks in the ninth chapter as "the mosque founded on piety."[1] The Holy Prophet and the companions erected it with their own hands, all working as ordinary masons and labourers. This was followed by his entry into the city of Madīnah, which was wearing a look of jubilation. People came out to greet him, clad in their gayest attire. Women sang in chorus from the housetops to welcome their noble guest. Everyone was eager that he should stop at his house. Slackening the reins of his camel, he let it have its own way. Wherever it stopped, he said to the eager crowds around him, there would he lodge. The camel moved on till it reached an open space in front of Abū Ayyūb's house, where it halted.

Muslim brotherhood

The courtyard belonged to two orphan boys. They offered it as a free gift for the erection of a mosque, but the Holy Prophet would not accept it without payment. They had therefore to take the price. The first thing done was the construction of a mosque, the Holy Prophet and his comrades working at it with their own hands. Each looked upon this labour of love as a proud privilege and, as they worked, all chanted in chorus after the Holy Prophet, "O Lord! there is no felicity, but the felicity of the Hereafter; O Lord! help the Helpers and the Refugees." The mosque was a monument of simplicity - walls made of mud bricks, the roof supported by trunks of palm-trees, and covered over with palm leaves and twigs it could not keep out rain, which made the unpaved floor muddy. To remove this difficulty, the floor was strewn with gravel. In a corner of the courtyard, a sort of platform with a roof was raised to accommodate those who had neither family nor home. Those who lived there were known as the residents of the *Ṣuffah (aṣḥāb al-Ṣuffah)*. This was, so to speak, a kind of seminary attached to the mosque for those accommodated

1 The Qur'ān, 9: 108.

there, devoting their whole time to the study of religion. Adjoining the mosque were erected two apartments for the household of the Holy Prophet.

In Makkah Muslims could not say their prayers openly in congregation. Now that the peaceful conditions of Madīnah permitted public prayers various ways were one day considered to summon the faithful to prayers at the fixed hours. 'Umar had seen a vision of a man repeating the words, *Allāh-u-Akbar, Allāhu-Akbar* (Allah is Great) and so forth - the full text of the Muslim call to prayer. Next morning he narrated his vision to the Holy Prophet. Another of the companions had had exactly the same vision. This was approved by the Holy Prophet as the call to prayer. The first Friday congregational prayer was held here on the day when the Holy Prophet left Qubā' and entered into the city of Madīnah.

Prayers being thus regulated, the Holy Prophet next turned to the question of providing for the Refugees. Most of them, while in Makkah, had lived in ease and plenty, but they had had to abandon their wealth and property. So he established a brotherhood between Helpers and Refugees – a brotherhood unique in the history of the world. Each of the Refugees was bound to one of the Helpers in a bond of brotherhood. The fellow-feeling and love on which this new brotherhood was created found wonderful expression. Each one of the Helpers took a brother Refugee home with him, placed half his house at his disposal and equally divided all his goods and chattels with him. The Helpers were an agriculturist people, and wished to divide their farms equally with their new brethren. The Refugees were tradesmen by profession, quite unused to farming. On realising this, the Helpers said they would do the whole labour themselves and give half the produce to the Refugees. So strong, in short, was this new tie that it surpassed even the relationship of brothers. When either of the couple thus joined passed away, his property was inherited not by his brother-in-blood, but by his brother-in-faith. But the Holy Qur'ān forbade that the tie should have so far-reaching an effect and enjoined the inheritance to go in the natural course to the blood-relations.[1]

1 The Qur'ān, 8 : 75.

Such was the genuine sacrificial spirit with which the Helpers embraced their brethren-in-faith, but the Refugees did not take undue advantage of their sympathy.[1] One 'Abd al-Rahmān ibn 'Auf, when offered half of everything owned by his Helper brother, expressed his gratitude for the kindness, and asked him only to show him the way to the market so that he could manage his own living; and in a short time he developed a flourishing business. Similarly the rest of the Refugees also took to trade. Those who could find nothing to set their hand to, worked as ordinary porters, thereby not only maintaining themselves, but also sparing something to contribute towards the Public Treasury *(Bait al-Māl)* to be expended on community welfare. Before long, their business flourished to such an extent that the merchandise caravans of some of them consisted of seven hundred camels each. There was a time - a time of want - when, on the arrival of a guest, the Holy Prophet, finding no provisions in his own house, asked Abū Ṭalḥah, one of the companions, to entertain him. On going home with the guest, Abū Ṭalḥah found that the food was hardly enough for his own children. To meet the awkward situation the light was put out and such food as there was was served to the guest, Abū Ṭalḥah and his wife, who had to bear him company as hosts, taking nothing but moving their hands and mouths as though they were also partaking of the food. The food being just enough for the guest, the whole family went hungry.

But the Muslims worked so hard that poverty soon changed to plenty and prosperity, and they began to live a comfortable life. Under these fluctuations of fortune, however, they conducted themselves admirably. Neither in the state of indigence did they ever grumble, nor in the time of affluence did they become extravagant. They spent it in the way of Allāh - in helping the poor, the needy, the orphans and the residents of the *Ṣuffāh,* whose sole occupation was to attend throughout the day to the teachings of the Holy Prophet and spend their nights in prayers. Out of these sprang the band of religious teachers and preachers who carried the torch of Islām far and wide to different countries and different peoples. The well-known Abū Hurairah, through whom a vast number of the

1 "Surely those who believed and fled (their homes) and struggled hard in Allāh's way with their wealth and their lives, and those who gave shelter and helped – these are friends one of another" (The Qur'ān, 8 : 72).

Holy Prophet's sayings have come down to us, was one of them. As they had no means of livelihood, the well-to-do among the Muslims used to invite them to take food with them. It is recorded that Sa'd alone sometimes took home as many as eighty guests.

A pact between various tribes

The third important matter to which the Holy Prophet addressed himself was to establish friendly relations among the various tribes living in Madīnah. The Jews were a considerable power there. In alliance with the tribes of Aus and Khazraj they took part in their internecine warfare. They were Arabs by descent but formed a distinct unit by their adoption of Judaism. They were subdivided into three clans, Banū Qainuqā', Banū Naḍīr and Banū Quraiẓah. The other inhabitants of the town were the Aus and the Khazraj, always at war with each other. Of the two chief clans of the Jews, the Banū Quraiẓah were the allies of the Aus, while the Banū Naḍīr joined the Khazraj. Now it so happened that the major portion of the Khazraj and the Aus embraced Islām. So the Holy Prophet concluded a pact between Muslims and Jews. The main terms were as follows: Firstly, Muslims and Jews should live as one people. Secondly, each party should keep to its own faith, and neither should interfere with that of the other. Thirdly, in the event of war with a third party, each should come to the assistance of the other, provided the latter were the party aggrieved and not the aggressors. Fourthly, in the event of an attack on Madīnah, both should join hands to defend it. Fifthly, peace should be made only after consultation with each other. Sixthly, Madīnah should be regarded as sacred by both, all blood-shed being forbidden therein. Seventhly, the Holy Prophet should be the final court of appeal in cases of dispute.

CHAPTER VI

THE DEFENSIVE BATTLES

"Permission (to fight) is given to those on whom war is made, because they are oppressed. And surely Allāh is able to assist them – those who are driven from their homes without a just cause except that they say: Our Lord is Allāh." – 22: 39-40

The Battle of Badr

Having settled at Madīnah, Muslims were no longer molested in the observance of their religion. Mosques were erected and the call to prayer was freely made; but let it not be imagined that enmity to Islām had ceased to exist. While Muslims enjoyed perfect religious liberty within the walls of Madīnah, the same fire of malice kept smouldering in the hearts of Makkans. Hostility continued to grow both in intensity and extent. When even a small band had emigrated to Abyssinia, the Quraish were too jealous to leave them in peace there, and pursued them even to the court of the Negus to bring about their destruction. Now that the Holy Prophet and his followers were safely settled at Madīnah, and were steadily gaining in power and influence, the Quraish could not remain inactive.

'Abd Allāh ibn Ubayy, an important personality of Madīnah, possessed immense influence there. Before the immigration of the Holy Prophet, the people of Madīnah were thinking of making him their over-lord. Naturally enough, when the Holy Prophet arrived there, 'Abd Allāh ibn Ubayy was eclipsed. He felt the sting of jealousy and maintained a hostile attitude towards the Muslims. The Quraish also instigated him to expel Muslims. But a large number of his own tribesmen had already joined the fold of Islām and an attempt to offer open resistance to the Holy Prophet might have led to civil war among his own people. Disappointed in ‘Abd Allāh ibn Ubayy, the Quraish began to incite the inhabitants of the strip of land lying between Makkah and Madīnah. As custodians of the sacred House of Ka‘bah, they commanded the respect of the whole of Arabia and were in a position to exert considerable influence upon the tribes. The success of the Quraishite propaganda among these people set the Muslims once more on their guard. On all sides they were hemmed in by enemies, and even within the walls of Madīnah a deep undercurrent of opposition, set in motion by ‘Abd Allāh ibn Ubayy, was running. Notwithstanding the compact, no confidence could be reposed in the Jews. Nor could ‘Abd Allāh ibn Ubayy be relied upon. The Muslims, therefore, felt great concern for their safety. Attack was apprehended every moment from without and treachery from within.

Small detachments of the Quraish used to go out on marauding expeditions and scour the country right up to the outskirts of Madīnah. One such party lifted camels from the very pastures of the town. In fact, ever since the Emigration, they were anxiously looking for an opportunity to cause trouble and extirpate Islām with the sword. They had made every preparation for an incursion upon Madīnah. The situation called for every vigilance by the Muslims. Divine revelation had been received, permitting the unsheathing of the sword in self defence. The words of the Holy Qur’ān in this connection are significant enough, and deserve the close attention of critics who stigmatise Islām, in season and out of season, as the religion of the sword. The Holy Qur’ān says : “Permission (to fight) is given to those on whom war is made because they are oppressed.”[1] And elsewhere: “Fight in the way of Allāh against those who fight against you but be not aggressive.”[2] Thus warfare is restricted by two conditions. It must not be waged save in self-defence, and it must cease as soon as the necessity for it had passed. Under the behests of the Holy Qur’ān, therefore, a Muslim cannot play the part of an aggressor. He must wait till the enemy has struck the first blow. So much for the commencement of fighting: subsequently, at every stage in the course of action, he has to observe perfect self-restraint so that if the enemy should incline towards peace,

1 The Qur’ān, 22 : 39.; 2 Ibid., 2 : 190.

he is bound to meet them more than half way, suspending hostilities then and there. He must not "transgress the limits."

Precautionary measures

By way of precaution the Holy Prophet had to adopt certain measures. It was necessary to obtain accurate information of the plans and movements of the Quraish. The establishment of friendly relations with the various Bedouin tribes in the vicinity of Madīnah was also urgently called for. With these ends in view, the Holy Prophet despatched small reconnaissance parties to keep an eye on the movements of the enemy as well as to approach certain tribes to secure their neutrality. Besides, he hoped that such measures would perhaps serve as a check on the aggressive designs of the enemy. The Muslims, they would realise, were not off their guard, and they would consequently think twice before taking the fateful step. They might also hesitate to endanger their Syrian trade, to which they owed their whole prosperity. Situated as Madīnah was, on the trade route from Makkah to Syria, disruption of relations with the Muslims would seriously imperil their caravans. This, it was hoped, would be effective in keeping their hostile intention in abeyance. The parties thus sent out had strict orders to abstain from seeking quarrels.

Pacts with neighbouring tribes

In consequence of the negotiations referred to above, several of the neighbouring tribes entered into agreement with the Muslims, idolatrous like the Makkans though they were. These pacts, it must be noted, were of a purely defensive character. The terms of one for instance, which speak for themselves, were as follows: "This is the script of Muḥammad to the Banū Ḥamzah. Their life and property shall be safe. Should some enemy attack them, they shall be assisted by the Muslims, unless they wage war against Islām. They shall also come to the Prophet's help when called upon."

It so happened that about the end of the month Jumādī II, 2 A.H., one such party was sent out under 'Abd Allāh ibn Jaḥsh. They were given sealed orders by the Holy Prophet, with instructions not to open the cover until two days had passed. When opened as directed, after two days' march, orders were revealed that the party should proceed to a certain place, Nakhlah, and there gather information about the Quraish schemes. It was nothing more than a precautionary measure lest the enemy should take the Muslims by surprise. There could have been no other motive whatsoever, no intention of an attack on Makkah, for Muslims were much too weak to think of any such design. The test of the preservation of the small Muslim brotherhood devolved upon the Holy Prophet and, like a skilled general, he realized the importance of keeping a watch on the movements of the enemy.

On reaching Nakhlah, as directed in the sealed letter, 'Abd Allāh ibn Jaḥsh came across some Quraishite traders on their way back from Syria. In contravention of the express orders of the Holy Prophet, he fell upon them, killing one 'Abd Allāh ibn Ḥaḍramī and taking two captives. When the news reached the Holy Prophet, he severely reprimanded 'Abd Allāh for transgressing his orders. The Quraish, who had been anxiously looking for an excuse, were thus afforded the long-awaited opportunity to give vent to their wrath. No great importance, under the then conditions of Arab society, could be attached to a murder such as that of Ibn Ḥaḍramī. In fact it was a commonplace incident, of daily occurrence. The usual course followed in all such cases was to demand blood-money. But the Quraish wanted a pretext with which to rouse the general populace against the Muslims and Ibn Ḥaḍramī's murder furnished it. They took about two months in making the necessary preparations and fell upon Madīnah in the month of Ramaḍān in the year 2 A.H. Thus came about the event known in the history of Islām as the battle of Badr.

Quraish attack Madīnah

By strange coincidence, a Quraishite trading caravan under the leadership of Abū Sufyān was, about this very time, on its way back from Syria. Abū Sufyān sent word to Makkah to arrange for the protection of the caravan. This fact has led to the unwarranted confusion that the Muslims wanted to waylay the caravan, and that the battle of the Badr was thus occasioned. The idea is absolutely unfounded. This very caravan had on its way to Syria passed by Madīnah quite unmolested. Again, in all their attempts to rouse the people to the attack, and in all their preparations, the Quraish leaders never uttered a word as to the alleged insecurity of the caravan. The murder of Ibn Ḥaḍramī was the only incident they made use of for arousing great excitement for vengeance. Besides, the caravan, deviating its course from the usual route, and passing along the coast had safely reached Makkah before the two armies met at Badr. It is thus absolutely baseless to impute such motives to the Muslims. The long-standing anxiety of the Quraish to crush the growing power of Islām was the sole cause of the battle. The Muslims were in fact forced into it. The very fact that the Muslim strength aggregated only 313, including boys, all poorly armed, proves that there could have been little eagerness to fight a force 1,000 strong fully equipped. The Holy Qur'ān thus depicts their state of mind when they were called upon to stand up in their own defence: "A party of the believers were surely averse. ...As if they were being driven to death."[1] There were many who looked upon it, it says, as a great hardship, thinking they were being thrust into the very jaws of death. Nevertheless they had to strike a blow in self-defence. The Holy Prophet summoned them together, explained the situation to them, stressing the fact that they could not help taking the field against a foe who was bent upon striking at their very existence. The Helpers had promised to defend the Holy Prophet only within the walls of Madīnah, but now the situation required the enemy to be met before they attacked the town. When the Holy Prophet turned towards them to know their mind, he found them all ready to follow his lead and to stand by him under the severest trials. This small band of Muslims hastily recruited and ill-equipped, placing their reliance on Allāh, marched out on the road to Makkah to check the onslaught of the Quraish. It was inadvisable to let the flames of fighting approach their homes at Madīnah. Reaching Badr, so called after a well of the same name, they found the Quraish army already encamped there. They did the same.

The Prophet praying in the battlefield

Numerically the Muslim force was less than one-third of the Quraish. Besides, the latter were composed of skilled vet-

1 The Qur'ān, 8: 5, 6.

erans, while Muslims had recruited even inexperienced youths. Therefore, in respect of neither numbers nor strength and skill were the Muslims a match for the enemy. This caused the Holy Prophet the deepest anxiety. Retiring into a small hut, set up for him, he addressed Allāh with tearful eyes: "O Allāh! shouldst Thou suffer this small band of believers to perish this day, no one will be left on earth to worship Thee and carry Thy message to the world." Having offered special prayers he came out of the hut with a smile on his face, and loudly recited the Quranic verse, revealed long before: "Soon shall the hosts be routed and they shall show their backs."[1]

The Quraish were thoroughly equipped. In obedience to Quranic injunction, Muslims desisted from advancing to the attack until the enemy had struck the first blow. At last, three of the Quraish champions came forward and challenged an equal number from among the Muslims to meet them. It was the fashion in Arab warfare in those days before a general conflict to stage single-handed combat. The gauntlet was taken up by three from among the Muslims, and it so happened that all the three Quraish heroes were killed in the duels. This was followed by a few more duels, and then the fighting became general. The Quraish army fell upon the Muslims, but the latter firmly held to their position and repulsed them. A remarkable phenomenon of Divine assistance manifested itself. Almost all the Quraish chiefs, ringleaders of the deadly campaign against Islām, were slain in action. Abū- Jahl suffered death at the hands of two youths from among the Anṣār. In all, seventy of the hostile army fell in the field. Seeing their chiefs fall, the rank and file were seized with confusion and took to flight. The Muslims pursued them and took about seventy prisoners. On the Muslim side, the casualties were only fourteen.

Divine Help for Muslim cause

The conflict of Badr presents a striking scene of Divine help, in one respect perhaps unique in the annals of warfare.[2]

1 The Qur'ān, 54 : 45.
2 "And Allāh certainly helped you at Badr when you were weak" (The Qur'ān, 3 : 123).

It often happens that an army having smaller numerical strength but otherwise well-equipped, composed of valiant soldiers, well-disciplined and skilled in the use of arms, defeats larger hosts, outnumbering it by far, but not possessing equal advantages. But what makes the battle of Badr unique is the fact that every form of weakness on one side was ranged against every form of strength on the other. The Quraish army was three times as large as the Muslim army. The position taken up by the Quraish was advantageous. Their ranks comprised soldiers of fame, with whom fighting had been a lifelong profession. Their equipment too was more than ample and all were in full armour. They had a hundred horsemen as well as seven hundred camels. And what of the Muslim strength? Their number was one-third of the enemy's army. Their ranks were composed of a number of raw youths, of Refugees of advanced age and of some Madinite Helpers, in no way a match for the war-like Makkans. And what of their horsemen and camels? They had no more than two and seventy respectively. In respect of equipment, there was no comparison at all. Thus utter weakness was pitched against overwhelming might. But the Divine hand comes to the succour of the weak, inspiring them with strength – strength other than that of numbers, equipment or arms – and worldly might was routed. To this phenomenon the Holy Qur'ān invites attention in the following verse: "Indeed, there was a sign for you in the two hosts which met together in encounter – one party fighting in the way of Allāh and the other disbelieving ... and Allāh strengthens with His aid whom He pleases. There is a lesson in this for those who have eyes."[1]

Treatment of prisoners of war

Those who were taken prisoners received kindly treatment at the hands of the Muslims, which impressed many of them with the nobility of Islāmic spirit. One of them, when he later accepted Islām remembered with gratitude the treatment he had received in captivity. Those, he would recount, to whom he was entrusted served him the best food in the house, the family contenting themselves with dates and other common

1 The Qur'ān, 3: 13.

eatables. Notwithstanding the fact that hostilities had not ceased, prisoners of war were repatriated on receipt of ransom. The poor who could not afford to pay their ransom were freed. Those who could read and write were each required to teach ten children, this being considered ample ransom to secure them liberty. To forgo the considerable sum of 4,000 dirhams as ransom money per head and accept the teaching of reading and writing instead, furnishes ample testimony to the value which learning had in the eyes of the Holy Prophet. The vanquished foe was never treated harshly by him. This was the first opportunity for the Muslims after their long and bitter sufferings at the hands of the Quraish to wreak vengeance on them, if they had so chosen. But how they were treated in fact is well illustrated by the following incident. There was one among the captives possessing a remarkable eloquence, which he used to exercise unsparingly while in Makkah to arouse opposition to Islām. He was brought before the Holy Prophet, and it was suggested that two of his teeth should be knocked out as an appropriate punishment and to incapacitate him from stirring up agitation against Islām. "If I disfigure any of his limbs," replied the Holy Prophet, "God will disfigure mine."

Fulfilment of Divine Promise

In short the battle of Badr dealt on the one hand a smashing blow to the power of the Quraish while, on the other, it strengthened the roots of Islām. It also produced a marvellous effect on the Jews as well as neighbouring Bedouin tribes. How could the Muslims overpower such large hosts, they thought to themselves, if they had not been strengthened by Divine aid? Then they were surprised to see how the worst and the most deadly enemies of Islām were each and all, picked out and slain. Did this not clearly point to the Divine hand at work? Another interesting fact in the battle of Badr was that the Holy Prophet had prayed to God with tears in his eyes on the very field of battle while the Quraish, even before marching out from Makkah, had made a solemn prayer at the Ka'bah that God might be pleased to grant victory to those who were in the right. Thus the result of the battle was, in fact, a Divine judgment against wrong while right received Divine support and triumphed. The designs of the enemy were frustrated, while the Muslims saw in their destruction the fulfilment of Divine promises held out to them all these twelve years that Truth would prevail. Throughout the prolonged period of trial and hardship, they had received Divine consolation that all opposition would break down and Islām would emerge triumphant. What they had implicitly believed, they now saw actually come to pass and naturally enough, the righteousness of the cause of Islām became manifest.

The Battle of Uḥud

The defeat of Badr was an ignominy which Quraishite pride could not leave unavenged. The contemptible little band of ill-equipped heretics had inflicted a crushing blow on them. Revenge was therefore the watchword all over Makkah. Most of the Quraishite chiefs having fallen at Badr, Abū Sufyān was elected leader, and he solemnly pledged himself to avenge the disgrace of Badr. The profit of the caravan which had at the time of the battle of Badr returned from Syria under his command was, by general consent, set aside to be devoted to the contemplated expedition of revenge. An army of 3,000 soldiers was collected twelve months after the defeat of Badr, including two hundred cavalry and seven hundred mail-clad veterans. Women were also allowed to accompany the force in order to rouse the spirits of the soldiers with their war songs. In the year 3 A.H. this army marched out towards Madīnah, and on Thursday, the 9th of Shawwāl encamped at the foot of the Uḥud, a hill three miles north of Madīnah. They took possession of the pastures of Madīnah, luxuriant crops were cut to serve as forage for their horses and camels were let loose to graze in the fields and devastate them.

The Holy Prophet holds a war council

The next day, Friday, the 10th of Shawwāl, the Holy Prophet summoned his companions to discuss a plan of action. It was his habit to take counsel with his friends before every great undertaking. He related some of his visions. In one he had seen that his sword was somewhat broken at the point; this was interpreted to portend some injury to his own person. In another he had covered his body with a coat of mail; this was taken to signify that they should keep within the walls of

Madīnah. Another vision in which cows were seen being slaughtered was interpreted to mean damage to his people. On the strength of these visions, the Holy Prophet was of opinion that they should not venture out to meet the enemy in open conflict, but rather stay within the four walls of Madīnah and repulse their onslaughts. Companions of age and mature judgment were at one with him in this suggestion. Even 'Abd Allāh ibn Ubayy, who had hypocritically embraced Islām after the battle of Badr, held the same view. But the majority consisting chiefly of ardent youths, favoured giving the enemy open battle. Keeping within the walls, they argued, would convey the impression of weakness and would embolden the enemy. Moreover, it was shocking to their self-respect to watch with complacence their fields being laid waste. Out of deference to the opinion of the majority, the Holy Prophet yielded to their plan and, putting on his armour, marched out of Madīnah, about sunset at the head of a party 1,000 strong, among whom were only two horsemen and a hundred men in armour.

Muslim Army led to Uḥud

The night was spent at a short distance from the city, the march being resumed at dawn next morning. On coming within sight of the enemy, 'Abd Allāh ibn Ubayy deserted with his three hundred men, thus reducing the Muslim strength to only seven hundred to meet four times their number. Even these were by no means skilled in warfare. Their only strength lay in their enthusiasm for the defence of Truth.[1] That zeal had instilled into the hearts even of the aged the vigour and spirit of youth. The same was the case with those who were minors. It is related of one boy that, on being refused enlistment on the score of youth, he stood on tip-toe to look taller. His zeal secured him a place in the ranks. Another of the same age stepped forward, asserting his claim to be enrolled. In a wrestling contest, he urged, he could throw his fellow. He was given a chance to make good his pretensions and, on succeeding he also was taken in. An aged man then came forward. "I am, O Prophet of Allāh," he

1 "And be not weak hearted, nor grieve, and you will have the upper hand if you are believers" (3 : 139).

pleaded "already on the verge of my grave. What glory would be mine should my life come to an end while striking a blow in the defence of Allāh's Apostle!" The seven hundred were thus recruited, their lack of strength and skill being made up for by their intense zeal for the cause so dear to them. Advancing to encounter the three thousand stout and well-equipped warriors, the Holy Prophet, like a skilled general, took up a position of vantage on the field, with the rocks of Uḥud to protect his rear, and in person drew up his men into ranks. There was, however, on one side an opening through the rocks by which the enemy could fall upon the Muslim ranks from the rear. Fifty archers were therefore posted on an eminence at the mouth of the outlet, with strict orders not to leave their posts on any account, however the day might go.

Besides the women who accompanied the Quraish army to rouse their martial spirits, there was also a Christian monk, Abū 'Āmir, to play a similar role. Once he had lived in Madīnah where he was held in deep veneration for his pious and abstemious life. On the arrival of the Holy Prophet at Madīnah, the Helpers accorded him so warm a reception that Abū 'Āmir could not bear to see it. He was disgusted and went over to Makkah. His presence in the Quraish ranks, he boasted, would by itself overawe the Madinites, who would surely desert the Muslim Refugees. Now that the two armies took the field and faced each other, women came to the front of the Makkan army and used all their arts to rouse the spirits of the soldiers. Then Abū 'Āmir made his appearance, reminding the Helpers who he was. He was, however, received with contempt and was forced to retire.

Quraish defeated and pursued

After a series of duels, in which Ḥamzah killed Ṭalḥah, the Quraishite flag-bearer, the conflict became general. The Muslims fell furiously upon the enemy. Abū Dujānah, a famous athlete, and Ḥamzah displayed prodigies of valour. As they swept along facing death on all sides, they threw the ranks of the Makkans into confusion, Ḥamzah at length fell to the javelin of a negro slave, Waḥshī, hired by Hindah, Abū Sufyān's wife, for that express purpose. Yet the Muslims fought desperately. Seven Makkan flagbearers fell one after another, till utter confusion seized the enemy. At last they took to flight, the Muslims closely pursuing them. Thus, once more the Muslims were on the point of securing a glorious victory over the Makkans. But a single act of indifference to duty on the part of the Muslim archers posted at the point where the surprise attack was apprehended turned the scales against them. Beholding the Makkans put to flight, the archers asked their commander's permission to join the rest of the Muslim army in the pursuit. Notwithstanding his refusal, they quitted their position which the Holy Prophet had so strictly ordered them to hold to the last, only 'Abd Allāh ibn Jubair with a few others keeping to their posts.

Khālid's attack from the rear

Khālid, who had the command of the Makkan cavalry, and who was keenly watching the situation, perceived the weak point, now left almost undefended. Losing no time, he wheeled round to the rear at the head of his two hundred men and, sweeping aside the few Muslim archers left at the opening, fell upon the Muslim army at a time when their line had become loose and irregular in consequence of their hot pursuit. The broken and fleeing ranks of the Makkans, seeing Khālid fall upon the Muslims from the rear, also turned back, and the handful of Muslims were thus encompassed on both sides. The overwhelming numbers of the enemy would have utterly crushed them had not a tactical precaution been taken beforehand by the Holy Prophet. When drawing up his army in battle array, he, like a vigilant general, had taken good care to provide for an adverse turn of fortune and the position with the mountain at his rear had been taken up with the express object of utilizing it as a refuge in the event of a disaster.

The Holy Prophet's bold action

While the Muslim army was busy pursuing the enemy, the Holy Prophet was keeping behind with Ṭalḥah and Sa'd. No sooner did he see Khālid advance and take up the position deserted by the archers, then he perceived the critical nature of the danger to which the Muslim army was exposed. Alternative courses were, under the circumstances, open to him – either to secure his own safety by betaking himself to a place of shelter, leaving his friends to their fate; or to call out to them at personal risk, in order to take them out of the danger. He chose the latter. Finding them hard pressed, he shouted at the top of his voice: "Rally to me, I am the Messenger of Allāh." As soon as the Holy Prophet's voice reached their ears, they turned their faces towards him, cutting their way through the ranks of the enemy. But while the shout attracted the Muslims towards him, it also signalled his whereabouts to the enemy. In a moment he became the target of the enemy's attacks. But his companions, devoted heart and soul to him, defended his precious life at the cost of their own, falling one by one around him. In the meantime, Muṣ'ab ibn 'Umair, who resembled the Holy Prophet in appearance, was slain. The news spread like wild fire that the Holy Prophet had been killed. This caused still greater consternation in the already confused ranks of the Muslims. One of them was so deeply struck with grief that he could no longer wield his sword. Another, Anas ibn Naḍar, was amazed to see him stand listless. He explained that it was no use fighting when the Prophet was dead. "Of what worth is life then," replied Anas, "if the Prophet is no longer in our midst? Let us fight on for the cause which he fought for."

Muslim rally

Thus cheering each other and piercing through the enemy's ranks, the companions mustered strong around their beloved Leader. By that time he had sustained serious wounds and had fallen to the ground. His devoted friends protected him, making a human wall around his body. The enemy bore down in all force upon this point, but the wall of Muslim soldiers proved invulnerable. A gap created by the fall of one was instantly filled by another rushing in to take his place. Recovering from the shocks, the Muslims again closed their ranks and once more gave the enemy a good fight, meeting blow with blow. Besides, they had now retreated to a position which defied all attempts at assault. The Quraish exerted their utmost and made repeated attacks but they were repulsed every time. They lost all hope of smashing the Muslims, now once more rallied into a compact body. The shots of Abū Ṭalḥah, the famous archer, kept pouring down on them with unerring accuracy. He broke three bows. Sa'd emptied the

Holy Prophet's quiver and took heavy toll of the enemy. Besides, they were now more exposed to the arrows and stones of the Muslims, who held a position of advantage. Thus, partly because of the well-directed Muslim archery and their better position, and partly because of the reckless daring which the Quraish knew to be characteristic of the Muslims, they thought it advisable to retreat.

Quraish atrocities

Thus frustrated in their attempts at the destruction of the Muslims, the Quraish gratified their passion for revenge on the field. Terrible acts of barbarity were committed on the slain. Their bodies were mutilated. Hindah tore out Ḥamzah's liver and chewed it; she strung his intestines together and garlanded herself. Abū Sufyān shouted from a distance: "Is Muḥammad there among you?" The Holy Prophet forbade a reply. Then he called aloud: "Is Abū Bakr there among you?" No reply again. "Is 'Umar there among you?" And he added: "All of them are slain; were they alive, they would have responded." 'Umar could no longer restrain himself "O thou enemy of Allāh," replied he, "they are all alive yet to bring woe to thee." Then Abū Sufyān shouted: "Glory to *Hubal!*" On this the Holy Prophet asked 'Umar to reply: "Allāh is the Most High and the Most Mighty." So long as it was a personal question, the Holy Prophet cared little for Abū Sufyān's ravings and would rather ignore them than give a reply. But when the honour of Allāh was involved, he could not keep quiet. Respect for His exalted Name urged him to give Abū Sufyān a befitting retort. Again, the latter cried out: '*Uzzā* is ours, *'Uzzā* is not yours." Again, at the bidding of the Holy Prophet, 'Umar replied: "Allāh is our Protector; there is no protector for you." Nevertheless, the Holy Prophet had a heart full of tender mercy even for the enemy. When asked to pray for the destruction of the Quraish, he thus implored to Allāh in all humility: "O Allāh! forgive my people, for they do not know."

Some of the Muslims, when they were once cut off from the rest in the general confusion that seized the Muslim ranks on Khālid's surprise assault, could not make their way back to the main body and left the field under the false impression that their army had been defeated. But their wives, on learning that they had left the Holy Prophet in the field, threw dust in their faces. A number of women-folk made straight towards the field, all enquiring about the welfare of the Holy Prophet. They felt more anxious on his account than for their own kith and kin. It is related that on being informed of the death of the father, a woman from among the Helpers simply recited the usual Quranic verse: "For we are Allāh's and to Him shall we return,"[1] and anxiously asked if the Holy Prophet was safe. She was then told that her brother had also fallen. She repeated the verse, but put the same question with the same concern on the Holy Prophet's fate. But yet more painful news – her husband too had been slain. With a deep sigh she uttered the same words, and on being informed that the Holy Prophet was quite safe, all her grief disappeared. When she saw him with her own eyes, she exclaimed with immense relief: "Now that you are alive, every calamity seems small." With the same dignified resignation, all other women bore the loss of their slain and mutilated relations. Some, 'Ā'ishah among them, had kept with the army on the battlefield and given drink to the wounded and nursed them while the battle was raging.

With the retreat of the Muslims to the cover of the mountain, Madīnah was left entirely exposed. But Abū Sufyān and his hosts had no courage to turn thither nor to pursue hostilities to a finish, which, they had good reasons to fear, might mean disaster to them. In hot haste, they turned towards Makkah, marching several miles the same day. On the way they discussed whether they could fairly claim to have been victorious. They had no spoils of victory to show nor had they a single prisoner of war. Was that a victory? The Muslim army was still in possession of the field. Was that a victory? They had not been able to overrun Madīnah, undefended though it was. Was that a victory? These were the various thoughts that occurred to them. Suggestions were made that they should return and decide the issue, but they could not summon up courage to do so. While they were wavering, news reached them that the Holy Prophet was on their heels with his army. The pluck of the Muslims on this occasion has been spoken of in the Qur'ān in highly commendatory terms.[2]

1 The Qur'ān, 2 : 156.; 2 The Qur'ān, 3 : 153.

Despite so many troubles and afflictions, it says, when the Holy Prophet called on them to come out to chase the enemy, they cheerfully responded. They followed the enemy, the very next day, right up to Ḥamrā' al-Asad, eight miles from Madīnah. But Abū Sufyān, thinking discretion the better part of valour, marched off with his army as soon as the news of the Muslim pursuit reached him.

Uḥud was not a defeat for Muslims

It betrays a lack of knowledge of historical facts to conclude that the Muslims were defeated at the battle of Uḥud. It is no doubt true that the Muslims sustained a heavy loss, but it is not less true that the Quraish had to turn back disappointed. Does history record a single instance of victory, in which the vanquished foe kept to the field and the victorious army marched off homeward without taking a single captive; at which the fallen foe had the pluck to pursue the victors the next day only a few hours after the battle and the victors took to flight on hearing of the chase? No doubt the Muslims had to pass through grave crises in this battle. The Holy Prophet in person was severely wounded and the rumour even went forth that he had been slain; and with that it was thought that Islām had, as a matter of course, come to an end. But all this had to come to pass in the life of the Holy Prophet to serve as a beacon of hope and courage for succeeding generations of Muslims, lest in times of distress and disappointment they should ever lose heart. The enemy may make jubilation over what appears to him as the overthrow of Islām but the Muslim heart must rest at ease. Islām is imperishable. Every calamity, however great, must turn out to be its real triumph in disguise.

It may be added that the battle of Uḥud had a very disquieting effect on the Arab tribes in general. It stirred them to open hostilities against Islām. They felt convinced that the Quraish meant to destroy the faith or else they would not have undertaken the trouble and cost of so big an expedition. Thus assured of the Quraishite resolve, the malice of the several tribes, so far suppressed, began to manifest itself. They thought the Muslim cause was ruined and they must not lag behind in participating in the honour of its overthrow. Here, there and everywhere, tribes made preparations to fall upon the Muslims.

The moral and spiritual culture of the people was no doubt the sole mission of the Holy Prophet. This great object could not, however, be achieved but through the small noble band he had prepared for the purpose. Now that the very existence of those who were intended to devote themselves to the spiritual purification of humanity was in danger, was it not his duty to adopt all possible measures to safeguard them? The interest of the ideal he had set before him called for resolute action. Besides, the Holy Prophet was the head of the community, and as such was responsible for their weal and woe. His position as their leader laid on him the obligation of looking after their good. In this respect too, he is an example to those placed in authority over others. As demonstrated by that perfect exemplar for mankind, the leader of men must not accept his position for the pleasant privileges it affords; he must face the irksome responsibilities it entails. It is his moral duty to think out ways and means to defend his people against aggression and adopt measures conducive to their welfare. Had the Holy Prophet no other record of brilliant achievements, this one great deed would have entitled him to a unique position in human history. He found his people hemmed in on all sides by deadly foes. Their existence was perpetually in danger. Through his foresightedness and self-sacrifice he rescued them from all perils and enabled them to win the laurels of success. The building-up of a nation comes under the category of great deeds in human history, and the success the Holy Prophet achieved in creating a mighty nation in the face of stupendous obstacles is unequalled in the annals of nation-building.

Insecurity of Muslims

As a result of the battle of Uḥud, the Jewish communities of Madīnah, disregarding their agreement, entered into conspiracies with the Quraish to injure the Muslims. The attitude of the hypocrites as well now became more openly inimical. They made it a point to cause trouble to the faithful in every way. The neighbouring tribes had also resolved to strike a death blow at Islām, thinking it was already on the verge of extinction. There was no security left for the Muslims, neither within nor without the city of Madīnah. Intelligence was daily received of an attack, now from this side, now from that. It was a very anxious time. The Muslims could not move about without arms. We learn from a report that they could not part with their arms even at night. The continuous strain at last exhausted their patience and they opened their hearts to the Holy Prophet, stating how unbearable things had become. He comforted and consoled them, assuring them that the dawn of peace was at hand. He shared the strain and stress of these days of hardship in person, and took every precaution to avert the danger of attacks threatening on all sides. One day, while it was yet dark, there was some uproar and it was feared that an enemy had come to assault the city or that a raid had been committed. The Muslims rallied from all parts and were prepared to march out in resistance. But to their amazement they beheld the Holy Prophet coming back on a saddle-less horse, having scoured the outskirts. There was no danger, he informed them, and no cause for anxiety. He thus demonstrated that he was not merely a wise superior but at the same time a brave soldier with a daring contempt for danger.

Butchering of Innocent Muslim Preachers

But, Madīnah was in the grip of constant peril and Muslims had to remain every moment on the alert. Every precaution was taken to nip the slightest danger in the bud. If trouble was reported to be hatching in one quarter and an attack upon Madīnah was apprehended, a detachment was forthwith despatched to deal with the danger before it grew. What might have resulted in the terrible conflagration of war was thus averted by timely precautions. Hostile critics accuse Islām of proselytizing at the point of the sword – an allegation diametrically opposed to the real state of things. Conversion was never secured by the sword. Not a solitary instance of conversion has been reported as a fruit of warlike expeditions. For the propagation of religion, the Holy Prophet appointed preachers prepared expressly for this purpose. These teachers, who had committed the Holy Qur'ān to memory, used to spread the light of Islām among the various tribes. Treacherous people would sometimes invite these teachers under the pretext of seeking instruction in the teachings of Islām and, having them at their mercy, would kill them without compunction. One such treacherous barbarity took place at Bi'r Ma'ūnah in the month of Ṣafar in the year 4 A.H. Abū Barā', chief of the tribes of Banū ʻĀmir and Banū Sulaim, came to the Holy Prophet with presents, asking for a few teachers to be deputed to his people, who, he hoped, might accept the message of Islām. The Holy Prophet did not accept the presents and said he feared treachery from the people of Najd. But on Abū Barā's undertaking responsibility for their safety, he consented and sent seventy select missionaries with him. On reaching a place called Bi'r Ma'ūnah, they found themselves surrounded by a large army. These emissaries of the Divine message were all put to the sword with the solitary exception of one, ʻAmr Umayyah, who managed to escape and narrated the heart-rending tale to the Holy Prophet, who was severely shocked at the brutal treachery.

A similar tragedy is recorded to have been enacted at another place, Rajīʻ. Certain tribes sent word to the Holy Prophet that they had embraced Islām and were anxious to have some teachers. The Holy Prophet thereupon sent ten preachers who met with the same fate. They offered some resistance. Eight were slain while struggling in self-defence whereas two, Khubaib and Zaid, relying on the traitors' word of honour, surrendered. They proved false to their word and, instead of setting them free as pledged, they sold them as slaves to the Makkans. Khubaib was taken by his masters, the tribe of Ḥarīth, out of the limits of the *Ḥaram,* the sacred area where violence of every form was forbidden even in pre-Islāmic Arabia and was slain. Before meeting his death he said his prayers, and then recited these verses:

> *"While I am killed as a Muslim, I do not mind on which side I fall for the sake of Allāh.*
>
> *"All this is in Allāh's path. He may shower His blessings on my mutilated limbs, should it so please Him."*

Zaid was purchased by Ṣafwān ibn Umayyah with the same intention. Abū Sufyān and the leading Quraish chiefs were all present at his execution. When the sword was unsheathed to cut off his head Abū Sufyān threw an irresistible temptation in his way. "Do you desire," he said, "that your life may be spared on condition that Muḥammad be slain in your stead." How noble and dignified was Zaid's reply at this critical hour of his life, when death was staring him in the face! "My life is nothing as compared with the Prophet's. I would not like to see him suffer the pain of even the prick of a thorn, even though it were to save my life." This is a typical illustration of the deep attachment the companions of the Holy Prophet cherished for him.

The Prophet forbidden to pray against tyrants

Such ruthless butchering of innocent Muslim teachers by the perfidious Arab tribes was indeed very painful to the Holy Prophet. He could put up with all sorts of hardships so far as his own person was concerned, but he could not bear the tortures of those who had accepted the Truth and never failed to stand by him in the hour of danger; who had cheerfully sacrificed their all in the path of Allāh, and thus had won exalted positions in the eyes of the Lord. The murder of the preachers was an unbearable shock to him, and he prayed to God to punish the offenders for these heinous crimes. As a matter of fact, these tribes deserved the same form of torturous punishment, but the Holy Prophet, when so deeply grieved, contented himself with praying to God to deal with them. But God had sent him as a mercy to the whole mankind.[1] He did not approve of his being so harsh as to invoke Divine wrath even upon such arch-criminals. He was to be the embodiment of universal mercy – making no distinction between friend and foe. Hence the Divine revelation: "Thou hast no concern in the matter whether He turns to them mercifully or chastises them; surely they are wrongdoers."[2] No sooner was this Divine reproval received than he gave up harbouring ill-will towards the treacherous perpetrators of cold-blooded murder on harmless preachers. Can history show a parallel?

Smaller engagements

To cut short a long tale of woe and misery the whole of Arabia was seething with spite against Islām. Jews, hypocrites, idolaters, each and all were out to annihilate Islām. Were it not for watchfulness on the part of the Holy Prophet in suppressing every storm of opposition before it gained strength, it would have been impossible for Muslims to stay a single day in Madīnah. There was thus only one practical policy in the circumstances left for Muslims – to scatter the enemy's forces

1 The Qur'ān, 21 : 107.; 2 Ibid., 3 : 128.

before they united and became strong enough to crush Islām. The situation called for a forward policy. They could not afford to sit quietly by, watching with complacence the enemy's hosts gathering till they had grown too strong for them. Obviously, this would have spelt the sure and certain extinction of Islām. Compelled by sheer force of circumstances, the instinct of self-preservation impelled them to take the bull by the horns. Of the several petty skirmishes that took place in this period one is known as the battle of Badr Ṣughrā (Smaller Badr) or Badr Ākhirah (Second Badr). Departing from the field of Uḥud, the Quraish had thrown out a challenge to the Muslims, that their fate would be tried again at Badr, the following year. Accordingly, when the time came, the Muslims marched to Badr but, not finding the Quraish there, peacefully returned, after disposing at the fair annually held there of whatever merchandise they had taken with them. The battle of Dūmat al-Jandal and Dhāt al-Riqā' in the year 5 A.H. and the "battles" of Banū Liḥyān and the Dhū Qarad in 6 A.H. were all of this nature. On the receipt of intelligence as to the enemy's war-like preparations, a body of Muslim troops was forthwith despatched and the hostile forces scattered either immediately or, in some cases, after a little skirmishing.

There are a number of other small skirmishes of which the one known as the battle of Muraisī' or Banū Muṣṭaliq, which took place in 5 A.H., is of some note. The Banū Muṣṭaliq came of the Khuzā'ah, a tribe which was in strong alliance with the Quraish. They inhabited a place called Muraisī', nine days' journey from Madīnah. Their chief, Ḥārith ibn Abī Ḍirār, made preparations to attack Madīnah, possibly on the instigation of the Quraish. Intelligence was brought to the Holy Prophet, who found it to be correct. He thereupon ordered counter-preparations to scatter the forces of Ḥārith. The latter fled with his army, but the inhabitants of Muraisī' gave the Muslims a battle and were defeated. Six hundred prisoners of war, including Juwairiyah, the daughter of Ḥārith, fell into the hands of Muslims. The Holy Prophet paid the ransom of Juwairiyah out of his own pocket and took her in marriage at her own request. In consequence all the six hundred prisoners of Banī Muṣṭaliq were released without ransom.

Slander against 'Ā'ishah

It was on the return journey from Muraisī' in the year 5 A.H. that 'Ā'ishah was accidentally left behind on the last stage of the journey. When the army started, she had gone out to search for a necklace which she just discovered to be lost, and her camel-driver started with an empty *howda,* thinking that she was in it. When 'Ā'ishah came back from the search, there was not a man left. It being dark, she sat down, thinking that when the mistake was discovered, her camel-driver would come back. Ṣafwān ibn Mu'aṭṭal had orders to remain in the rear to see that nothing was left behind when the march took place. It was day-light when he discovered 'Ā'ishah and, seating her on his camel, he joined the army at midday. The hypocrites, always on the look-out for some opportunity to injure the cause of Islām, made this unfortunate accident the basis of a slander against the noble lady, 'Abd Allāh ibn Ubayy being the chief source of the slandering rumours. The Holy Prophet made an enquiry which showed that there was not the least ground for casting aspersions on 'Ā'ishah's chastity. He further received Divine revelation establishing her innocence.[1] There is nothing strange in the Holy Prophet receiving a revelation clearing a righteous woman of baseless slander; for the Holy Qur'ān had already cleared another righteous woman, Mary, the mother of Jesus, of a similar charge brought against her by the Jews, denouncing them "for their having uttered against Mary a false calumny".[2]

The Battle of Aḥzāb

While the Holy Prophet was engaged in suppressing mischief on the part of the Arab tribes in order to obviate war on a large scale, the Quraish were busy preparing for another campaign against Madīnah. The Jewish clans exiled from Madīnah, now settled at Khaibar, were also allied with them in the common cause of the extirpation of Islām. They succeeded in rousing the Bedouin tribes in the vicinity of Makkah so that they also joined the anti-Islāmic alliance. Thus Quraish, Jews and Bedouins all combined to deal a crushing blow to Islām.

1 The Qur'ān, 24 : 11-20.; 2 Ibid., 4 : 156.

A large army, estimated at from ten to twenty-four thousand, was brought together in the 5th year of the Hijrah. Even the Jewish tribes within the walls of Madīnah turned false and joined hands at the last moment with the assailants. Humanly calculating, there was little chance for the Muslims to survive the onrush of these overwhelming hosts.

Intelligence of this impending attack on an unprecedented scale was brought to the Holy Prophet, who immediately summoned his companions to take counsel as to how to meet the situation. On one side, the city had a natural barrier of rugged rocks; on the other, it was protected by the stone walls of houses, built compactly together in unbroken continuation, which constituted by themselves a strong fortification. There was thus only one side open to attack and Salmān, a Persian Muslim, suggested that that side should be fortified by a broad and deep ditch. The work of digging the ditch was at once undertaken. The Holy Prophet apportioned the labour amongst parties of ten men each, himself participating like an ordinary labourer. Covered with earth and dust, they sang these verses in chorus: "O Allāh! had it not been for Thy mercy, we could not have had guidance. We would not have given alms, neither would we have prayed. Send down tranquillity upon us, and establish our steps in battle. For they are against us and they wish to pervert us by force, but we refuse."

The last words, "but we refuse" formed the burden of the song, and were repeated again and again. At the same time the Holy Prophet invoked Allāh's blessings on the Refugees and the Helpers in these words: "O Allāh! there is no felicity but the felicity of the Hereafter; O Allāh have mercy on the Refugees and the Helpers!"

The Prophet sees vision of a great future

History records but this sole instance of a personage who held spiritual as well as temporal sway over a nation, and yet worked as an ordinary workman, side by side with them, in the hour of extreme national danger. It is a distinguishing feature of the Holy Prophet's character that he conferred lustre on whatever he set his hands to. Placed in whatever position, he acquitted himself with marvellous grace. The manliest of kings, he was at once the kingliest of men. In the course of the digging operations they came upon a hard stone. All exerted themselves to the utmost but could not break it. The Holy Prophet, who had marked out the limits with his own hands, was therefore asked to allow a slight deviation from the original plan. Taking up a pick axe he addressed himself to the task at which others had failed. Getting down into the ditch, he struck hard at the stone which gave way emitting at the same time a spark of fire, on which the Holy Prophet, followed by the companions, raised a cry of *Allāh-u-Akbar* (God is Great), and said that he saw in the spark that he had been awarded the keys of the palace of the Syrian king. A second stroke and the stone was split, another spark being emitted. Once more the *takbīr*, "God is Great" was shouted aloud, the Holy Prophet observing that he had been given the keys of the Persian kingdom. The third attempt broke the stone to pieces and the Holy Prophet announced that he had seen the keys of Yaman coming into his possession. Then he explained that on the first occasion, he was shown the palace of the Caesar, on the second that of the Chosroes of Persia, and on the third, that of Ṣan'ā, and that he had been informed that his followers would gain possession of all these countries. What a phenomenon! A huge force, 24,000 strong, was at the very gates of Madīnah, determined to crush out Islām. The whole of Arabia was thirsting for Muslim blood. And in the midst of these dark clouds of misfortune, the Holy Prophet's eye perceived a distant ray of the future power of Islām. Was this not something passing the wildest stretch of human imagination? Who but the All-Wise and All-Knowing God could reveal such mysteries of the future at a juncture when Islām itself was threatened with utter extinction?

It was an hour of terrible consternation for the Muslims when the confederate hosts fell in full force upon Madīnah. The very foundations of the city were shaken. The Holy Qur'ān depicts the anguish and perplexity of the moment in these words: "When they came upon you from above you and from below you, and when the eyes turned dull and the hearts rose up to the throats, and you began to think diverse thoughts about Allāh. There were the believers tried and they were shaken with a severe shaking."[1]

1 The Qur'ān, 33 : 10-11.

But through the seeming scene of dread and terror, the hearts of true Muslims could read the fulfilment of what had been promised to them by Allāh and his Messenger. Their thoughts are thus set forth in the Holy Qur'ān:

> *"And when the believers saw the allies, they said: This is what Allāh and His Messenger promised us, and Allāh and His Messenger spoke the truth. And it only added to their faith and submission.*[1]

Notwithstanding the enormously overwhelming odds bent upon their destruction, and their fears in the grim situation, Muslims perceived that this was the last desperate attempt of a dying enemy. This would break up the enemy's power once and for all, and usher in the happy era of the triumph of Islām.

Muslim sufferings in siege

By way of precaution against a possible attack from without, or Jewish treachery from within, the females and children were removed to well-fortified places. The siege lasted for about a month, during which period the Muslims, including the Holy Prophet, suffered a great deal from hunger. For days they received no food and tied stones on their stomachs to mitigate the pangs. But their spirit was not a whit subdued. One day the Holy Prophet suggested buying off the tribe of Ghaṭafān by offering them one-third of the produce of Madīnah. This would have gone a great way to weaken the enemy's strength. Notwithstanding their starvation and the straits to which they had been reduced by a prolonged siege and perpetual vigil, Muslims thought it below their dignity to submit to such humiliation. The Helpers, who were directly concerned in the proposed bargain, said they had never paid subsidy to the Ghaṭafān even in pre-Islāmic days and would not cow down before them now, especially when the honour of Islām was involved. Come what might, they would fight to the last man.

Confederates routed

The Jews and hypocrites were on the lookout for an opportunity to rise from within, simultaneously with an attack from without. Duels were tried first in which the Muslims had the

1 The Qur'ān, 33 : 22.

upper hand. 'Amr ibn Wudd, a famous Arab hero believed to be a match for a thousand, was slain at 'Alī's hands. At last, the Quraish made a general attack in full force, but they could not press their way across the ditch. Their arrows and stones, however, came down in terrible showers, and had it not been for the well-disciplined steadfastness of the Muslims, the enemy would have won the day. Muslims' firmness was at last crowned with success. The large army, 24,000 strong, could not succeed in breaking through their defence and became exhausted. The siege became tiresome to them. Besides, they ran short of provisions. A storm which blew down their tents and overturned their cooking pots was the final straw. The Holy Qur'ān thus alludes to the incident: "We sent against them a strong wind and hosts that you saw not."[1] The wind accomplished for the Muslims what they could not do by the strength of their own arms. Finding the very elements of nature against them, the Quraish and their confederates were much overawed. They took it as an evil portent. Losing heart, they marched off the same night so that, to the great joy and thanksgiving of the Muslims, not one of them could be seen the following morning. Was it anything but the Divine hand at work behind the scenes, frustrating the attempts of overwhelming odds to crush the handful of Muslims and setting at naught the treacherous schemes of Jews and hypocrites?

Thus ended in utter disappointment and dismay the most powerfully organised expedition against Islām.

Relations with the Jews

The Jews, as already observed, formed a potent element of the population of Madīnah. Trade coupled with usury had made them rich. The Aus and the Khazraj generally borrowed money from them. In point of education and in almost every respect the Jews were ahead of their neighbours.

On the arrival of the Holy Prophet at Madīnah, the Jews entered into an agreement with the Muslims. But the growing prosperity of Islām kindled the spark of jealousy in their hearts. Keeping secretly in touch with the hypocrites, they

1 The Qur'ān, 33 : 9.

made much mischief against the Muslims.[1] They did not spare even the Holy Prophet whom they addressed in insolent and derogatory words. For instance while speaking to him, they would twist the word *rā'inā*, which means "listen to us", into *ra'ina*, meaning, "he is a fool." Likewise the words *al-salām-u-'alaikum, i.e.,* peace be to you, would be muttered *al-sām-u-'alaikum, i.e.,* death overtake you. Various ingenious plans were adopted to injure the cause of Islām. Some embraced the faith with the set purpose of bringing many more out of the fold.

What was only jealousy in the beginning grew in course of time into positive enmity. Insinuations against Muslim women in obscene verses were also freely indulged in. They even stooped so low as to molest them in the streets. One such incident in a street of Madīnah resulted in the murder of a Jew and a Muslim and ultimately led to actual fighting between the two communities. The Jewish tribe of Banū Qainuqā', with whom the trouble arose, warned the Muslims to bear in mind that they were not like the Quraish, they would give them a lesson. Thus breaking their compact, they resolved upon fighting out the issue with the Muslims and betook themselves to fortified strongholds. The Muslims too had to prepare for war and laid siege to their forts. After a siege of fifteen days, the Jews offered to surrender and to bear whatever penalty the Holy Prophet might choose to impose upon them for their breach of the agreement. They were required to quit Madīnah which they did, settling in Syria. This came about a month after the battle of Badr.

Another Jewish tribe, the Banū Naḍīr, notwithstanding their agreement with the Muslims maintained secret negotiations with the Quraish from the very beginning. Before the battle of Badr, the Quraish wrote asking them to murder the Holy Prophet. Once they invited the Holy Prophet and made a vain attempt on his life. Jewish treachery becoming manifest through such acts, the Holy Prophet could not safely allow such a dangerous element to remain in the very heart of Madīnah. They were consequently offered the alternatives of renewing their agreement with the Muslims as an assurance of

1 "Vehement hatred has already appeared from out of their mouths, and that which their hearts conceal is greater still" (The Qur'ān, 3 : 118).

their peaceful intentions or settling elsewhere. The Banū Quraiẓah, who had been so far not guilty of serious treachery against Islām, willingly renewed the agreement. But the Banū Naḍīr, bent on mischief, refused to do so. They now became open enemies of Islām. 'Abd Allāh ibn Ubayy also promised them help, which confirmed them in their opposition. Islām, it must be borne in mind, was at this time passing through a very critical stage. It was the period of the battle of Uḥud, when enemies on all sides were up in arms to strike a deathblow at the faith. An external assault was dangerous but an internal outburst, which might come any moment, was still more so. To be forewarned is to be forearmed. This was possible in the case of an external attack, which would allow the Muslims time to prepare themselves to meet the situation. But an unexpected explosion in Madīnah itself would mean a sure blow at the very heart of Islām. The Banū Naḍīr had friendly relations with the enemies of Islām. Their refusal to renew the agreement was therefore tantamount to a declaration of war. Besides, they were guilty of having attempted to take the Holy Prophet's life. In view of all these considerations, the only course left was to treat them as avowed enemies. Siege was therefore laid to their strongholds and it was raised only on condition that the Banū Naḍīr left Madīnah. Some of them went to Khaibar and settled there. This took place in the fourth year of the Flight.

The Banū Naḍīr played an important part in connection with the battle of Aḥzāb. Besides rousing the Quraishite tribes they roamed about the desert, visiting the haunts of the Bedouins and stirring them up against Islām. The Banū Quraiẓah whose attitude towards the Muslims had so far been friendly were also affected. At first, they refused to join in a war against Islām, but they were given repeated assurance that the Muslims stood no chance of survival. They could not possibly withstand the combined force of the vast forces springing up like mushrooms on every side to put an end to Islām. It was, they were told, time that they made their choice between throwing in their lot with the Muslims or joining hands with the confederates. The Banū Quraiẓah were thus prevailed upon to make common cause with the rest of the anti-Islāmic tribes. Breaking their pact with the Muslims, they entered into an alliance with the confederates, promising them help in the ensuing conflict – the battle of Aḥzāb. The new and secret compact did not remain a dead letter. The Banū Quraiẓah actually took part in the battle. The Holy Qur'ān refers to this in the following words: "Those of the people of the Book who backed them (the confederates)"[1]. History too, furnishes testimony to their participation in the battle. They had planned an attack on Muslim women as well. It was an hour of grave danger for the Muslims. With twenty-four thousand enemies on the other side of the ditch exerting themselves tooth and nail to crush Islām, and with the hypocrites busy making mischief within, the treachery of the Banū Quraiẓah added enormously to the difficulties of the Muslims. Hence when the battle of Aḥzāb ended it was deemed right to inflict due punishment on them as a preventive against the recurrence of such underhand treachery. Siege was laid to their fastnesses and after some resistance they surrendered. This took place in the fifth year of the Hijrah.

Their punishment

Sa'd ibn Mu'ādh, formerly their ally, was chosen by themselves to determine, as an arbitrator, what punishment they deserved. Had they left the decision to the Holy Prophet, they would most probably have received the same treatment as their sister tribes, the Banū Qainuqā' and the Banū Naḍīr. At worst, they would have been exiled. But Sa'd the arbitrator of their own choice, viewed their treachery in the hour of peril with great abhorrence. The gravity of their offence, he believed, called for exemplary punishment, in the absence of which solemn agreements would in future command little respect and be treated as worthless scraps of paper by any of the parties concerned. Hence he came to the conclusion that punishment in no way milder than that prescribed for a vanquished foe in their own Scripture, the Old Testament, was their just deserts. This is what the Old Testament lays down on the point: "And when the Lord, thy God, hath delivered it into thine hands, thou shalt smite every male thereof with the edge of the sword. But the woman and the little ones and the cattle and all that is in the city, even all the spoil thereof, shalt thou take in to thy-

1 The Qur'ān, 33 : 26.

self and thou shalt eat the spoils of thy enemies which the Lord thy God has given thee" (Deut., 20 : 13-14).

By the verdict of Sa'd, therefore, in accordance with Mosaic law, the male portion of the Banū Quraiẓah, numbering three hundred, were sentenced to death and the females and children to captivity, and the property was confiscated. Harsh as the punishment may appear, it was exactly the judgment the Jews used to pass under the law of their Book, against their fallen foes. Besides the heinous crime of treachery of which the Banū Quraiẓah were guilty would in like circumstances be visited with no lighter punishment even in this age of civilization. The judge was one of their own choice, and the sentence was in strict conformity with their own sacred law. Again, they were guilty of treachery of a dangerous nature. Is the Holy Prophet to be criticised on this account? The objection against the harshness of this punishment is an objection against Mosaic Law. It is, in fact, an unconscious censure of that law as well as an admission that a more humane law had to supersede it. A contrast with Islāmic law on this point will bring into clear relief what a tender, sympathetic and compassionate law Islām came to inaugurate.

Conquest of Khaibar

The battle of Khaibar comes after the truce of Ḥudaibiyah in the seventh year of the Flight, but inasmuch as it has a bearing on Islāmic-Jewish relations, it is not out of place to treat it here. When banished from Madīnah the major portion of the Banū Naḍīr, especially their ring-leaders, settled at Khaibar, the strong-hold of the Jews in Arabia, at a distance of about 200 miles from Madīnah. Here they held independent sway, and had fortified the place strongly. On the arrival of the Banū Naḍīr, the seed of enmity against Islām was sown in their hearts. On the occasion of the battle of Aḥzāb, they roused against Islām the Makkans, the tribe of Ghaṭafān and the Bedouin tribes and even enlisted the cooperation of the Banū Quraiẓah. With the unsuccessful expedition of Aḥzāb, the Muslim power took firm roots in Madīnah. The Jewish malice, however, grew in bitterness. They held secret negotiations with 'Abd Allāh ibn Ubayy, head of the hypocrites, who gave them every assurance that they could yet crush the power of Islām. In the year 6 A.H. the Holy Prophet was debarred by the Makkans from performing the pilgrimage and had to conclude a truce with them on rather humiliating conditions. This deepened the impression of the Jews of Khaibar as to the weakness of the Muslim power and they began to cherish fresh hopes of bringing about the destruction of Islām. They took to conspiring once more with the tribe of Ghaṭafān with a view to directing another expedition against Madīnah. Intelligence of their designs came to the Holy Prophet who, after due verification of the report, directed a body of 1,600 men to advance on Khaibar. Midway between Khaibar and Ghaṭafān lay a place called Rajī'. On strategical grounds this was chosen as the base and this move cut off all intercourse between the two places. No help from the Ghaṭafān was thus forthcoming. The latter conscious of their guilt apprehended an attack upon themselves and felt concerned on their own account. It was thought that the Jews would abandon the idea of resistance and would surrender. But as the Muslims advanced on Khaibar, it was found that the Jews had made every preparation to offer a hard battle. Fighting commenced; several fortresses were captured by the Muslims. But one fortress called Qamūṣ, which was very strongly fortified and manned, held out for about twenty days, when at last this too fell before a fierce assault directed by 'Alī. After their surrender the Jews requested that they might be left in possession of their lands on condition that half of the produce would be made over as tribute. The request was granted and the Jews were allowed to retain possession of the place though the Holy Prophet knew they would not refrain from mischief-making.

Jewish plot against the Holy Prophet

Immediately after the settlement, the leading Jews conspired against the life of the Holy Prophet. Zainab, wife of Ḥārith, a Jewish chief who had fallen in the action, was instigated to invite the Holy Prophet to dinner and poison him. By Divine Providence, however, the Holy Prophet had hardly lifted a morsel to his mouth when, suspecting treachery, he withheld his hand. But one of his companions, Bishr ibn Barā', who took the food, died of the effect of poison. Treacherous and mischievous as they were, the generous treatment accorded them by the Muslims had no effect. It failed to extinguish the fire of enmity in their hearts. They proved a source of perpetual trouble, ever plotting treachery to injure the Muslims. Down to the time of 'Umar's Caliphate they continued their mischief. Once they cast 'Umar's own son, 'Abd Allāh, from the top of a house. Every attempt at conciliating them having proved futile, they were at last exiled by 'Umar to Syria.

The Prophet's lenient dealing

The Holy Prophet, however, dealt with the Jews of Khaibar mercifully. He did all in his power to conciliate them. Their attempts to poison him would have justified the most drastic measures against the whole people. But he was anxious to see them united in a bond of friendship with the Muslims and no punitive measures were adopted against them. Only the immediate perpetrator of the base crime, Zainab, was punished with death, and that for the murder of Bishr. The conspirators – and in fact the whole nation was involved in the foul attempt – were all allowed to go free. They all deserved death, but the Holy Prophet hoped that forgiveness might change their hostile attitude.

Marriage with Ṣafiyyah

He took a further step to make friendship with them. Among the captives who had fallen into the hands of the Muslims was Ṣafiyyah, the daughter of their Chief. The Holy Prophet liberated her and in order to conciliate the Khaibarites took her in marriage. Fabulous treasures, it is alleged came into the possession of the Muslims at the conquest of Khaibar. These are however, merely imaginary tales, the worth of which can well be gauged from the fact that at his marriage ceremony with Ṣafiyyah, the Holy Prophet had not the means to entertain his friends to the customary feast. They were asked to bring their own meals and these constituted the wedding feast. What was placed before the assembly comprised only of dates and ground barley. In this simple manner was celebrated the wedding of a triumphant monarch with a princess.

CHAPTER VII

THE TRUCE OF HUDAIBIYAH

"Surely We have granted thee a clear victory, that Allāh may cover for thee thy (alleged) shortcomings in the past and those to come, and complete His favour to thee and guide thee on a right path, and that Allāh might help thee with a mighty help"
- 48 : 1-3.

Islām spread in spite of the sword

The battle of Ahzāb established the fact that Islām was supported by the Divine hand. The Quraish did their utmost in two successive battles, Bādr and Uḥud, but could do little harm to Islām. The various Bedouin tribes too, exerted themselves severally but failed to shake the firm foothold of Islām. The hypocrites and the Jews in vain sought to undermine Islām from within. At last, Quraish, Bedouins, hypocrites and Jews, enemies both external and internal all made a combined attempt against Islām, but with the same result. This was the final struggle and never thereafter did the enemy gather courage to assail Madīnah. These are historical facts, admitted alike by friend and foe; yet the cry is raised that Islām owes its propagation to the instrumentality of the sword. The facts recorded on the pages of history point exactly to the reverse. The truth is that Islām spread not by the sword but in spite of the sword. No other religion has displayed such mettle. The sword fell on the Faith from all sides but, instead of destroying it, it helped as it were to extol it. Three successive attacks of increasing power were made on Madīnah with a view to extirpating Islām. But what was the result? Was the power of Islām weakened in any way? On the contrary, each time there was a considerable increase in the number of Muslims put in the field. At Badr, the Muslim army consisted of barely 300, while a year later, at Uḥud it rose to 700, and lastly at Aḥzāb, to about 2,000. A gradual growth is thus visible in the power of Islām in proportion as the attacks upon it grew in fury. The greater the attempt to crush it the more it flourished. The more it was suppressed, the more it rose. Day by day it went on thriving; no storm could uproot it, no hot wind could blight it. The Divine hand was supporting it.

The Holy Prophet sets out on pilgrimage

About a year had elapsed since the battle of Aḥzāb when the Holy Prophet saw in a vision that he, with his companions, was performing the pilgrimage at the Ka'bah. It was thought that the Quraish as well as the Bedouins, who had done their utmost against Islām, were at last impressed with its inherent strength. It was also thought that they might likewise be impressed with its truth and would not offer resistance to Muslims performing the pilgrimage. Besides, the pilgrimage to the Ka'bah was a privilege never denied even to the worst of enemies. There was thus no reason why the Quraish should stand in the way of the Muslims. Consequently in the year 6 A.H., the Holy Prophet with about 1,400 of his companions, started on an 'Umrah to Makkah.[1] By way of precaution, lest their motive should be misunderstood, it was strictly forbidden to carry arms. This, it was thought, would lay the Quraishite suspicions at rest, assuring them of the Muslims' peaceful intentions. A sheathed sword was the only arm that was allowed to be carried. A sword in those days was almost a part of every-day dress, no matter how peaceful the state. Taking sacrificial animals with them as usual, they set out for Makkah. On approaching the vicinity of the town, they found the Quraish ready to offer armed resistance. Budail, the chief of the tribe of Khuzā'ah, not a Muslim but well-disposed towards Islām, brought this intelligence to the Holy Prophet, who sent him

1 Pilgrimage is performed only in the month of Dhu-l-Hijjah 8th to 10th. A visit to the house attended with some of the ceremonies of pilgrimage proper at any other time is called 'umrah or a minor pilgrimage, lit. a visit. In this case, only 'umrah was intended.

back to tell the Quraish that the Muslims had come to perform the pilgrimage and not to fight. The Quraish, it was also proposed, might conclude peace with them for a certain period. Having sent this word to the Quraish, the Muslims halted at Ḥudaibiyah, a day's journey from Makkah.

Failure of negotiations

Budail communicated the message to the Quraish. The wiser and more experienced element was in favour of accepting the proposal of peace. They had good reasons to believe that they were unable to harm Islām. They had already done their best more than once in its opposition, but to no purpose. Besides, with the conclusion of peace, they would be in a position to resume their trade with Syria, suspended in consequence of hostilities with the Muslims who commanded the route. 'Urwah was sent as a plenipotentiary to discuss terms with the Muslims. In the course of the discussion he remarked that it was better for the Holy Prophet not to place much reliance in his followers for they would disappear should a calamity befall him. Abū Bakr was greatly enraged at this and treated him rather harshly. The negotiation ended in fiasco, but he carried away with him an impression of the high esteem in which the Holy Prophet was held by his friends. "I have been to the courts of the Caesar as well as the Chosroes," he told the Quraish, "but have never witnessed a semblance of the devotion Muḥammad commands."

Bai'at al-Riḍwān

Another emissary was sent to the Quraish by the Holy Prophet, but he was maltreated and the camel on which he rode was killed. An armed Quraish detachment also came out to take the Muslims by surprise, but was itself taken captive. The Muslims, however, had no desire to fight, and hence let them all go. At last 'Uthmān was commissioned to negotiate with the Quraish. The latter arrested him and kept him in custody. A rumour went forth that he had been murdered. The Muslims had reason to believe that the Quraish were bent upon fighting. It was a critical situation. The Muslims were practically unarmed and much smaller in number. The Quraish had every advantage on their side. But what a firm faith in Divine protection! When all negotiations had failed and the enemy was bent on bloodshed, it was not for a Muslim to turn his back. The Holy Prophet called upon his companions to pledge themselves afresh, in view of the inordinately critical nature of the situation, that they would fight to the very last man in the defence of their faith. Under a certain tree close by the pledge was cheerfully taken. In the history of Islām this goes by the name of *Bai'at al-Riḍwān.* It was an act of dauntless self-sacrifice in the cause of Truth and as such a red-letter event in the annals of Islām.[1]

Terms of the Truce

The Muslims' resolve to shed the last drop of their blood in the defence of their faith brought the Quraish to their senses. Their past experience made them realize what such a resolve meant. Unarmed though the Muslims were and numerically weak besides, the Quraish could foresee that disaster was in store for them should battle be joined. Thus chastened in spirits, they deputed one Suḥail ibn 'Amr to resume peace negotiations. A truce was drawn up restoring a state of peace between the two parties for a period of ten years. The main clauses of the treaty were as follows:

1. The Muslims shall this year return without performing the pilgrimage.
2. Next year they may come but shall not stay at Makkah longer than three days.
3. They shall not take with them any of the Muslims already living in Makkah, and, on the other hand, they shall not stand in the way of any one from among themselves should he wish to remain behind at Makkah.

1 After the death of the Holy Prophet, the tree which commemorated this heroic resolve began to be much visited by the people. But, fearing lest credulity should later on invest it with some sort of sanctity, it was cut down at the bidding of 'Umar, the second Caliph. Such was the jealousy of the early Muslims for the principles of the unity of God. Anything savouring of superstition, no matter of what historical importance or interest, could not be tolerated.

4. Should any of the Makkans go over to Madīnah the Muslims shall hand him over to the Makkans; but if any of the Madinite Muslims should rejoin the Makkans, the latter shall not restore him to the Muslims.

5. The Arab tribes shall be at liberty to enter into alliance with whichever party they choose.

When putting the agreement in writing, 'Alī, who acted as a scribe, began with the words, *B-ism Allāh al-Raḥmān al-Raḥīm i.e.*, in the name of Allāh, the Beneficent, the Merciful. Suḥail objected to the adoption of this form of Muslim opening to the document, insisting that he must have the traditional form that had all along been in vogue in Arabia *viz., Bism-i-Allāhumma, i.e.,* in Thy name, O God. To this the Holy Prophet agreed. Further on, he again took exception to the words: "This is an agreement between Muḥammad, the Messenger of Allāh, and the Quraish." "If we were to admit," he remonstrated, "that you are the Messenger of God, why all this bloodshed?" But 'Alī said he would not expunge the words "the Messenger of Allāh" with his own hand. The Holy Prophet, however, attached no importance to such an insignificant detail. He asked to be shown where the words in dispute were. The spot being pointed out to him, he blotted out the words with his own hand, and dictated the words "Muḥammad, son of 'Abd Allāh" instead.

The terms were extremely distasteful to the Muslims, but out of regard for the Holy Prophet's attitude, they kept quiet. Meanwhile Abū Jandal, the son of Suḥail, appeared on the scene. He had embraced Islām at Makkah and the Quraish tortured him on that account. At last, he managed to escape from the hands of his persecutors and had now come to the Muslim camp expecting, of course, to find a warm welcome there. He showed the scars of his tortures to the Muslims. The Holy Prophet was moved and tried to secure an exception to the fourth term of the agreement in favour of Abū Jandal. But Suḥail was inexorable, so the Holy Prophet had to yield. Abū Jandal's miserable plight extremely moved the Muslims. They could not bear the idea of his being thrust back into the mouth of persecution. 'Umar was too deeply touched for self-control. As a spokesman of the general body of the Muslims, he earnestly remonstrated with the Holy Prophet. "Art thou not the true Messenger of Allāh?" he asked. "Is not ours a righteous cause?" On getting a reply in the affirmative, he argued, "Why then should we suffer so much humiliation in the matter of faith?" The Holy Prophet assured him that whatever he was doing was at the bidding of Allāh. "Did you not tell us," rejoined 'Umar, "that we shall perform the pilgrimage?" "But I never told you," replied the Holy Prophet, "that we shall do so this very year." In the same manner 'Umar had argued with Abū Bakr on the question, and he too had given him a similar reply that everything was done by the Holy Prophet in obedience to the will of Allāh.

In brief, the Muslims felt much troubled on account of Abū Jandal, but they could do nothing about it. The Holy Prophet observed that it was a crucial test of the Muslims' word of honour, and they must respect it at all costs. He also consoled Abū Jandal, telling him that Allāh would surely open a way for him.

On his return to Madīnah, the Holy Prophet received the Divine revelation, "Surely We have granted thee a clear victory..."[1] What was considered by the Muslims to be an ignominious peace was a real victory in the eyes of God. The Holy Prophet immediately sent for 'Umar to give him the happy news. The latter was afraid, for he had spoken rather harshly in discussion with the Holy Prophet concerning the terms of peace and he thought he was perhaps summoned in order to be reprimanded. On arrival, however, his fear changed into joy when he heard the Divine revelation. Did it pertain, he asked the Holy Prophet, to the truce of Ḥudaibiyah and, on being told that it did, he also believed with other Muslims that it was indeed a victory. So far everybody was smarting under the humiliating terms of the treaty, but now the Quranic chapter *al-Fatḥ* (the Victory) was on all lips. Was it in any way an act of ultra credulity on their part? Their own experience in the past convinced them of the truth of Divine revelation. The career of Islām so far had been replete with similar events.

Truce brings about triumph of Islam

That the truce of Ḥudaibiyah also turned out to be the triumph of Islām is borne out by the fact that on the occasion of

1 The Qur'ān, *Fatḥ*, Ch. 48.

his advance on Makkah about a year and a half later, the Holy Prophet was accompanied by 10,000 comrades instead of the 1,400 which was the number at the time of this truce. How to account for this remarkable rise in the number of Muslims? The fact is that the state of warfare which had so far prevailed between Muslims and non-Muslims had created a wide gulf between them. The general malice towards Islām would not permit Arabs to mix with Muslims. Hence they had so far no opportunity of coming into contact with Muslims and becoming acquainted with their Islamic virtues. For the first time since the inception of the Islamic movement the gulf was bridged over for a considerable length of time by the truce of Ḥudaibiyah. This afforded non-Muslims an occasion calmly to ponder over the inherent virtues of Islam. They came to realize how all those who had been under the Holy Prophet's moral influence were edified and raised to a higher plane. It is only human not to appreciate the ways of those against whom one harbours the slightest feelings of enmity. The Arabs were bent upon the destruction of Islām. They were therefore not well disposed to appreciate the teachings of Islām. Now that the barrier was removed and normal intercourse with Muslims had been resumed, they were in a position to carefully study the morals and manners of Muslims. The false impressions created by hostility concerning the Holy Prophet all vanished. They came to understand for themselves that he neither favoured cutting asunder blood ties nor was he a mischief-monger as they had supposed. The nobility of his nature and the beauty of his morals were now revealed to them. They realized that they had been the dupes of misrepresentation and that the Holy Prophet's character was far above what had been depicted to them. Thus impressed with the sublimity of the Holy Prophet's ideals and the purity of his comrades' lives, a large number of them joined the brotherhood of Islām.

Divine promise fulfilled

Thus the words of the Divine revelation, which the Holy Prophet had received on his way back from Ḥudaibiyah found fulfilment: "That Allah may cover for thee thy (alleged) shortcomings in the past and those to come." The faults imputed to him through malice were all removed and his glorious personality was unveiled once more in all the richness of its beauty. The words "and those to come" also contain a promise for the future. Any accusation brought against him at any future time, announce the prophetic words, shall not be allowed to stand, but shall similarly be washed away. One has only to watch the daily changing angle of vision of Europe towards the Holy Prophet to appreciate the truth of this portion of the verse. The ugly caricature of his character that has been so far drawn, either through misconception or misrepresentation, is undergoing a marked change. Europe is daily awakening to the nobility and purity of his character. General recognition of the true sublimity of the Holy Prophet's life is bound to come, sooner or later, as foretold in the Qur'ān. The time has come when closer contact with the Muslim world may disillusion Europe of its wrong notions concerning Islām; when it may come to realize, as did the enemies of Islam thirteen centuries ago, that the fair face of Islām is free from the stigmas with which ignorance and prejudice have disfigured it. It may realize, groping as it is for light which it cannot find in the Christian religion, that its salvation lies in the same Islām which it has all along painted in the darkest colours. Strange are the ways of God and little wonder that the history of Islām should repeat itself. Those bent upon its destruction may fall victim to its moral force, as happened at the conclusion of the truce of Ḥudaibiyah. The power of God may once more manifest itself and what appears to all human calculations the final overthrow may turn out to be the real triumph of Islām.

Prophet's love of peace

That such harsh terms should have been accepted by the Holy Prophet was not without a set Divine purpose. The incident is eloquent testimony to the fact that warfare was held in abhorrence by him. So far, Muslims had ever had the upper hand in the various conflicts with the Quraish. Not once were they defeated, notwithstanding the united might of several tribes. They regarded the terms derogatory to their faith and insisted on rejecting them. They had pledged to fight to the last man to vindicate the honour of Islām. In spite of this, wherever there is the slightest indication on the part of the enemy towards peace, the Holy Prophet welcomes it with open arms.

The Muslims were not defeated, but the terms of the treaty seemed to treat them as the vanquished party; yet the Holy Prophet accepted them. Can such be the attitude of one bent upon domineering over others, as is alleged? Is it not a conclusive testimony to show how peace-loving the Holy Prophet was? The Qur'ān too enjoins this attitude when it says: "And if they (the enemy) incline to peace, incline thou also to it."[1]

Sad plight of Makkah converts

But what, after all, is the outcome of the truce which appeared so humiliating? Does it put a check upon conversions in Makkah? Humanly speaking, it should have done so. The truce is fresh testimony to the helplessness of the Muslims. So far, converts could count upon the help of their Muslim brethren at Madīnah. But under the terms of the truce, Muslims were deprived of their right to succour converts, who were in the grip of their oppressors; moreover if the latter managed to make good their escape to Madīnah, even then Muslims could not give them shelter. It is a great relief to be in the company of friends in time of distress, even though the friends themselves be in no better plight. But even this last source of solace was denied to Muslim converts by the truce of Ḥudaibiyah. How, under these circumstances, could courage be found to embrace Islām? At home, the Muslim is put to untold tortures; now, even at Madīnah, he fares no better. The example of Abū Jandal is there to damp the spirits of the most enthusiastic. Such being the situation, the progress of Islām should have come, as a matter of course, to a standstill. But is it not remarkable that, on the contrary, Islamic light spreads during this period at a ten-fold pace? What is the one logical conclusion? Only that the intrinsic worth of Islām outweighs by far the prospects of all tortures. The charm and beauty of Islām make its lovers disregard all pains its acceptance may entail. Rejection at Madīnah (any more than persecution at Makkah) could not discourage them. Sufferings and afflictions sank into insignificance before the power and beauty of Truth. Here is another occasion for the critic to ponder. Should he

1 The Qur'ān, 8 : 61.

call this the spreading of Islām by the sword, or the spreading of Islām in spite of the enemy's sword?

'Utbah, another daring convert to Islām, tortured no less ruthlessly by the Quraish, followed the example of Abū Jandal and decamped to Madīnah. Two envoys of the Quraish followed close upon his heels and demanded his extradition according to the truce of Ḥudaibiyah. Like his predecessor, he also was advised by the Holy Prophet to return to Makkah, "Dost thou force me back to idolatry," remonstrated 'Utbah in amazement. A trying situation again 'Utbah pleading in the name of religion on the one hand, the Quraish insisting on the observance of the treaty on the other. This time, being in Madīnah, the Holy Prophet's position is far more secure than it was with Abū Jandal at Ḥudaibiyah, when the Muslims were but a handful, as well as unarmed. But a word once pledged could not lightly be set aside according to the Holy Prophet's code of honour, even though a Muslim were to turn apostate on that account. " 'Utbah," said the Holy Prophet, "we cannot help making you over to the Quraish. Allāh will open a way out for you." The Holy Prophet's regard for his word is marvellous, but 'Utbah's love for Islām is no less so. Why on earth should he bother about Islām any longer when the Holy Prophet himself is thrusting him back into the hands of the infidels? But, captivated as he is by the charm of Islām, it is not for him to question why. Humbly and implicitly he submits to the Holy Prophet's behest and accompanies the two Makkans back to the place where death is staring him in the face. There is no earthly power to shield him against the wrath of the Quraish. The instinct of self-preservation impels him to work out his own salvation. Come what may, he thought, he must strike a blow to save his life. Seizing upon a favourable opportunity, he kills one of the guards, and the other runs for his life. But still Madīnah is a forbidden land for him. He must find a resting place elsewhere. So he takes up his sojourn at 'Iṣ, a place on the seashore - a sort of neutral zone. The rest of the afflicted at Makkah, against whom the gates of Madīnah were shut, resorted to the same place, which grew by and by into a fairly big settlement of Muslim refugees. They were not subject to the terms of the truce of Ḥudaibiyah. Their growing strength alarmed the Quraish who feared lest they should some day obstruct their trade with Syria. Hence they thought it expedient to withdraw the clause that required the extradition of fugitives from Makkah, for they thought the withdrawal would go a long way to weaken the 'Iṣ settlement.

Message of Islām carried beyond Arabia

That the truce of Ḥudaibiyah was indeed a signal triumph of Islām was amply borne out by subsequent events. The numerical strength of the Muslims waxed manifold. Conquerors of fame such as Khālid and 'Āmr ibn al-'Aṣ, who were once the pride of the enemy's ranks, now rallied to the standard of Islām. Peace thus achieved what no victory on the battlefield, however great, could have accomplished. The Holy Prophet looked upon it as the harbinger of splendid achievements, and adjusted the programme of his activities accordingly. Immediately after his return from Ḥudaibiyah he summoned all the Muslims together, and explained to them that Islām had come as a mercy to the whole of mankind. The time had arrived, he told them, for the message of Islām to be carried far and wide to the sovereigns of the neighbouring kingdoms, the Caesar in Rome, the Chosroes of Persia, the king of Egypt, the Negus of Abyssinia and certain Arab chiefs, inviting them to Islām[1].

Muqauqis, the king of Egypt, received the messenger with great honour, and though he did not accept the faith, sent presents to the Holy Prophet. These included a mule on which the Holy Prophet himself rode, and two maids, of whom one Mary, was married to the Holy Prophet and thus raised from the state of a slave-girl to the status of a queen. The other was married to Ḥassān, the poet.

Caesar's attitude towards Islam

Diḥyah Kalbī- was sent to the Caesar with an epistle.[2] It so happened that at this time, Abū Sufyān was also in Syria,

1 Of these, the original despatch addressed to Muqauqis, king of Egypt, has only recently been discovered preserved to this day. Tradition says that Muqauqis took care to preserve the epistle within a precious casket. Its facsimile has now been published and reads exactly as reported in Ḥadīth.

2 This epistle to the Caesar, as well as the epistles addressed to other sovereigns, contained the Quranic verse, "Say: O people of the Book, come to an equitable word between us and you, that we shall serve none but Allāh and that we shall

where he had taken a mercantile caravan. The Caesar summoned him to his court and enquired of him about the Holy Prophet. In reply to various questions, Abū Sufyān, though still in deadly hostility to Islām, testified to the righteousness of the latter. The Holy Prophet came, he said, of a high family. His followers were daily growing in number. Never in his lifetime had an untruth escaped his lips nor had he ever been guilty of breaking a promise. When a person once embraced his faith, nothing could shake him. His teachings, in brief, were, to worship but one God, not to associate other gods with Him, to say prayers, to lead a life of continence, to speak truth, and to do good to relations, neighbours and fellow-men in general. The Caesar was much impressed with the account given by Abū Sufyān, an opponent of Islām. He had also seen a significant vision about the matter. So he called a conference of the prominent priests of his kingdom, and tried to win them over to his view of Islām, the adoption of which, he tried to persuade them, would promote their welfare. When, however, he found that they all disliked the idea of renouncing their old creed, he calmed their resentment by assuring them that he only wanted to test their constancy to their own faith. Obviously, he could ill-afford to set the whole of the Church against him.

Chosroes orders Prophet's arrest

The despatch to the Chosroes was carried by 'Abd Allāh ibn Ḥudhāfah. It opened with the words: "In the name of

not associate aught with Him, and that some of us shall not take others for lords besides Allāh"(3 : 64). It calls upon the people of the Book to accept what is common between their faiths and Islām - that they should worship only one God and set up no associate with Him nor should they deify men like themselves. In fact the verse invites attention to a principle which, if adopted today, would end all religious strife, welding the various systems into one Universal Religion and humanity into one Universal Brotherhood. To eliminate all differences, it lays down that whatever is common to all religions should be accepted by all, as a basis, and on this foundation should be built the superstructure of details which are in harmony with this fundamental truth. In this way, all the religions of the world can meet on a common ground and settle their disputes in an amicable manner. The idea of an eclectic religion, which has of late sprung up, is in accordance with this very truth which was promulgated over thirteen centuries ago.

Allāh, the Beneficent, the Merciful," followed by the words "from Muḥammad." The Chosroes could not tolerate that any one else in the world should have his name placed above his own. He was enraged at the word Muḥammad (peace and blessings of Allāh be upon him) put above his own name. He raved at the messenger, and tore the letter to pieces. In this fit of anger, he sent orders to the governor of Yaman to arrest the Holy Prophet. Accordingly, the Governor, Bāzān by name, sent two men to Madīnah for the purpose. The Arabs had little weight in the eyes of these people. It was a commonplace thing for their soldiers to arrest any of the Arabs. These men, arriving at Madīnah, delivered their word to the Holy Prophet, who surprised them with the news that their King, the Chosroes, was himself no more. They went back and to their surprise, they learnt that the very night the Holy Prophet had uttered these words the Chosroes had been assassinated by his own son. This event led to the conversion of the Governor. The Province of Yaman threw off the yoke of Persia which before long broke up.

Negus Accepts Islām

The Negus of Abyssinia, when he received the Holy Prophet's epistle readily accepted Islām at the hands of Ja'far, a Muslim refugee who was still living there.

The Mūtah campaign

Of the epistles sent to Arab chiefs, that addressed to Shuraḥbīl-ibn 'Amr of Buṣrā on the Syrian border is of special note. He killed, against all inter-tribal usage, the messenger, Ḥārith ibn 'Umair - an act which was an open declaration of war against Islām, and was taken as such by the Muslims. It would have been unwise to allow them leisure to gather all their forces to fall upon the Muslims. An army 3,000 strong was forthwith collected to advance against the enemy. Zaid, the liberated slave of the Holy Prophet, was given command, - a typical illustration of the fundamental equality between man and man which Islām inculcates. Proud men of Quraishite descent and noble Helpers were placed under a freed man. The Holy Prophet in person accompanied the army up to the place called Thaniyyat al-Wadā'. Shuraḥbīl too had in the meantime raised a large army 100,000 strong. The Caesar was also making preparations for war. The armies met at Mūtah, after which the battle is named. Zaid falling in the action, Ja'far took over the command. He too fought desperately and was killed, receiving as many as ninety wounds. He was succeeded by 'Abd Allāh ibn Rawāḥah, who was also slain. All this succession of command had been prearranged by the Holy Prophet himself; such was his habit of thoroughness. After this Khālid was chosen as the commander, and he very skilfully saved his small army, which was insignificant as compared with the vast hosts of the enemy. This battle took place in the month of Jumadī I, in the year 8 A.H.

Prophet's deep-rooted conviction

The circumstances under which all these epistles were issued to the various sovereigns is a point worth consideration. Had the Holy Prophet done so after the subjugation of the whole of Arabia it could have been regarded as a measure inspired by ambition. But what was the state of things actually obtaining at the time? Twelve months before Madīnah had been besieged, and there was little hope of the survival of a single Muslim soul. Even now the Muslims were too weak to venture to go to Makkah to perform such an important religious duty as the pilgrimage. Non-Muslims were still in power, so much so that they had just dictated terms to the Muslims. On all sides in Arabia, Islām was surrounded by enemies, and the sprinkling of Muslims here and there did not count for much. Yet in the face of all these depressing circumstances, the Holy Prophet's faith in the ultimate triumph of Islām was never for a moment shaken. He had full confidence that Islām would prevail in the long run and could foresee the day when its light would illumine every nook and corner of the world. Despite present weakness, the Holy Prophet invites the mighty potentates of the world to accept the faith. Such was his deep rooted conviction in the force of truth.

Herein lies a useful lesson for those Muslims of to-day who are sceptical regarding the success of the propagation of Islām in the West, for they think there is no mighty empire to back it up. Truth does not depend upon force for its maintenance. It is in itself potent enough to hold its own. For the anti-Islamic critic as well, the point is worth consideration. Is it possible for an impostor to have so firm a faith in his final success? Let those who are inclined to attribute these ambitious despatches to a perverted mentality ponder over the phenomenal success which followed only a few years later. If these facts point out that Muḥammad (peace and blessings of Allāh be upon him), was neither an impostor nor insane, then there is but one conclusion irresistibly forced upon an unbiased critic - that he was a Prophet of God.

These epistles also establish the fact that, from its very inception, the Holy Prophet looked upon Islām as a cosmopolitan religion. For Christianity, universality was not at first claimed. Jesus himself laid no such claim. He clearly said that he had come for the lost sheep of Israel. He even refused the favour of prayer to a non-Israelite woman. Muḥammad, peace and blessings of Allāh be on him, on the contrary proclaimed from the very inauguration of his dispensation that it was meant for the whole of mankind. It was not an empty claim. He spared no pains to realize the ideal in his own life-time, inviting the various monarchs to accept the truth of Islām.

These epistles were despatched in the year 7 A.H. They all bore the seal of the Holy Prophet, with the words "Muḥammad, the Messenger of Allāh". Certain records mention also the order in which these words were engraved on the seal. At the top came "Allāh", at the bottom "Muḥammad" and between the two *Rasūl* or "Messenger." The letter to Muqauqis, which has now come to light, bears the same impression as has been described in these records.

In the same year, 7 A.H., the Holy Prophet went, as stipulated in the truce of Ḥudaibiyah, on a minor pilgrimage (*'umrah*) to the Ka'bah. And this same year, the remaining Muslim refugees in Abyssinia came over to Madīnah.

CHAPTER VIII

THE CONQUEST OF MAKKAH

"No reproof be against you this day. Allāh may forgive you, and He is the most Merciful of those who show mercy" – 12 : 92.

Quraish contravened terms of truce

The aggressions of the Quraish reached their climax in the eighth year after the Flight, now drawing to a close. The truce of Ḥudaibiyah had been in force for about two years. The restoration of an atmosphere of peace had proved marvellously favourable to the growth of Islām and the Quraish could no longer view with a complacent mind the daily growing power of Islām. At last they contravened the truce. The tribe of Khuzā'ah, availing itself of the discretion allowed by the truce of Ḥudaibiyah, had entered into alliance with the Muslims, while their hereditary enemies, the Banū Bakr, had become partisans of the Makkans. It so happened that the Banū Bakr with the help of the Quraish chiefs one night fell upon the Khuzā'ah who sought shelter within the precincts of the *Ḥaram,* where bloodshed was strictly forbidden according to Arab tradition. Even there they were not spared. Many were put to the sword. The Quraish not only did not prevent their allies' aggression but actively helped them in utter disregard of the terms of the truce of Ḥudaibiyah. Consequently a deputation of the Khuzā'ah came to Madīnah to ask the Holy Prophet to rise in their defence, as required by the terms of the alliance. The Holy Prophet sent word to Quraish telling them to accept either of these three conditions – that they should pay blood money for those slain from among the Khuzā'ah; or that they should dissociate themselves from the Banū Bakr or that they should declare the truce of Ḥudaibiyah null and void. In reply, the Quraish said they accepted the last one though, later, Abū Sufyān tried to gloss over this imprudence of his people. Abū Sufyān realized that such a glaring breach of agreement was fraught with grave danger and consequently came to Madīnah for a renewal of the truce. The Holy Prophet, however, saw through the trick, for Abū Sufyān turned a deaf ear to all the Muslim demands. Hence the Prophet refused a renewal, and Abū Sufyān had to return to Makkah with his designs frustrated.

Preparations for attack on Makkah

The Holy Prophet accordingly made preparations for an expedition against Makkah, summoning together all the tribes that were in alliance with the Muslims. For twenty-one long years, the Quraish had been tyrannizing the Muslims. Thrice had they attacked Madīnah to extirpate Islām and the Muslims. One would have judged from these preparations that the oppressors would now be duly punished for their offenses. And it was but natural to expect that the people who had perpetrated cold blooded crimes against Islām should meet their deserts. A certain Muslim, Ḥāṭib, anxious on account of his relations in Makkah, secretly despatched a letter by messenger to apprise them of the contemplated Muslim incursion. Had it reached its destination, the Makkans would have also made preparations to oppose the Muslims. But Divine purpose had ordained that this great conquest should be carried out without bloodshed. The Holy Prophet was informed of Ḥāṭib's letter. Men were despatched at once to arrest its bearer, who was overtaken and brought back with the letter. It caused great excitement among the Muslims against Ḥāṭib who had attempted to betray his fellow-Muslims. He was arrested and brought up for judgment. In ordinary circumstances a soldier guilty of such conduct would have been court-martialled. But the conquest of Makkah was to be an example of forgiveness. If even the deadliest enemies were to be forgiven - *there shall be no reproof against you this day* - how could a friend who had made a mistake, grievous though it was in the extreme, be treated otherwise. His excuse was accepted and he was forgiven.

Ten thousand holy ones

At last, at the head of ten thousand righteous followers, the Holy Prophet set out for Makkah on the tenth of Ramaḍān,

8 A.H. Two thousand years before this came to pass, Moses seems to have had a clear vision of this when he said: "He came with ten thousands of holy ones" (Deut., 33 : 2). Post-Mosaic history cannot point to any other event fulfilling these prophetic words. It is not only the number of the Prophet's soldiers at the conquest of Makkah that fits in with the two thousand years old prophecy; their description as "holy ones" points to a still greater truth. The object with which these ten thousand soldiers gathered round the Holy Prophet's banner was not conquest and bloodshed but the establishment of righteousness even though at the expense of their own blood. They encamped at Marr al-Ẓahrān, a day's journey from Makkah. Every member of the whole body of Muslims was directed to kindle his own fire in order to impress the Quraish with the numerical strength of the Muslim force, and thus obviate armed resistance and consequent bloodshed. The Makkans surrendered without resistance.

Abū Sufyān accepts Islām .

The foremost of the Quraish brought before the Holy Prophet was, strange to say, no other than Abū Sufyān, the head of the opposition after Abū Jahl. Time and again he had done his utmost to extirpate Islām. An arch-offender like Abū Sufyān was presented to be pardoned! It appeared simply impossible. But nothing is impossible before the magnanimity of a Great Mind. He was granted pardon. A year and a half before, when called upon at the court of the Caesar to testify to the character of the Holy Prophet, it seemed as though the truth of Islām had already made its way into his heart. Now, his own utter helplessness notwithstanding all the power he since enjoyed, the final triumph of Islām in spite of its want of resources, and above all the generous forgiveness of the Holy Prophet - all these considerations convinced him of the inherent force of Islām. The heart which had remained sealed against Islām for twenty long years, now opened to the Truth, and Abū Sufyān embraced the faith.

General amnesty

Impressed with the strength of the Muslim force, Abū

Sufyān hastened back to inform his people that any resistance would be futile. At the same time he apprised them of the Holy Prophet's word, guaranteeing safety to all those who should enter Abū Sufyān's house, or close the doors of their own houses, or enter the Ka'bah. At last the Muslim army advanced on the city from various directions. One detachment was under the command of Sa'd ibn 'Ubādah who, when passing by Abū Sufyān, shouted: "To-day is the day of fighting. It is not a day of safety for Makkah." This displeased the Holy Prophet, who took the standard from him and entrusted it to his son, Qais, in order to avoid bloodshed.

Khālid was to enter that part of the town which was the stronghold of the worst enemies of Islām. It was the people of this part who had participated in the attack on the Khuzā'ah. Among these lived 'Ikrimah, the son of Abū Jahl. Notwithstanding the proclamation of general security guaranteed to all citizens, these people would not let Khālid pass unmolested, but, on the contrary, met his army with a shower of arrows. Khālid was thus constrained to attack them. The casualties that took place in the skirmish are reported to have been from thirteen to twenty-eight on the side of the enemy and two on that of the Muslims. The Holy Prophet in the meantime had reached a rising ground of the town and was much shocked on seeing the swords of Khālid's men flashing at the further end. "Had I not issued strict orders," he exclaimed, "that there should be no bloodshed on my account?" Khālid was then called upon to account for this act of seeming disobedience, but the explanation was found quite reasonable.

Ka'bah purified of idols

Then the Holy Prophet proceeded towards the Ka'bah, the Sacred House, which was an emblem of the Unity of God, to purify it of idols. As he touched each idol with his stick, he recited this verse of the Qur'ān revealed long since: "Say, the Truth has come and falsehood vanished. Surely falsehood is ever bound to vanish."[1] Never since has an image or an idol found its way into the holy precincts of that house, dedicated to the Oneness of God. Then he turned to the "place of

1 The Qur'ān, 17 : 81.

Abraham" and offered his prayers there. 'U<u>th</u>mān ibn Ṭalḥah, the key-bearer of the Ka'bah, was then sent for, the house was opened and entering therein, the Holy Prophet said prayers again. The key was then returned to 'U<u>th</u>mān with the words that the charge of the sanctuary would ever remain with him and his descendants.

Unparalleled Magnanimity

This done, the Holy Prophet delivered a sermon urging the unity of God and the universal brotherhood of man. Thereafter he addressed a special gathering of the Quraish. They were before him in the position of offenders. What tortures had they not inflicted upon the Muslims! What horrible pains the Muslims had been put to, in utter disregard of all moral and traditional laws! The very recollection of the fantastic forms of persecutions sends a shudder into one's heart. Again, their tyranny had not been confined to the soil of Makkah; they had pursued the Muslims wherever they fled to take shelter. Repeated attacks had been led against Madīnah to crush them. So heinous was the guilt of the Makkans now standing for justice before the Holy Prophet! Malicious, vindictive, destroyers of the fundamental rights of man, oppressors of the innocent, the Makkans deserved the most exemplary punishment under the most humane laws. If the ringleaders had been put to the sword, and others thrown into jails to serve as a warning and a lesson for the future, no one could have questioned the justice of the verdict. The most civilized way of dealing with offenses of this nature is to mete out exemplary punishment to some of the offending party, whether really guilty or not. And the rest are reduced to a state of abject servility. This had been the treatment ever accorded to the vanquished foe by the victors, and the same is the method of dealing with a subject people today, under the most civilized Governments. Strong is the instinct of revenge in the nature of man, and it is apt to run riot, particularly when the foe lies at one's sole mercy.

But the Quraish had an implicit faith in the noble and merciful nature of the Holy Prophet. They never expected harsh treatment at his hands. So, when the Holy Prophet asked them what treatment they expected, they replied: "Thou art a noble brother, and the son of a noble brother". They were not unfamiliar with the generosity of the Holy Prophet. They were persuaded that the magnanimity which had distinguished his character during a period of forty years before his claim to prophethood was not in the least changed. But the treatment he accorded them exceeded even their own expectations. "This day," he said, "there is no reproof against you." What a generosity! To say nothing of punishment, they were exempted even from reproach for their black crimes. Not even a pledge as to their future behaviour was demanded from them. The property of the exiled Refugees, which the Makkans had taken possession of, was not recovered from them. The refugees were asked to forgo all their previous rights. Even the worst offenders were not punished. 'Ikrimah, Abū Jahl's son, who had attacked Khālid's detachment at the time of the entry into Makkah fled for his life elsewhere. In a state of great distress, his wife came to the Holy Prophet and asked forgiveness on behalf of her husband. He was granted pardon. To Waḥshī, murderer of Ḥamzah, the Holy Prophet's uncle, and to Hindah, who had chewed his liver, was also extended this generous clemency. Habbār, who had stoned the Holy Prophet's daughter while on her way from Makkah to Madīnah so badly that the injuries led ultimately to her death, was also forgiven. World history fails to produce the like of the Holy Prophet's generous forgiveness of such arch-enemies. No example of such magnanimous forgiveness is met with in the life of any other prophet. Christ indeed preached forgiveness to enemies, but he had no occasion to exercise the quality of forgiveness, for he never acquired power to deal with his persecutors.

Makkans embrace Islām

Makkah was conquered, but a far greater conquest, and one beyond the reach of Muslim arms, was accomplished by the general amnesty granted to the denizens of the town. It captivated the hearts of the people. Even enemies of Abū-Sufyān's bitterness had been impressed with Islāmic morals. This final scene of Islāmic magnanimity disarmed all opposition. Makkans witnessed with their own eyes how all those Divine promises held out to the Muslims, while the latter were yet groaning under the tortures of their enemies, had at last come true. The combined forces of opposition could do little harm to Islām. This furnished conclusive testimony to the righteousness of the cause and removed whatever doubt was still lurking in their hearts.[1] In brief, all opposition vanished. The truth of Islām went deep into Makkan hearts. They entered the fold in flocks. The Holy Prophet seated himself on a Spur of Mount Ṣafā to receive them into the Muslim brotherhood. Males were followed by females, who also embraced the faith in large numbers. All these conversions were spontaneous. There was not a single instance of conversion by force. There were some who did not accept Islām, but not the slightest molestation was caused to them on that account. They still clung to their own idolatrous creed, but Muslims treated them kindly. Friendly relations existed between them - so much so that they fought shoulder to shoulder with Muslims at the ensuing battle of Ḥunain. The conquest of Makkah is conclusive refutation of the charge that Islām was ever propagated at the point of sword; for could there have been a more favourable opportunity for such conversion? Not a single instance of compulsion, however, can be pointed out. Here is Muir's confession on the point: "Although the city had cheerfully accepted his authority, all its inhabitants had not yet embraced the new religion, nor formally acknowledged his prophetical claim. Perhaps he intended to follow the course he had pursued at Madīnah and leave the conversion of the people to be gradually accomplished without compulsion."

The battle of Ḥunain

Scarcely a month had elapsed since the Holy Prophet had left Madīnah, when intelligence was brought to him that the tribe of Hawāzin, occupying the slopes to the east of Makkah, was gathering in great numbers to undertake an offensive against the Muslims. The advancement of Islām after the truce of Ḥudaibiyah had already made them restless. Long before

1 To-day, when Islām is once more in the straits, when enemies are bent upon its extirpation, when all the powers of the world have combined to sweep it off of the face of the earth, it seems as though Divine power will again manifest itself, even as it did in days of yore, so as to convince the world that human hands are too weak to crush Divine Truth.

the conquest of Makkah, they had been stirring the Bedouin tribes to rise against Islām. Now with the fall of Makkah, they thought they must take the earliest opportunity to strike a blow at Islām, lest it should grow too strong for them. War-like as they were, it took them but a few days to bring together a large army. The Holy Prophet, on being apprised of their preparations despatched an officer to make enquiries and the latter confirmed the news. An army was therefore drawn up to scatter the Hawāzin forces. Ten thousand were already around the Muslim standard; two thousand volunteers came forward from among the Makkans to swell the number, and at their head the Holy Prophet marched towards the valley of Ḥunain, where the Hawāzin had assembled. In addition to man-power, a good deal of equipment was supplied by the Makkans.[1]

Retreat and rally of Muslim forces

The Hawāzin were skilled in archery and they had occupied every point of vantage. They had posted the flower of their archers on the various hills. The Muslims had to take up a disadvantageous position. Showers of arrows poured down upon them from all sides, while the main enemy army fell upon them from the front. Khālid was leading the van of the Muslim army. Under his command were placed the Makkan auxiliaries, including non-Muslims. They faced the brunt of the onslaught and could not withstand its fierceness. Their retreat caused confusion throughout the Muslim ranks. All fell back in utter disorder. Even the detachments of the Refugees and the Helpers joined the general retreat. The Holy Prophet with 'Abbās and a few others, was left entirely exposed to the advancing hosts of the enemy. He saw the Muslim army turn back, but firmly kept to this dangerous post with marvellous equanimity. The enemy was fast sweeping upon him, and he was almost alone, but that did not cause the faintest ripple on the serenity of his mind. Was he not secure under the omniscient protection of the Mightiest of the mighty? The same unfailing source of solace – unswerving faith in Divine help

1 "Certainly Allāh helped you in many battlefields, and on the day of Ḥunain, when your great numbers made you proud, but they availed you nothing and the earth with all its spaciousness was straitened for you, then you turned back retreating" (9 : 25).

and implicit conviction in the final triumph of his cause - sustained him now as ever. With the enemy storm whirling along on to him, he shouted repeatedly at the top of his voice: "I am the Prophet; there is no untruth in it. I am the son of 'Abd al-Muṭṭalib." 'Abbās also called out with his stentorian voice: "O hosts of Helpers! O companions of the Tree!" *"Labbaik,"* (Here we are at thy command) was the reply from all sides as the scattered forces rallied to the Holy Prophet. Jumping off their horses and camels, the Muslims fell upon the advancing foe in such fury that the latter could not keep their ground. Some took to flight; others offered resistance for some time. But on the fall of their standard-bearer, they also took to their heels.

While marching out towards the field, the commander of the Hawāzin, Mālik, an impetuous young man of thirty, had ordered that females and children should accompany the forces. Their presence, he thought, would keep up their spirits and prevent them, if hard pressed, from turning their backs. However, when the fateful hour came, they left everything - women, children, cattle and all. The booty that fell into Muslim hands included twenty-four thousand sheep and four thousand ounces of silver. Besides, six thousand prisoners were taken. Having taken the booty to a place of security, the Muslims continued their advance. A part of the defeated army took shelter in their stronghold of Autas, whither the Holy Prophet despatched a handful of Muslims to scatter them. The main body secured themselves within the walls of Ṭā'if well-fortified with battlements. They were skilled in the art of warfare, and well conversant with the latest weapons such as the catapult. They had also stored a year's provisions within the walls and posted strong garrisons all round. The Holy Prophet pushed straightaway thither and laid siege to the town. With the help of certain tribes, the Muslim army also made use of the new weapons. The siege dragged on. At last the Holy Prophet conferred with his friends. An experienced Bedouin chief made the significant observation that the fox had entered into its den and could not be caught very quickly; however, if left alone, it could do little injury. Being assured that the enemy was no longer capable of doing any harm to the Muslims, the Holy Prophet ordered the siege to be raised, since the protection of Islām from hostile attack was the only object of the whole expedition. While retiring, the Holy

Prophet was asked to invoke Divine wrath on the foe. This was the very place where he had once been pelted with stones. Instead of cursing them, however, the Holy Prophet prayed for them: "O my Lord! grant light to the tribe of Thaqīf and bring them to me," *i.e.,* to Islām. The prayer was granted and before long these people voluntarily accepted Islām.

On his return from Ṭā'if, the Holy Prophet divided the booty among the Muslim rank and file, setting apart the usual one-fifth for the national treasury. Among the captives was his foster-sister, Shaimah. She was brought before him, and as he recognised her he spread his own mantle for her to sit upon and showed her kindness and consideration. Shaimah was not his real sister. But never was even a real sister better honoured. He persuaded her to accompany him to Madīnah, but she said she would rather stay among her own people. So she was sent off with handsome presents.

A deputation of the Thaqīf waited upon the Holy Prophet for the purpose of securing the release of the prisoners. The spokesman laid all the troubles of his people before him.[1] The Prophet's heart was cast in nobler mould. His mercy knew no bounds. The enemy had as good a claim on the Holy Prophet's extensive mercy as any other human being. His heart melted at the sight of the smallest human misery. How could he bear the sight of the sufferings of thousands? At once he ordered the release of the prisoners that had fallen to his own and his family's share. But, he said, he could not interfere with the rights of other individuals who were entitled to dispose of their share of the prisoners as they chose. What a splendid example of the equality of human rights! Surely, those who had been cheerfully sacrificing their wealth, their property, even their lives for him, would not dream of denying him the privilege of setting at large their prisoners. But it was not for the Holy Prophet who had come to establish human equality to encroach upon the free exercise of others' rights. A king or an over-lord has no right, in Islām, on an individual's prop-

1 What would have been the reply of a most civilized modern conqueror? "I quite realize your difficulties. But now it is too late. You should have thought of it before taking the offensive against us. Had you won the struggle, you would have treated us even worse." Is not this the typical reply with which the entreaties of a vanquished foe are rejected in these days of civilization?

erty. But at the same time, his heart was aching within him on account of those woe-stricken people. He was anxious to help them out of their distress. He told them to call on him again at the time of afternoon prayers, and he would commend their request to the Muslim congregation for sympathetic consideration. Accordingly, at the hour fixed the release of six thousand prisoners was secured through the intercession of the Holy Prophet. And these people were still idolaters! Is it not unique in the annals of the world?

The booty having been distributed, the Holy Prophet made generous grants to certain Quraishite and Bedouin chiefs, out of the share set apart for the Treasury. This gave rise to suppressed murmurs amongst some of the youngsters among the Helpers. The Holy Prophet, they grumbled, had been partial to his own kinsmen in the distribution of the booty. How ruthlessly an autocrat would have dealt with such insolence can easily be imagined. But the Holy Prophet sent for the Helpers and spoke to them in a very kindly manner. "I have been told," said he, "that you are dissatisfied at my ostensible partiality towards the Quraish chiefs." Brought up under the influence of the Holy Prophet himself, the Helpers had the moral courage to tell the plain truth. "Yes," they replied, "there are some amongst us who are talking like that." Then the Holy Prophet said: "Is it not true that I came to your midst while you were misguided; so Allāh guided you to the right path. You were indigent; Allāh made you prosperous. You were ever at daggers drawn with one another; Allāh created mutual affection in your hearts." The Helpers replied that all that was true. "You could also give me a different reply and you would be quite justified in doing that," continued the Holy Prophet. "You could say that I came over to you when I was belied and rejected by my own people and you accepted me. I came to you when I had no one to help me, and you stood by me. I was turned out of my home, and you gave me shelter. O Helpers! did it make you suspicious that I gave away a portion of worldly riches for the purpose of conciliation, thinking that Islām was already ample reward for you. O Helpers! are you not satisfied to take home with you the Messenger of Allāh, while others drive goats and camels to their homes. By Allāh, Who holds my soul in His hands, if all the people go one way while the Helpers take another, I will tread along the path of the Helpers." This spontaneous outburst of the Holy Prophet's heart shows how little weight worldly riches carried with him. The audience were deeply moved, many of them bursting into tears of joy, knowing that they were to be accompanied by the Holy Prophet himself and thus were wealthier than booty could make them.

Spread of Islām in Arabia

On his way back from Ṭā'if in the month of Dhī-Qa'd in the year 8 A.H., the Holy Prophet visited Makkah and, having performed the minor pilgrimage *('umrah)*, returned to Madīnah about the close of the year.

Makkah was known as *Umm al-Qurā' (the mother of towns)*, and though it was not the temporal capital of the peninsula, it commanded the spiritual allegiance of the whole of Arabia. During the months of pilgrimage, people flocked to this city, year after year, from every part of the country. Naturally the people of Makkah had great influence upon the country which looked to the Quraish as leaders in the matter of faith. Formerly when during the pilgrimage the Holy Prophet preached to a tribe, he invariably met with the reply that he should first convince his own people. Consequently, when after the fall of Makkah, the inhabitants of the town joined the Muslim brotherhood in large numbers, it made a marvellous impression on the general populace of Arabia. Besides, they witnessed with their own eyes how the Prophet, single-handed as he was and discarded on all hands, had at last triumphed in the teeth of all opposition. The truth became manifest, with the result that people began to join Islām in large numbers. This is the reason why in the years 9 and 10 A.H. Islām spread all over Arabia. This period of the general acceptance of Islām began with the year 9 A.H., when tribe after tribe declared its adherence. During the same year the Holy Prophet organised the collecting of a poor-rate from all the tribes within the fold of Islām. A separate establishment was organised for this purpose and collectors were sent out to various places. The payment of this poor-rate is obligatory on every Muslim. This tax, the main item to replenish the *Bait al-Māl* (Treasury), was controlled by the central authority. Once the tax-collectors visited a certain tribe, and realised a flock of sheep and cattle, which was usurped by a neighbouring non-Muslim tribe.

'Uyainah, a Muslim chief, made an attack on them by way of reprisal, taking fifty prisoners.

The Banī Tamīm had rendered assistance to the Holy Prophet in the battle of Ḥunain. They sent a deputation to Madīnah to wait upon the Holy Prophet. A controversy was held here between speakers and poets from both sides. But the Banī Tamīm had to admit the superiority of the Muslim speakers and poets, whose one theme was now no other than Islām. This made a considerable impression on them and, having already been in close contact with the Muslims, they made up their mind to join Islām. Thus was Islām spreading rapidly. The only hindrance was the old-standing prejudice; and wherever this disappeared, Islām took a foothold.

During this period, mischief-making tendencies were manifested by the Banī Ṭayy. 'Ali, at the head of 200 mounted soldiers, was commissioned to suppress them. Among those who were taken prisoners was the daughter of Ḥātim Ṭā'ī, a man famed for his generosity. Her name was Safānah. When the Holy Prophet came to know of it, he sent for her and wanted to set her free with all respect and honour. But the worthy daughter of an illustrious father had no desire to avail herself alone of the privilege. So long as her fellow female prisoners were not liberated she would remain in captivity, she said. Her request was granted and all the prisoners were set at large. Her brother had run for his life towards Syria. She went thither in search of him and informed him of the breadth of the Holy Prophet's generosity. He immediately came to the Holy Prophet, accepted Islām, and was restored to the chieftaincy of his tribe.

During these days, Ka'b ibn Zuhair, a famous poet and once a bitter opponent of Islām, came into the fold and composed the well-known eulogy, called *Burdah,* in praise of the Holy Prophet. The eulogy has immortalized his name.

Deputations from Arab tribes

By this time, Islām had won general popularity throughout Arabia. News of its final triumph spread far and wide to the distant corners of the country. The people were not altogether unaware of what had so long been passing between the Prophet and the Quraish. They had been eagerly watching the whole course of the struggle. They knew how the Quraish had tormented him and his followers for preaching virtue and the Oneness of God and how, after their flight to Madīnah, attempts had been made for eight long years to crush them. Those who attended the annual gatherings on the occasions of pilgrimage carried this news to all parts of the country. The people were also aware of the Holy Prophet's prophecy that all opposition to Islām would ultimately vanish.[1] Hence deputations began to pour into Madīnah from every part. The Holy Prophet received them with great honour, and taught them the principles of Islām with the utmost kindness. With those who embraced the faith, a teacher was sent in order to instruct them in the religion. Thus in the first half of that very year, delegations from far off places like Yaman, Ḥadzramaut, Baḥrain, 'Umān and the Syrian and Persian borders called at Madīnah.

Ignorance and prejudice attribute the spread of Islām to the instrumentality of the sword. While the fact is that the progress of Islām was at a standstill so long as a state of warfare prevailed. As soon as settled conditions of peace were restored, Islām spread by leaps and bounds on all sides. It seemed as though some unseen power was at work in bringing host after host within the fold of Islām. Never was a military expedition sent to any of the places whence these deputations came. This is a fact which has, by an irony of fate, been to this day intentionally misrepresented. Religious freedom and peace have ever favoured and will ever favour the spread of Islām.

Expedition of Tabūk

The rise of Islām in the land of Arabia alarmed the neighbouring Christian Empire. She viewed with a jealous eye its rapid growth. The sympathies of Muslims were always ranged on the side of Jews and Christians as opposed to idolaters and fire-worshippers. At the time when the Persian hosts, sweeping over the Asiatic possessions of the Roman Empire as well as Egypt, were at the very gates of Constantinople and it seemed that the fateful hour for the Empire was in sight, the Holy Qur'ān prophesied that the Roman Empire would over-

1 "He it is Who has sent His Messenger with the guidance and the religion of Truth that He may make it prevail over all religions" (48 : 28).

power Persia within a period of nine years: "The Romans are vanquished in a near land and they, after their defeat, will gain victory within nine years ... and on that day the believers will rejoice."[1] In accordance with this prophecy, when the Muslims won their victory at Badr, the same year the Roman Empire recovered her lost territory and pushed right into the boundaries of Persia herself.

Impending danger on the Syrian frontier

The Roman Empire, however, could not tolerate the growing power of Islām. A skirmish had once already taken place at Mūtah. Now that the news reached Syria that the whole of Arabia was giving allegiance to Islām the religious jealousy of the Romans was aroused. They had cherished the hope of converting Arabia to their own faith. They thought that an attack upon the country would at least hamper the spread of Islām. Intelligence was received that the Caesar had assembled a large force to crush the power of Islām, and that all the Christian tribes in Arabia had joined hands with him. The tribe of Ghassān was particularly a source of danger to the peace of Arabia. On the strength of this information, the Holy Prophet directed the despatch of an expedition to the border of Syria. The Holy Qur'ān enjoins fortification of borders as a safeguard against sudden incursions. The Holy Prophet was awake to all dangers, whether spiritual or physical. He, therefore, could not lightly disregard incessant news of vast preparations by the Caesar for the extirpation of Islām.

Expedition to the northern frontier

The best method of defence was to keep the enemy outside the boundaries of Arabia; hence the necessity of sending an expedition to the frontier. The Holy Prophet summoned all the tribes to come to the defence of their motherland. The impending danger was threatening the peace of the whole of Arabia. But a number of obstacles stood in the way. The journey was long and the weather burning hot. Crops were ripe and ready for the sickle; and, above all, fear of facing the

1 The Qur'ān, 30 : 2-4.

well-disciplined and trained forces of the Roman Empire lurked in many hearts. Besides, such a long journey could not be undertaken on foot. There were many who could not afford to provide themselves with horses or camels, nor could the Holy Prophet afford to make such arrangements for them. At this juncture 'Uthmān offered one thousand camels and ten thousand dīnārs for the expedition. An army 30,000 strong was equipped, and it marched out of Madīnah in the month of Rajab 9 A.H.

Muslim army at Tabūk

Midway between Madīnah and Damascus at a distance of fourteen days' journey from the former, lies the place known as Tabūk. Here the Muslim army encamped and awaited news of the enemy. It seems that the available Muslim strength, coupled with a recollection of the daring of the three thousand facing a hundred thousand on a previous occasion at Mūtah, damped the spirits of the tribes of Sassān, Lakhūm, Judhām and others. The Caesar also dropped the idea of an attack. When the Holy Prophet got to the border he found it quite peaceful. If conversion was to be secured, as alleged in season and out of season, at the point of the sword, could there have been a more promising opportunity? Thirty thousand men, well-equipped and daring and devoted, were there at the Holy Prophet's bidding. But not a single conversion is reported as an outcome of this stupendous expedition.[1] Even if he had had a passion for territorial aggrandizement, could there have been a more favourable opportunity? He had undergone the hardships of a long and tedious journey in the trying climate of the Arabian summer. At last he reached the very gates of the enemy's country and found them unprepared for resistance. A dash onward into Syria lying before him, and a large tract of rich land was undoubtedly his. But his heart was as free from passion for territorial conquest as from that for conversion by force. Despite all the expense and trouble, when he felt satisfied after a halt of twenty days that there was no cause for apprehension, he returned in accordance with the Quranic injunction: "And fight in the way of Allāh against

1 "Had it been a near gain and a short journey, they would certainly have followed thee, but the hard journey was too long for them" (9 : 42).

those who fight against you, but be not aggressive."[1] The enemy did not want to fight. How could the Holy Prophet fight with him? Accordingly agreements were concluded with a number of petty Christian states, and peace was secured on the border, after which the Holy Prophet returned to Madīnah.

The hypocrites in Madīnah

Though emigration to Madīnah had given the Holy Prophet a certain amount of freedom, it increased opposition to his cause ten-fold. While at Makkah, the malice of the Quraish found vent in tormenting the Muslims, but now it was bent on the latter's destruction. The Bedouin tribes, who had so far been mere spectators of Muslim persecutions, were also stirred at the growth of Islām in Madīnah. The Jews, being at a distance, had remained quiet so far, but now that the Muslims were their next-door neighbours in Madīnah, they could not watch the steady growth of Islām without a sting of jealousy and rose in opposition. Distinct from all these, and of a singular nature, another wave of opposition set in, within the camp, known in Islāmic phraseology as that of *the hypocrites.*[2] These were the men who had not the pluck to come out into the open. So they joined the faith with the object of undermining it from within. A certain man, 'Abd Allāh ibn Ubayy, was at their head. This was the man who, before the immigration of the Holy Prophet, wielded immense power and influence in Madīnah. The people were thinking of making him their king. But the Holy Prophet's presence eclipsed his personality, and he dwindled into a nonentity. In the beginning he offered some opposition but, beholding the rapid growth of Islām, he thought hypocrisy would be the best policy. Thus he put on the mask of Islām, but thenceforward till his last breath in the year 9 A.H., he left no stone unturned to bring Islām into trouble. One can keep on one's guard against an open enemy but enemies disguised as friends are very dangerous and hard to deal with. They lull one into a sense of security by their friendly appearance, and when an opportunity comes they strike unexpectedly. They also have access to one's inner

1 The Qur'ān, 2 : 190.

2 "If We pardon a party of you, We shall chastise a party, because they are guilty" (9 : 66).

thoughts, which renders them all the more dangerous. They keep in secret contact with one's enemies, apprising them of all plans and movements. Islām was thus confronted with every conceivable form of opposition and intrigue. Its final triumph is therefore a concrete illustration of the fact that a plant tended by the hand of God Himself will survive the worst fury of storms.

Hypocrites' plans against Islām

The malice of 'Abd Allāh assumed a manifest form on the occasion of the battle of Uḥud. Making sure that the Quraish, 3,000 strong, were resolved upon crushing the Muslims, he deserted with his 300 men and returned to Madīnah. This, he thought, would weaken not only the Muslim strength of arms but also their morale, and the Quraish would be able to crush them all the more easily. He also promised to help the Banī Naḍīr in their mischief against Islām. At the battle of Aḥzāb, when, an army of 24,000 strong laid siege to Madīnah, the hypocrites did not participate in the defence of the town on the lame excuse that they had to look after their own houses which were exposed to the enemy's attacks. On the occasion of the expedition against the Ban-ī Musṭaliq, 'Abd Allāh's malice was once more brought into play. He made a futile attempt to create a split between Helpers and Refugees. On the Holy Prophet's return from this expedition, 'Abd Allāh and his partisans fabricated a grave accusation against the chastity of 'Ā'ishah, the Righteous. On every occasion they hoped the worst would befall the Muslims. They were ever on the lookout for an opportunity to rise from within, should an enemy from without win the slightest advantage over Islām. At the battle of Tabūk, the excessive heat afforded them ample pretext to refrain from enlisting. Their real motive in staying behind was to stir up mischief at Madīnah in the absence of the Muslims. But all their efforts to harm Islām came to nought.

The Prophet's love for enemies

The ethical and the religious history of the world presents perhaps but one instance of acting up to the idealistic saying "Love thy enemy." The Holy Prophet had nothing but the tenderest treatment to mete out to such dangerous enemies as the hypocrites. He never punished them for their offenses. When 'Abd Allāh's mischief in bringing about a rupture between Helpers and Refugees came to light, 'Umar proposed his execution. "I do not like," replied the Holy Prophet, "that people should say that Muḥammad puts his own comrades to death." When, however, the hypocrites erected a mosque in Madīnah at the instigation of Abū 'Āmir, with a view to providing a rendezvous for the conspirators against Islām, the Holy Prophet ordered it to be burnt down. The mosque was built before the expedition of Tabūk. The Holy Prophet was invited to perform the opening ceremony by saying his prayers therein. He replied that he would see to it on his return from the Tabūk expedition. In the meanwhile he came to know through Divine revelation that it was not a mosque but in reality a hot-bed for hatching plots for the ruination of Islām.[1] Hence on his return, it was set on fire. 'Abd Allāh died about two months later. Among the Muslims he was known as "Chief of the hypocrites," and his deep-rooted enmity to Islām was beyond the shadow of doubt. But apparently, he used to repeat the Muslim formula of faith, and called himself a Muslim. His son, also named 'Abd Allāh, but a sincere Muslim, came to the Holy Prophet on his father's death, and asked him on behalf of the deceased for two favours - firstly, to grant his own shirt for a shroud; and, secondly, to perform the funeral service in person. Such treatment was normally reserved for dearest friends. But the Holy Prophet's heart was too generous to grudge a favour, even to a bitter enemy. He granted both requests, and gave his shirt to enshroud the deceased. When he got ready for the funeral prayers, 'Umar tried to dissuade him, emphasising that 'Abd Allāh had been a great enemy of the faith. But the Holy Prophet said he must say prayers over his body. On this 'Umar further remonstrated, inviting the Holy Prophet's attention to the Quranic verse which says, "If thou shouldst ask forgiveness for them even seventy times, God will not forgive them."[2] "Then I would ask forgiveness more than seventy times," rejoined the Holy Prophet. His boundless generosity shown to the Makkans has already been mentioned, and now towards this greatest internal enemy his treatment was no less generous.

1 The Qur'ān, 9 : 107, 108.; 2 Ibid., 9 : 80.

What breadth of sympathy! Doubtless he is the one personage in human history who is entitled on the score of facts and deeds to be acclaimed as the "Mercy for Nations".[1] His heart was overflowing with tenderness and mercy not only for his friends but equally for the bitterest of his foes.

End of the hypocrites

The fury of the hypocrites' hostility abated with the death of 'Abd Allāh ibn Ubayy. The righteousness of Islām gradually dawned upon them, as all attempts at its suppression failed one by one. So far they had exerted themselves to their utmost to injure Islām, but all to no avail. Now that their chief had passed away, they began to perceive that the Divine hand was surely behind Islām. Many of them, convinced of the truth of the faith, became sincere and devout Muslims. A few who were still left unreclaimed were excluded from the brotherhood in accordance with Divine behest. It is particularly noteworthy here that these men were given no punishment whatsoever. They were not executed, nor were they exiled. All that was done was openly to warn Muslims against their mischief. No poor-rate was demanded from them.[2] This attitude of the Holy Prophet throws a flood of light on the real significance of jihād in Islām. Here is the Quranic injunction concerning jihād: "O Prophet! Resort to jihād against the disbelievers and the hypocrites."[3] If we interpret it in the light of the Holy Prophet's practical treatment of the hypocrites we are driven to the conclusion that jihād means anything but bloodshed for the propagation of religion.

Thus, in the very life-time of the Holy Prophet, the trouble caused by the hypocrites came to an end. Islām attained security from the designs of external as well as internal enemies. Not only was enmity obliterated from all over the country but these enemies themselves were converted into devoted friends. Was this something within human accomplishment? It was done by the hand of Him Who had spoken long since: "Before long Allāh will bring about friendly relations between you and those whom you regard as your enemies. And Allāh is powerful; and Allāh is Forgiving, Merciful.[4]

1 The Qur'ān, 21 : 107.; 2 Ibid., 9 : 103.; 3 Ibid., 9 : 73.; 4 Ibid., 60 : 7.

Year of Deputations

Towards the close of the ninth and throughout the tenth year A.H. deputations from various clans and tribes kept pouring into Madīnah.[1] The deputation from Tā'if waited upon the Holy Prophet about the end of the 9th year. It has already been noticed that at the battle of Hawāzin, when a portion of the discomfited foe took refuge in Ṭā'if, the Holy Prophet had to lay siege to the town. When, however, he had made sure that they were no longer capable of inflicting injury on the Muslims, the siege was raised. 'Urwah, the chief of the Thaqīf, was absent on this occasion, having gone to Yaman to qualify himself in the arts of warfare. On his return he made straight for Madīnah. He was already acquainted with the merits of Islām and had also seen the Holy Prophet on the occasion of the truce of Ḥudaibiyah. Arriving at Madīnah, he accepted Islām, and his foremost concern thereafter was to see his own people benefited with its blessings. The Holy Prophet dissuaded him from going in their midst, for he had had personal experience of their bitterness. But 'Urwah was over-confident of his influence among his people. He assured the Holy Prophet that he commanded very high respect among them and would therefore be quite safe. Reaching Tā'if, he summoned all the people together and invited them to accept Islām. At early dawn he sounded the Call to prayer, on which certain hot-headed members of the tribe surrounded his house and showered arrows upon him till he was slain.

'Urwah's murder led to a skirmish between the people of Ṭā'if and the tribe of Hawāzin, who had by now joined the faith. At last, when they saw Islām prevailing on all sides, and opposition seemed useless, they decided to accept the faith. A deputation consisting of six chiefs and about twenty others was formed to call at Madīnah. The Holy Prophet did not even demand an explanation regarding the murder of 'Urwah. They showed their willingness to accept Islām, but requested that the idol Lāt should not be destroyed for three years for the ignorant and the women-folk would not like it. The Holy

1 "When Allāh's help and victory comes, and thou seest men entering the religion of Allāh in companies, celebrate the praise of thy Lord and ask His protection. Surely He is ever Returning (to mercy)" (110 : 1-3).

Prophet rejected the demand. At last they asked for a respite of one month. But how could Islām and idolatry go together? The Holy Prophet sent Mughīrah to pull down the idol; for the people feared they would come to grief should they do it with their own hands.

During this year, a deputation from Banī Tamīm, as already stated, came to the Holy Prophet. Before the expiry of the 9th year, Islām had spread all over the southern and eastern part of Arabia. The majority of the chiefs of Yaman, Mahrah, 'Umān, Baḥrain and Yamāmah joined Islām, through either delegations or epistles. The Arabs were by tradition a freedom-loving race. A tribe would look upon it as a disgrace to pay tribute to another. Hence the payment of the poor-rate stood in the way of some of the tribes. They liked Islām, but they could not reconcile themselves to submit to the humiliation, as they regarded it, of paying a tax even though Divinely ordained. The Christians of Mahrah and Yaman also joined towards the close of this year. A preacher was sent to Mundhir, the chief of Baḥrain, who accepted Islām without the slightest hesitation. The Christian tribe, Banī Ḥanīfah, also sent a delegation thereabout. Another was received from the tribes of Yamāmah.[1]

The Najrān deputation

A deputation consisting of sixteen persons was also sent by another Christian tribe, the Banī Taghlib. But the best known Christian delegation was that from Najrān, consisting of seventy members. Their chiefs were 'Abd al-Masīḥ and 'Abd al-Hārith, coming of the tribes of Banī Kindah and Banī Ḥārith respectively. These people belonged to the Roman Catholic church. Whereas other delegations were lodged at the houses of various Muslims, this one was allowed to put up at the Prophet's mosque where they were also allowed to hold services in accordance with the ritual of their own faith. They were invited to Islām, but they were desirous of holding a discussion. When, however, they rejected the clear and valid arguments advanced, the Holy Prophet summoned them to

1 This was the one which included the notorious imposter, Musailimah. He thought that mere idle talk of Divine things had made Muḥammad a Prophet; why should he not try the same himself? This led to his claim to prophethood, but finally he fell in a battle during Abū Bakr's Caliphate.

what is known as *mubāhalah*[1] in Islāmic phraseology. But the Christian chiefs had already perceived the righteousness of Islām. They dared not accept the Holy Prophet's challenge to a *mubāhalah,* nor did they want to give up their own faith. At last they went away after entering into an agreement with the Holy Prophet, peace and blessings of Allāh be upon him.

In the year 10 A.H. deputations from certain other Yamanite tribes waited on the Holy Prophet, of which that of Bajlah was the most noteworthy. This tribe had a temple of its own called the Dhul Khalaṣah which was regarded as the Ka'bah of Yaman. The idol *Khalaṣah* after which the temple was called was demolished.

Wail and Ash'ath, two chiefs of Ḥadzramaut, came with a large following. They were clad in silk garments. The Holy Prophet asked them if they would like to embrace Islām. They had come, they said, with that express object. Then the Holy Prophet told them to put off their silk dress, which was forthwith done, and all were admitted to Islām. It was not merely to teach certain formals that the Holy Prophet had been commissioned. His mission was to uproot every moral and social evil. He abolished all long-prevailing corruptions, and gave a distinct Islāmic tone to the whole fabric of society. At a single stroke he raised a fallen humanity from the depth of ignominy, purified them of all their evil habits and imbued them with the pure and simple ways of Islāmic life. In fact, he infused an altogether new life into them.

In this manner, tribe after tribe and clan after clan sent their deputations to the Holy Prophet desiring to be admitted into the Islāmic brotherhood. Then they asked the Holy Prophet to depute a teacher for their instruction in religion as well as a collector for the realization of the poor-rate.

There were, however, still some left who had not lost hope of striking a blow at Islām. Two of them, 'Āmir and Arbaḍ, decided on a sudden assault on the Holy Prophet. 'Āmir, according to the plan, was to engage the Holy Prophet in conversation while Arbaḍ was to strike him dead with his sword.

1 The Qur'ān, 3 : 61. A *mubāhalah* consists in invoking divine decision through prayer after argumentation has failed. Both parties pray to God that whichever of them intentionally rejects the truth, may be visited with a heavenly calamity to serve as a warning to others.

They went out with this intention and, happening to meet the Holy Prophet, 'Āmir began talking to him as pre-arranged, but Arbad could not summon enough courage to fulfil his part. At last, when 'Āmir saw that no such plan could succeed, he asked the Holy Prophet to grant him an interview in private which, to his utter surprise, was refused. 'Āmir was the chief of a very mighty tribe. When departing, he threatened the Holy Prophet that he would bring down upon him an overwhelming force of mounted and foot soldiers. The Holy Prophet, thereon, only prayed to God for protection, saying, "O Allāh! suffice me against 'Āmir ibn Ṭufail." And strange to say, this enemy of Islām died of plague on his way back, before he could get to his people.

Whole of Arabia converted

In short, the period of warfare was over. People joined Islām in multitudes. In the course of some two years there was one and but one religion - Islām – throughout the vast Arabian Peninsula with a few Jewish and Christian exceptions, here and there. The cry of *Allāh-u-Akbar* resounded on all sides. A marvellous phenomenon! There was a time when the Holy Prophet would, on occasions of pilgrimage, go round the various tribes inviting them to Islām, but nobody would listen to him. And now the same tribes sent in their deputations and regarded it a great honour to be admitted into the fold of Islām. As soon as the state of warfare was over, it took the Holy Prophet but two brief years, not only to bring the whole of Arabia under the banner of Islām but at the same time to work a mighty transformation, sweeping away all corruptions and uplifting the nation to the loftiest heights of spirituality.

Islāmic principles of war

In dealing with the different important battles which the Holy Prophet had to fight with the Quraish, it has been shown that they were all defensive and three times did the Quraish advance on Madīnah to give Islām a crushing blow. The wars with other tribes or those with the Jews and the Christians belong to the same category, and it has been shown that the Holy Prophet never sent an expedition for proselytizing or political aggrandizement. But there exists such a misconception on this point that a review of the whole situation in the light of what is said in the Holy Qur'ān seems to be necessary.[1] That the Holy Prophet preached his faith with the sword is no more than a myth. The basic principle of Islām, a faith in all the prophets of the world, is enough to give the lie to this allegation. The great and liberal mind that preached not only love and respect for the founders of all the great religions of the world but much more than that - *faith in them* could not shrink to the narrowness of intolerance for those very religions. Tolerance is not in fact the word that can sufficiently indicate the breadth of the attitude of Islām to other religions. It preaches equal love for all, equal respect for all, equal faith in all.

Compulsion in religion interdicted

Again, intolerance could not be ascribed to a book which excludes compulsion from the sphere of religion altogether. "There is no compulsion in religion" (2 : 256), it lays down in the clearest words. In fact, the Holy Qur'ān is full of statements showing that belief in this or that religion is a person's own concern and that he is given the choice to adopt one way or another; that if he accepts truth, it is for his own good, and that if he sticks to error, it is to his own detriment. A few of these quotations are: "We have shown him the way, he may be thankful or unthankful" (76 : 3). "The truth is from thy Lord, so let him who please believe and let him who please disbelieve" (18 : 29). "Indeed there have come to you clear proofs from your Lord; so whoever sees, it is for his own good, and whoever is blind it is to his own harm" (6 : 104). "If you do good, you do good for your own souls. And if you do evil, it is for them" (17 : 7).

Fighting allowed conditionally

The Holy Prophet was allowed to fight indeed, but with what object? Not to compel the unbelievers to accept Islām, which was against all the broad principles which he had

1 "Permission (to fight) is given to those on whom war is made, because they are oppressed. And surely Allāh is able to assist them - those who are driven from their homes without a just cause except that they say: Our Lord is Allāh" (22 : 39, 40).

taught. No, it was to establish religious freedom, to stop all religious persecution, to protect the houses of worship of all religions, mosques among them.

> *"And if Allāh did not repel some people by others, cloisters and churches and synagogues and mosques in which Allāh's name is much remembered, would have been pulled down" (22 : 40). "And fight with them until there is no persecution and religion is only for Allāh" (2 : 193). "And fight with them until there is no more persecution and all religions are for Allāh" (8 : 39).*

The conditions under which the permission to fight was given to the Muslims have already been described. Every student of Islāmic history knows that the Holy Prophet and his companions were subjected to the severest persecutions as Islām began to gain ground at Makkah; over a hundred of them fled to Abyssinia, but persecution grew still more relentless. Ultimately the Muslims had to take refuge in Madīnah but they were not left alone even there and the sword was taken up by the enemy to annihilate Islām and the Muslims altogether. The Qur'ān bears express testimony to this: "Permission (to fight) is given to those on whom war is made, because they are oppressed. And surely Allāh is able to assist them – those who are driven from their homes without a just cause except that they say: Our Lord is Allāh" (22 : 39, 40). Later, the express condition was laid down: "And fight in the way of Allāh against those who fight against you but be not aggressive. Surely Allāh loves not the aggressors" (2 : 190).

Peace to be preferred

The Qur'ān therefore allowed fighting only to save a persecuted community from powerful oppressors, and hence the condition was laid down that fighting was to be stopped as soon as persecution ceased: "But if they desist, then surely Allāh is Forgiving, Merciful. And fight them until there is no persecution" (2 : 192, 193). If the enemy offered peace, peace was to be accepted, though the enemy's intention might be only to deceive: "And if they incline to peace, incline you also to it and trust in Allāh. He is the Hearer, the Knower. And if they intend to deceive thee, then surely Allāh is sufficient for thee" (8 : 61, 62). The Holy Prophet made treaties of peace with his enemies; one such treaty was the famous Truce of

Ḥudaibiyah, the terms of which were not only disadvantageous but also humiliating to Muslims. According to the terms of this treaty "if an unbeliever, being converted to Islām, went over to the Muslims, he was to be returned, but if a Muslim went over to the unbelievers, he was not to be given back to the Muslims." This term of the treaty cuts at the root of all allegations of the use of force by the Holy Prophet peace and blessing of Allāh be upon him. It also shows the strong conviction of the Holy Prophet, that neither would Muslims go back to unbelief, nor would new converts to Islām be deterred from embracing Islām because he gave them no shelter. And these expectations proved true, for while not a single Muslim deserted Islām, a large number came over to Islām and, being refused shelter at Madīnah, formed a colony of their own in neutral territory.

It is a mistake to suppose that the conditions related above were abrogated at any time. The condition to fight "with those who fight with you" remained in force till the end. The last expedition led by the Holy Prophet was the famous Tabūk expedition and, as already stated, though he had marched a very long distance to Tabūk at the head of an army of thirty thousand, yet when he found that the enemy did not fulfil the condition laid down above, he returned, and did not allow his troops to attack enemy territory. There is not a single instance of an expedition being sent to convert a people by force; nay, there is not a single case in which the Holy Prophet ever asked a man to believe on the pain of death. The waging of war on unbelievers to compel them to accept Islām is assuredly a myth. It was the enemy that waged war on the Muslims to turn them away from their religion, as the Holy Qur'ān asserts: "And they will not cease fighting you until they turn you back from your religion, if they can" (2 : 217).

Relations with non-Muslims

It is also asserted that the Qur'ān forbids relations of friendship with the followers of other religions. How could a book which allows a man to have as his wife a woman following another religion (5 : 5) say in the same breath that no friendly relations can be had with the followers of other religions? The loving relation of husband and wife is the friendliest of all relations and when this is expressly permitted, there is not the least reason to suppose that other friendly relations are forbidden. The fact is that wherever there is a prohibition against making friends with other people, it relates only to the people who were at war with Muslims, and this is plainly stated in the Qur'ān:

"Allāh forbids you not respecting those who fight you not for religion, nor drive you forth from your homes, that you show them kindness and deal with them justly. Surely Allāh loves the doers of justice. Allāh forbids you only respecting those who fight you for religion, and drive you forth from your homes and help (others) in your expulsion, that you make friends of them; and whoever makes friends of them, these are the wrong-doers" (60 : 8, 9).

How apostates were dealt with

Another widely prevailing misconception may also be noted here. It is generally thought that the Qur'ān provides the death sentence for those who desert the religion of Islām. There is not the least ground for such a supposition. The Qur'ān speaks repeatedly of people going back to unbelief after believing, but never once does it say that they should be killed or punished:

"And whoever of you turns back from his religion, then he dies while an unbeliever - these it is whose works go for nothing in this world and the Hereafter "(2 : 217).

"O you who believe, should any one of you turn back from his religion, then Allāh will bring a people, whom He loves and who love Him" (5 : 54).

"Those who disbelieve after their believing, then increase in disbelief, their repentance shall not be accepted, and these are they that go astray" (3 : 90).

On the other hand, the Qur'ān speaks of the plan of the Jews to adopt Islām first and then desert it, thus creating the impression that Islām was not a religion worth adopting (3 : 72). Such a scheme could never have entered their heads while living at Madīnah where the government was Muslim if apostasy according to the Quranic law were punishable with death. The misconception seems to have arisen from the fact that people who, after becoming apostates, joined the enemy were treated as enemies; or where an apostate took the life of a Muslim he was put to death, not for changing his religion but for committing murder.

CHAPTER IX

THE FAREWELL PILGRIMAGE

"This day have I perfected for you your religion and completed My favour to you" – 5:3.

Prophet's last pilgrimage

The ninth year A.H. was drawing to its close, but Arabia had not altogether been purged of idolatry. There were yet certain people who clung to their ancestral form of religion. Hence the Holy Prophet's pilgrimages so far had been all of the kind known as *'umrah* (the minor pilgrimage). By this time, however, Islām had spread far and wide and the idolatrous tribes were comparatively few; so a party of Muslims, with Abū Bakr at their head, was sent to Makkah, to perform the pilgrimage proper. Soon after, 'Ali was sent thither to proclaim that thenceforward no polytheist would perform the pilgrimage. This was, in fact, a sort of a prophecy, foretelling the conversion of the whole of Arabia, so that no polytheist would be left to perform the pilgrimage. The entire country, joined Islām in the year 10 A.H., when the Holy Prophet in person set out on pilgrimage. What an impressive spectacle! As many as 124,000 persons from various corners of Arabia assembled on this occasion without a single polytheist among them. The very spot where the Prophet was, at the beginning of his mission, discarded and rejected, was now the scene of marvellous devotion to him. To whichever side he turned his eye, he saw hosts of devoted friends. What an inspiring manifestation of Divine Power! How all those assembled there must have been impressed with Divine awe and majesty may well be imagined.

But whereas the Holy Prophet saw this remarkable sight of the final triumph of Truth, he was at the same time given to understand that his mission on earth had been fulfilled. His efforts had been crowned with such success as had never fallen nor will ever fall to the lot of another man. Thus the time had come when he should retire from this earthly life, the grand object of which had been accomplished. On the one hand, the whole of Arabia had embraced Islām, while on the other, religion itself had attained its highest point of perfection. "This day," the Divine word came to tell him, "have I perfected for you your religion and completed My favour to you."[1] It was thenceforward unnecessary that another messenger should ever arise. All the religious requirements of man had been provided for in the Holy Qur'ān. This would be the one fountain of Divine knowledge at which humanity would drink for all time to come. No doubt, no better occasion could have been chosen to proclaim the momentous and happy news of the perfection of religion. This was the place which had never, in the history of the world, witnessed any temporal fights or bloodshed. This was an assembly which had met there for the sole object of Divine glorification, cutting asunder all worldly ties for the time being. This was a congregation where human equality ruled supreme, where no mark of distinction between king and peasant was to be noticed, where all met as brethren to do homage to their Lord, and where every heart was filled with Divine awe.

Sermon at Minā

The sermon that the Holy Prophet delivered on this occasion was remarkable. He was mounted on a camel, and the people assembled all around him on the field of Minā. The words that fell from his lips were repeated aloud in order to reach the farthest ends of the vast assembly. Every Arabian tribe and clan was represented on this occasion, and thus the message was conveyed throughout the length and breadth of the peninsula. It ran thus:

"O people! lend an attentive ear to my words; for I know not whether I shall ever hereafter have the opportunity to meet you here."[2]

1 The Qur'ān, 5:3.

2 Obviously the Holy Prophet had perceived the approach of his end from the verse announcing the perfection of religion, which was revealed to him on the

"Do you know what day it is to-day? This is the *Yaum al-Naḥr* or the sacred Day of Sacrifice. Do you know which month is this? This is the sacred month. Do you know what place is this? This is the sacred town. So I apprise you that your lives, your properties and your honour must be as sacred to one another as this sacred day in this sacred month in this sacred town. Let those present take this message to those absent. You are about to meet your Lord Who will call you to account for your deeds.

"This day all sums of interest are remitted, including that of 'Abbās ibn 'Abd al-Muṭṭalib. This day, retaliation for all murders committed in the days of ignorance is cancelled, and foremost of all, the murder of Rabī' ibn Ḥārith is forgiven.

"O people! this day Satan has despaired of reestablishing his power in this land of yours. But should you obey him even in what may seem to you trifling, it will be a matter of pleasure for him. So you must beware of him in the matter of your faith.

"Then, O my people! you have certain rights over your wives, and so have your wives over you... They are the trust of God in your hands. So you must treat them with all kindness ... And as regards your slaves, see that you give them to eat of what you yourselves eat, and clothe them with what you clothe yourselves.

"O people! listen to what I say and take it to heart. You must know that every Muslim is the brother of another Muslim. You are all equal. You are all members of one common brotherhood. It is forbidden for any of you to take from his brother save that the latter should willingly give. Do not tyrannize over your people."

Then the Holy Prophet cried at the top of his voice: "O Lord! I have delivered Thy message," and the valley resounded with the reply from the myriads of human throats with one accord: "Aye that thou hast". No doubt the message was sublime, but the zeal with which it was delivered was no less so. Here is another Sermon on the Mount in the history of the world, grander than the first and more practicable.

9th of Dhu-l-Ḥajj, in the plain of 'Arafāt. He had been raised, he was well cognizant, in order to bring religious truth to perfection. Evidently, when he was informed that that perfection had been attained, he came to the conclusion that his presence on earth was no longer needed.

The Holy Prophet's last illness

On his return from the Farewell Pilgrimage, when he received the happy tidings of the perfection of religion and delivered his final message, the Holy Prophet was every moment looking forward to meet his Lord. About the end of the month of Ṣafar, 11 A.H. he fell ill. He had already ordered the despatch of an army towards the Syrian border, under the command of Usāmah, son of Zaid, whose father had been slain in a previous expedition sent thither. Notwithstanding his illness, in person did he entrust Usāmah with the standard, and men of position such as Abū Bakr and 'Umar were placed under him as ordinary soldiers. By so doing he intended to emphasize, on the very evening of his earthly life, the principle of human equality. The army encamped outside Madīnah. But the Holy Prophet's illness growing alarming, its departure was postponed. With the consent of all his wives, it was agreed upon that the Holy Prophet should stay on at 'Ā'ishah's house for the period of his illness. Till his last breath 'Ā'ishah kept to his bed-side and nursed him. Even in the course of his illness he went to the mosque to lead prayers as usual, but felt too weak to speak. One day much water had to be poured over his head before he could come out, and he had a bandage round his head. After the prayer, he addressed the congregation, saying that Allāh had offered a servant of His choice between this earthly life and the life with Him, and he chose the latter. Abū Bakr was quick enough to realize that the Holy Prophet was referring to his approaching end, and tears came into his eyes. Then the latter directed that all the doors opening into the courtyard of the mosque should be closed, except that of Abū Bakr. After this, he advised the Refugees to show every kindness to the Helpers.

Abū Bakr appointed Imām

The following day the Holy Prophet grew weaker. When at Bilāl's call to prayer, he tried to rise and make his ablutions, he found himself unable to do so. So he said that Abū Bakr should be asked to lead the prayers. 'Ā'ishah excused her father by saying that he was a man of tender heart and would burst into tears in reciting the Qur'ān. Besides his voice was too low. But the Holy Prophet repeated the same direction.

Again 'Ā'ishah put forward the same excuse on behalf of her father, but the Holy Prophet was persistent, so Abū Bakr, thereafter, led the prayers. One day when the Holy Prophet felt a little relief, he moved the curtain of his house aside and stepped into the mosque. The congregational prayer was at that moment going on, beholding which a ripple of joy passed over his face. He saw with his own eyes how devoutly and humbly those whose guidance was entrusted to him bowed and prostrated before Allāh, even in his absence. This was, indeed, a matter of no small happiness to him. But his strength failed him, and he had to retrace his steps.

The Holy Prophet's Demise

This happened on Monday, and it gave the assembly the impression that he was convalescent. So they all resumed their various pursuits. Abū Bakr departing to visit his family at Sunḥ. But soon afterwards the Holy Prophet collapsed, and 'Ā'ishah supported him. In the meantime, one of her relations entered the room with a green twig in his hand. The Holy Prophet asked for it with a gesture and rubbed his teeth with it, cleaning his mouth well. Then came a sudden change. His strength failed rapidly. "Lord! blessed companionship on High," were the last whispered words of his earnest prayer. Having faithfully rendered his obligations towards his earthly companions, he now returned to the loving bosom of companionship on High. It was on Monday, the twelfth of Rabī' al-Awwal, that he breathed his last, at the age of sixty-three. May the Lord shower His choicest blessings on him.

News of the Holy Prophet's death spread like wildfire, and people thronged into the mosque. 'Umar thought the rumour had been given out by malicious mischief-mongers. Was not the Holy Prophet with them in the mosque but a little while ago? Did he not look convalescent? Under this impression, 'Umar addressed the assembly and insisted that the Holy Prophet was not dead. Whosoever, he continued, with his sword drawn, should say that the Holy Prophet was dead, would do so at the peril of his life. All were attending to 'Umar when Abū Bakr appeared on the scene and made straightaway for 'Ā'ishah's chamber. Uncovering the Holy Prophet's face, he found that the unhappy news was true. Then kissing the forehead of his departed Master, he exclaimed, "God will not bring death twice upon thee".

Abū Bakr's sermon

Abū Bakr then went out into the mosque and mounting the pulpit, he began to address the assembly. "O people," he said, "verily, whosoever worshipped Muḥammad, behold, Muḥammad is indeed dead. But whosoever worshipped Allāh, behold! Allāh is alive, and will never die." It required no small moral courage to utter these words in the atmosphere of excitement then prevailing. 'Umar was standing there with his sword unsheathed to strike off the head of anybody who should dare say so. But the Muslims brought up under the influence of the Great Prophet, were devoted heart and soul to the worship of One God. Had it not been for the fact that they were too jealous for the Unity of God, they must have greatly resented the blunt words of Abū Bakr. Then Abū Bakr proceeded to recite the Quranic verse: "Muḥammad is but a Messenger - messengers have already passed away before him. If then he dies or is killed, will you turn back upon your heels?"[1] The Prophet's mission, the communication of Divine will to mankind, had been fulfilled. His death could, therefore, mean no harm to religion. There was no reason to feel so much grieved. Had not prophets before him passed away, one and all? Muḥammad, peace and blessings of Allāh be upon him, too was mortal and must share the common lot of mankind. Prophets could claim no exception to the law of nature which was applicable to all alike. Had a single one of the forgoing prophets escaped death, there would have been cause for Muslims to grieve. But all his predecessors had passed away and there was nothing extraordinary in the death of Muḥammad, peace and blessings of Allāh be upon him. The sermon had a very soothing effect upon the assembly, and this Quranic verse was on the lips of everyone. It brought solace to the wounded hearts of Muslims in this unbearably sad bereavement. They submitted with a cheerful resignation to the will of Allāh. Prophet or non-prophet, everybody must depart from this earthly abode, sooner or later; Allāh alone is Everlasting.

1 The Qur'ān, 3 : 144.

CHAPTER X

THE PROPHET'S SUBLIME MORALS

"And surely thou hast sublime morals". "Certainly you have in the Messenger of Allāh an excellent exemplar" - 68 : 4; 33 : 21.

The Prophet, an exemplar

The Holy Prophet's "morals are the Qur'ān", are the words in which his wife 'Ā'ishah, the most privy to his domestic life, has summed up the whole range of his morals and manners. In other words, his daily life was a true picture of the Quranic teachings. He was an embodiment of all that is enjoined in the Holy Qur'ān. Just as the Book of God is a code of high morals for the development of the manifold faculties of man, similarly the Holy Prophet's life is a practical demonstration of all those morals. Thus a Muslim had a twofold guidance - the Holy Qur'ān in the way of precept, and the Holy Prophet's life as a perfect example.

No work was too low for him

Sincerity was the key-note of the Holy Prophet's character. He loved virtue for its own sake. High morals which formed an attractive feature of his character, were not an acquisition with him, but were ingrained in his very nature. He would do all things with his own hands. If he wanted to give alms to a beggar, with his own hands would he place it directly in those of the latter. He would assist his wives in their household duties. He would milk his own goats, patch his own clothes, and mend his own shoes. In person would he dust the house and he would tie his camel and look after it personally. No work was too low for him. He worked like a labourer in the construction of the mosque. Again, when a ditch was being dug to fortify Madīnah against the impending incursion of the enemy, he was seen at work among the rank and file. In person would he do shopping not only for his household, but also for his neighbours and friends. In brief, he never despised any work, however humble, notwithstanding the dignity of his position as Prophet and King. He thus demonstrated through personal example that a man's calling, whether high or low, does not constitute the criterion of his status. It is his righteousness and treatment of others that determine whether he is noble or otherwise. A roadside labourer, a hewer of wood and a drawer of water is as respectable a member of Islāmic Brotherhood as a rich merchant or a high dignitary.

Simplicity

All his actions and movements were characterised by simplicity and homeliness. Anything savouring of artificiality was repugnant to his nature. When mounted, he would not mind seating another behind him.[1]

He did not like his companions to rise on his arrival. Once he forbade them saying, "Do not rise for me as do the people of 'Ajam (non-Arabs)", and added that he was a humble creature of God, eating as others ate, and sitting as others sat. Again, when a certain man wanted to kiss his hand, he withdrew it remarking that that was the behaviour of non-Arabs towards their kings. Even if a slave sent him an invitation, he would accept it. He would take his meals in the company of all classes of people. When in a congregation, he would sometimes keep quiet for a long while. If there was really anything to talk about, he would talk, but he did not like chatting for its own sake. He gave himself no preference over others. When walking, people would walk in front of him as well as behind him. When seated among people, there was nothing about him to make him conspicuous. A stranger could not distinguish

1 A report from Qais says that once the Holy Prophet paid a visit to his father Sa'd. For his return journey, Sa'd offered him his own ass to mount, and directed his son, Qais, to accompany him on foot. The Holy Prophet, however, insisted that Qais should share the animal's back with him, and should have the front seat, for the owner had a prior claim.

him from the rest, and had to enquire which of them was the Holy Prophet, peace and blessings of Allāh be upon him. Such was the humility of his disposition. When squatted on the floor, he was very particular to see that his knee did not project beyond others. He would never interrupt others talking. He would, in all simplicity, join others in smiling when there was occasion for it. He would talk so slowly that his words could even be counted. He walked so fast that his companions had sometimes to run to keep pace with him.

Food

His habit of living was also marked by simplicity. Whatever was offered to him, he would cheerfully partake of it. If, however, there was something wrong with it, he would not eat it, but would not find fault with it. Of dates, barley, wheat, meat and milk, whatever he could conveniently get, he would eat. If sumptuous food was placed before him, he would partake of it but, as a rule, he would take only one course at a meal. He loved cleanliness. He had a special liking for honey. Of vegetables, he liked vegetable marrow. He disliked things that give a bad smell such as onions. While seated at meals, he would not recline. If, when invited to dinner, some extra men accompanied him, he would not embarrass the host, but would politely drop a hint both for the host and the unconscious intruders. He would wash his hands before as well as after meals and would clean his mouth.

Dress

His dress was also simple. He did not mind putting on a patched garment, nor would he discard a handsome one. He did not like males to wear silk, for he wanted them to look manly. He was very particular about the neatness of his dress. He ordered for a seal-ring when it was needed for sealing his epistles to the various kings. Thereafter he wore it always.

No attraction for comforts

His dwelling consisted of small rooms, made of mud bricks, having a bedstead and a jar of water as furniture. This is how he lived even when he had conquered Khaibar. On the occasion of his marriage with Ṣafiyyah, he had not the means to entertain his friends to a feast. They were asked to bring their own meals, and the wedding feast served consisted of ground barley and dates. For days together, no fire was lit in his house. The whole family would have only dates and water for their meals. He looked upon this world only as a temporary abode. "My case," he once observed, " is like that of a mounted wayfarer who pauses at noon under the shade of a tree, just to rest for a while, and then proceeds on his way." Worldly things, riches and comforts, had no attraction for him.

Cleanliness

In all his habits, cleanliness was exquisitely blended with simplicity. He would make frequent use of a green twig crushed into a toothbrush, and clean his teeth a number of times daily. He would keep his body very clean, would often wash and comb his beard and hair, and always keep them tidy. He would also make use of perfume.

Love for friends

The Holy Prophet had a deep love for his friends. While shaking hands with them, he would never be the first to withdraw his hand. He met everybody with a smiling face. A report from Jarīr ibn 'Abd Allāh says that he never saw the Prophet but with a smile on his face. Sometimes he would enjoy witticism and innocent jokes with his friends. He would talk freely, never putting an artificial reserve to give himself an air of superiority. Nor would he ever talk big of himself. He would take up his friends' children in his arms like a father. Sometimes they soiled him but not a shadow of displeasure would pass over his face. He disliked backbiting and forbade his visitors to talk ill of any of his friends; for, he said, he would rather think well of them all. He would ever take the lead in greeting his friends and shaking hands with them. He would sometimes call them by their pet names by way of affection. He would remember with tender affection the fidelity of Khadījah even after her death. Zaid, his liberated slave, was so much attached to him that he preferred to stay on in his company rather than go with his father to his native town. He would overlook the shortcomings of others and would not even hint at them. In a general sermon, however, he would touch upon how to remove a particular drawback, without letting anybody feel a personal reference. He abhorred falsehood and loathed lies. Of mere offence, however great, he would take no notice. At the battle of Uḥud, when the archers abandoned the position at which he had posted them, with the consequent loss of those near and dear to him and injury to his own person, he neither court-martialled nor punished them. He did not even rebuke them. To those who fled from the field, he said no more than that they had gone a bit too far.

Generous to enemies

The Holy Prophet's generosity even towards his enemies stands unique in the annals of the world. 'Abd Allāh ibn Ubayy was a sworn enemy of Islām; his days and nights were spent in plotting mischief against the faith, ever instigating the Quraish and the Jews to crush the Muslims. Yet at his death the Holy Prophet prayed to the Lord to forgive him; he even offered his own shirt to enshroud his body. The Makkans who had all along subjected him and his friends to the most barbarous tortures were given a general amnesty. What treatment a worldly conqueror would have meted out to them can easily be imagined. But the Holy Prophet's forgiveness was unbounded. Thirteen long years of persecutions and conspiracies were absolutely forgiven and forgotten. Prisoners of war, sometimes numbering as many as 6,000, were generously set free. A report from 'Ā'ishah says that he never avenged any wrong to his own person. There were cases, no doubt, though very few and far between, in which punishment had to be inflicted. But all these were cases of ugly treachery by a people with whom forgiveness had lost its reformatory effect. To let such offenders go at large would have meant countenancing mischief. Punishment was never given where there was the least chance for the success of forgiveness as a deterrent, if not a reformatory measure. Generosity was extended to the followers of all persuasions - Jews, Christians, idolaters, all alike.

Equal justice for all

In the administration of justice, the Prophet was scrupulously even-handed. Muslim and non-Muslim, friend and foe, were all alike in his eyes. Even before he received the Call, his impartiality, honesty and integrity were of household fame and people would bring their disputes to him to settle. At Madīnah, idolaters and Jews both accepted him as the arbitrator in all their disputes. Notwithstanding the deep-rooted malice of the Jews against Islām, when a case between a Jew and a Muslim once came up before the Holy Prophet for hearing he decreed in favour of the former, regardless of the fact that the Muslims, even perhaps the whole of his tribe, might thereby be alienated. And what such a loss meant to Islām in those days of its weakness and hardship is obvious enough. In short, he was the embodiment of the Quranic verse which says: "Let not hatred of a people incite you not to act equitably. Be just; that is nearer to observance of duty."[1] He warned his own daughter, Fāṭimah that her own deeds alone would avail her on the day of judgment, and if she did a wrong she would be punished like any other member of the Muslim brotherhood. On his death-bed, immediately before he breathed his last, he had it publicly announced: "If I owe anything to anybody it may be claimed. If I have offended anybody he may have his revenge."

Humility

In his dealings with others, he never placed himself on a higher pedestal. He would conduct himself just as a man like others. Once, while he held the position of king at Madīnah, it so happened that a Jew whom he owed some money, came up to him and addressed him very harshly and rudely in demanding his dues. "You, Banī Hāshim," he tauntingly observed, "never pay back when you once get something out of another person." 'Umar was much enraged at the insolence of the Jew, but the Holy Prophet rebuked him saying: "O 'Umar, it would have been meet for you to have advised both of us – me, the debtor, to repay the debt with gratitude, and him, the creditor,

1 The Qur'ān, 5 : 8.

to demand it in a more becoming manner." Then he paid the Jew more than his due, and the latter was so impressed with the Holy Prophet's sense of justice and fair play that he accepted Islām.

On another occasion, when he was out in the woods with his friends, the time for preparation of food came. Everybody was allotted a piece of work, he himself going out to pick up some fuel. Spiritual and temporal overlord as he was, he would yet do his share of work like an ordinary man. In his treatment of his servants, he observed the same principle of equality. A report from Anas says that during the ten years that he was in the Holy Prophet's service, he was not once scolded by him. He would never rebuke his servants for their mistakes. He never kept anybody in slavery. As soon as he got a slave, he set him free. Throughout the whole of his life, never did he beat a servant or a woman.

Sympathy for the poor and the distressed

It is recorded that the Holy Prophet never disappointed a beggar. He would not give him a flat refusal. He would wait in the hope that perhaps something might yet come to his hand. He would meet such demands even at the sacrifice of his own comfort. He would feed the hungry, himself going without food. He never kept any money in his possession. While on the death bed, he sent for whatever there was in his house and distributed it among the poor. Even for the dumb creatures of God, his heart overflowed with mercy. He spoke of a man who drew water from a well to quench the thirst of a dog as having earned paradise with that act of kindness to a helpless creature of God. Once he remarked concerning a certain deceased woman that she was undergoing punishment for the offence that while alive, she would tie up her cat and keep it hungry. From his earliest days, he had a deep sympathy for widows, orphans and the helpless. "I and one who looks after an orphan," he would often say, "are as close to each other as these fingers," holding up his index finger and middle finger together. The Holy Qur'ān is also full of similar solicitude for orphans, the weak and the helpless. "Hast, thou seen him," it says, "who belies religion? That is the one who is rough to the orphan and urges not the feeding of the needy."[1] He himself would calmly bear the greatest calamity, but the slightest pain to another would melt his heart. He would ever stand by the oppressed. He vindicated the rights of women over men, of slaves over their masters, of the ruled over the rulers, and of the subject over the king.

He was very fond of children. While walking along, he would pat and stroke those he met on the way. Without fail would he visit the sick to enquire after their health and console them. He would also accompany funerals.

Hospitality

Hospitality reached its highest pitch with the Holy Prophet. He would take pains to entertain his guests as best as he could. In person would he wait upon them. When the number of guests was too great for him to accommodate, he would distribute the excess among his companions, who, like their Master, would show them every attention. Sometimes, they would serve all the food to the guests, themselves going to bed without any.

Gentleness

Never in his life, did abusive language escape the Holy Prophet's lips. He never uttered even a harsh word. He would prevent others also from harsh language. If he wanted to warn others, he would do so in a very mild and affectionate tone. The Jews accosted him with the words, *Al-sā'm-u-'alaikum (i.e.,* death on you) instead of *Al-salām-u-alaikum,* (i.e., peace on you). Hearing this 'Ā'ishah could not restrain herself and burst out involuntarily, "May God bring death on *you."* The Holy Prophet disapproved of this, saying, God did not like harsh words.

Faithfulness

His integrity, his righteousness and his sincerity were of universal fame throughout Arabia, so much so that he was

1 The Qur'ān, 107 : 1-3.

known as *al-Amīn,* the Trustworthy. His arch-enemy, Abū Jahl, had to confess that he did not call him a liar, but that he looked upon the message he brought as false. Another, Naḍr ibn Ḥārith, bore testimony to his righteousness in the presence of his own comrades: "Muḥammad was a boy amongst you, the most truthful and the most honest. Now that he has grown old and brought you a message, you call him an enchanter. By God, he is not an enchanter." When once he pledged his word, he kept it under the most trying conditions and even at a heavy cost. According to a term in the agreement at Ḥudaibiyah, he bound himself to make over to the Quraish any of the Makkan Muslims who should come to seek shelter at Madīnah. He observed the agreement faithfully under circumstances which brought blood to the very eyes of the Muslims. In respect of chastity and piety, he was a perfect model. He led a highly pure life as a bachelor till the age of twenty-five, and even the worst of his detractors cannot point to the faintest blot on the clean sheet of his character.

Forgiveness

Forgiveness was another most radiant gem in the Holy Prophet's character. It found its perfect manifestation in him. The Holy Qur'ān enjoined him to "hold fast to forgiveness,"[1] and this was explained to him from on High thus: "Whosoever should cut you off draw him to yourself Whosoever should deprive you, give him. Whosoever should do you wrong, pardon him." It did not remain with the Prophet a dead letter or a cheap homily. He lived up to it under the most trying situations. At the battle of Uḥud, when he was wounded and fell down, a comrade asked him to invoke Divine wrath on the enemy. "I have not been sent as a curse to mankind, but as an inviter to good and as a mercy. O Lord! grant guidance to my people; for surely they know not." Once a Bedouin felled him, throwing his wrapper round his neck, and when asked why he should not be repaid in the same coin, he pleaded that he (the Holy Prophet) never returned evil for evil. The forgiveness shown at the conquest of Makkah is indeed unparalleled in the history of the world. Every imaginable

1 The Qur'ān, 7 : 199.

attempt had been made to uproot Islām, and to take the Holy Prophet's life. But not a word of reproach was said about these deadly crimes. To an enemy like Abū Sufyān who had been doing everything he could against Islām, and to his wife Hindah who was guilty of the heinous barbarity of mutilating Hamzah's corpse was extended unstinted forgiveness.

Modesty

The Holy Prophet was exceedingly modest. According to him modesty was a part of religion. The Holy Qur'ān also bears similar testimony. The Holy Prophet was sometimes greatly hurt through ignorance on the part of others, but he would not utter a word of disapproval; concerning this the Holy Qur'ān says: "Surely, this gives the Prophet trouble, but he forbears from you."[1] He would never point out others' delinquencies by name. He would express his dislike in a general way.

In the matter of religion, however, he would at once point out if anybody was wrong. At the death of his son, Ibrāhīm, there was a complete solar eclipse, which the credulous among the Muslims took as a sign of heavenly mourning. The Holy Prophet did not like this superstitious idea. Forthwith he delivered a sermon, explaining that an eclipse had nothing to do with the birth or death of anyone.

Affection

The Holy Prophet was tender-hearted and affectionate. His heart ached within him at the corrupt state of his fellow-beings. The Holy Qur'ān testifies to it when it says: "Perhaps thou wouldst kill thyself with grief because they believe not."[2] He took great interest in the welfare of his followers. He would ever pray for them and even portrayed the misfortunes that were to befall them in later days, and gave them consolation under these calamities. If once he received any favour at the hands of anyone, he would ever thereafter remember it. Out of regard for the memory of Khadījah, he would ever send presents to her relations. When a deputation from the Negus of Abyssinia called at Madīnah, he in person attended to their comfort. His companions offered themselves

1 The Qur'ān, 33 : 53.; 2 Ibid., 26 : 3.

for every kind of service, but he said he loved to serve them with his own hands, for they had given shelter to his exiled friends. When the daughter of Ḥātim Ṭā'ī was taken prisoner among others, he said that the daughter of such a generous man should not remain a prisoner and consequently all the prisoners were released for her sake.

Respect for others

He would show consideration to both old and young. He would get up on the appearance of his foster-mother and foster-sister, and spread his own mantle for them to sit on. He had equal respect for his own daughter. "Respect your children," was one of his numerous teachings. He enjoined great respect for motherhood. "Paradise lies at the feet of mothers," he would say.

Courage

Humble and meek in the highest degree, he had the courage of the bravest of men. Never for one moment did he harbour any fear of his enemies. Even when plots to take his life were being hatched in Makkah, he would fearlessly move about, day and night. He told all his companions to emigrate from Makkah, but he himself stayed there in the midst of his enemies almost alone. When the pursuers, following up the track, arrived at the very mouth of the cave of Thaur, even then fear was unknown to his heart. "Be not grieved," he consoled his friend. On the field of Uḥud, when the whole of his army fell into a trap, he shouted aloud, regardless of all danger to his own person, to rally the confused soldiers. On another occasion, when the Muslim rank and file took to flight, he advanced alone towards the enemy, calling aloud: "I am the Messenger of the Lord." When one night a raid was suspected, he was the first to reconnoitre the outskirts of Madīnah. On a certain journey, while resting under a tree all alone, an enemy happened to come upon him. Unsheathing his sword, he shouted at him: "Who can save you now from my hands?" Not daunted in the least, he replied "God". And, strange to say, his enemy's sword fell from his hand. Taking up the same sword, the Holy Prophet put him the same question, on which he assumed a tone of abject humility. The Holy Prophet let him go.

Steadfastness

The biographies of the Holy Prophet, peace and blessings of Allāh be upon him, written by friends and foes, are all one in their admiration for his unflinching fortitude and unswerving steadfastness under the most trying calamities. Despair and despondency were unknown to him. Hemmed in, as he was on all sides by a gloomy prospect and opposition, his faith in the ultimate triumph of Truth was never for one moment shaken. The most furious storms of hardships, privations and persecutions failed to move him an inch from his post. He would make the best of all available God-given means, and then leave the rest to His grace. Unexpected turns of fortune could not depress or dampen his spirits. After the terrible disaster at 'Uḥud, the very next day he was again up in pursuit of the enemy. In a word, under the most adverse and trying circumstances, his heart was ever aglow with the firm conviction that Truth must triumph in the long run.

CHAPTER XI

THE PROPHET'S DISTINCTIVE CHARACTERISTICS AS A REFORMER

"And We have not sent thee but as a mercy to the nations: - 21 : 107.

The most successful of prophets

Ever since the dawn of human civilization this planet has been visited by prophets and reformers in different ages and at different places. The last of them was the Holy Prophet Muḥammad (may peace and the blessings of God be upon him!). We should like to mention a few important points which distinguish his dispensation. First of all comes the amazing success he achieved in his mission admitted on all hands by friend and foe alike. A single sentence in the *Encyclopedia Britannica*'[1] under its article on the "Koran", is sufficient to establish the truth of this statement: "Of all the religious personalities of the world, Muḥammad was the most successful." Never did a reformer find his people sunk so low as the Arabs were at the time of the Holy Prophet's advent. They were equally ignorant of the true principles of religion and of civic and political life. They had no great art or science to boast of, nor had they any intercourse with the rest of the world. National solidarity was a thing unknown to them, each tribe forming an independent unit and being at daggers drawn with the others. Judaism had done its best for their reformation, but to no avail. Christianity had also failed in similar attempts. Hanīfism, which had risen in a feeble wave, failed like the preceding movements, and died out without leaving any impress on Arab society. It was for the regeneration of

1 Cf. 11th Edition.

such a lost people that the Holy Prophet was raised. In the course of a few years he swept away long-standing religious, moral and social corruptions, and metamorphosed, so to speak, the very soil of Arabia. Debased forms of idolatry and superstition were replaced by the purest Unitarianism. The selfsame barbarous children of the desert were imbued with a new fervour for the cause of Truth, which carried them far and wide to the distant corners of the world to deliver the message of the Lord. In respect of Divine worship they excelled the greatest of ascetics and hermits, without renouncing the world. In the midst of their busy everyday life, no sooner did the call to prayer reach their ears, than they would leave off their worldly concerns, and fall prostrate in humble submission before the Lord. Their nights were also mostly spent in His worship. Thus, despite their being in this world, they were not of this world, and consequently their devotions to God were attended with a living conviction hardly ever experienced by a recluse in his hermitage.

Whereas such was the spiritual elevation to which they had attained, their temporal achievements were no less grand. They won a foremost position among the mighty conquerors of the world. Great empires melted away like snow before them. They not only conquered vast territories, but also developed a statecraft which preserved their strength for twelve long centuries, notwithstanding the negligence of later generations. In brief, they had attained to the heights of moral greatness and material prosperity. But hand in hand with their achievements in these two directions, they cultivated various branches of science which enlightened the whole of the world, then enshrouded in utter darkness. And what is still more surprising, all this was accomplished within a score of years. It is thus obvious that the Holy Prophet's teachings were all-comprehensive and were calculated to bring about all-round development of man's faculties.

There is no human ailment but they offer a cure for it. Just as the greatest physician is not the one who claims to be so, but the one who cures the most obstinate diseases in the greatest number of cases, similarly the greatest of reformers is not the one who might claim to be so, but the one who should bring about the greatest amount of reformation. And this is the criterion which raises the Holy Prophet above all other reformers in the estimation of thoughtful people.

Universality of the message

Another point which marks him out among the great spiritual reformers and prophets of the world relates to the universality of his message. Every prophet had his message confined to a particular people. Every prophet came with light and guidance but for the benefit of a particular nation or country. Purification of the human soul was, no doubt, the mission of each, but the mission was always limited. But the Holy Prophet's message was cosmopolitan, his light universal, and the sphere of his sympathies coextensive with humanity. "And We have not sent thee but as a mercy to the nations"[1]; "And we have not sent thee but as a bearer of good news and as a warner to all mankind"[2]; "That he might be a warner to the nations"[3]; "Say: O mankind, surely I am the Messenger of Allāh to you all,"[4] are a few of the numerous verses of the Holy Qur'ān which speak of the Holy Prophet being commissioned for the uplift of the entire human race. Again, the Holy Book speaks of itself as "a reminder to all the nations."[5]

There was a time when humanity was partitioned into numerous water-tight compartments, so to speak. Every nation, shut up within the confines of its own particular homeland, lived in entire isolation from the others. Means of communication were limited. Under such conditions of life no great expansion of mental outlook could be expected. The outlook of each was limited to its own immediate environments. Their own part of the race was all-in-all to each people. Thus Divine Wisdom could not but commission separate reformers to each people adapted to their particular needs and conditions. These various prophets played their specified role - the purification of a particular nationality. But like the field of their mission, their spiritual force was also limited in its range. The flame kept on for a period of time but grew gradually dimmer and dimmer, till it was ultimately extinguished altogether. Then would arise the need for another spiritual luminary to illumine the dark age, and hence the succession of reformer after reformer. But whereas Divine Providence thus provided for the spiritual welfare of man by raising prophets

1 The Qur'ān, 21 : 107.; 2 Ibid, 34 : 28; 3 Ibid, 25 : 1.; 4 Ibid., 7 : 158.
5 Ibid., 12 : 104.

from time to time among various peoples, this lead to a baneful impression. Each nation, ignorant of similar Divine favours shown to others, began to think that only they were the chosen ones of God. This fostered the mischievous idea of Divine favouritism, with a host of concomitant evils. To correct this sense of racial distinction, to remove prejudices created by geographical, social and other artificial barriers, and to weld humanity into one compact whole, Divine purpose decreed the commission of the World-Prophet, with a message for the whole of the human race. And just as his spiritual force knew no bounds, it was likewise to be above all limits of time - it was to maintain its efficacy for all time to come. Consequently when the chain of national prophets came to an end with its last link, Jesus, who was sent, to use his own words, "for the lost sheep of the house of Israel," the time was ripe for the Sun of spirituality to dawn on the religious horizon to illuminate the whole world. "The Mercy for the Nations"[1] made his appearance and emancipated humanity from the shackles of ignorance, superstition and corruption. The previous prophets resembled so many Divine lamps with light just enough for this or that room, and hence the necessity of different lamps corresponding to the numerous geographical and national spheres. They shed their lustre all around and everything within their range became radiant. But when the sun arose from the sands of Arabia, these lamps automatically ceased to be in demand. The light of the sun cannot be supplanted by any other light, and is itself sufficient to illumine the world till its end.

Unity of human race

It is self-evident that no kind of progress in any walk of life is possible unless there is a set object, a definite ideal before us to inspire us to self-exertion. Every previous prophet had the good of his particular people at heart, which was the specific mission of his life. If, following their example, the Holy Prophet Muḥammad had also the welfare of Arabia as the only goal of his life, he would have defeated the very purpose for which he was raised. He was to remove all these national and geographical prejudices, to lay the foundation of a

1 The Qur'ān, 21 : 107.

Universal Religion and weld the multitudinous communities into one homogeneous whole - a Universal Brotherhood of Man. Previous religions strove to unite individuals into communities – in itself a great service - but Islām, the Religion of nature, came to amalgamate these petty nationalities into one vast Brotherhood. Hence while the numerous prophets before the advent of the Holy Prophet Muḥammad addressed themselves to the creation of this or that denomination, to his lot fell the proud privilege of cementing these heterogeneous congeries of human beings into One Fraternity. Thus the third of the Prophet's distinctions consists of the fact that while others came to teach the secret of national unity and progress, he expounded the grand truth of the fundamental oneness of the whole of the human race and chalked out all the highways and byways along which lies the prosperity not of this or that nation, but of the entire human race.

Development of entire human nature

Again, the mission of each one of the preceding prophets was limited to the cultivation of a particular phase of human character. Thus, the life of each presents a model in this or that branch of human morals. But the Prophet Muḥammad came to develop human nature in its entirety, and to bring out and cultivate each one of its numerous faculties. In his own life, every phase of human morals found a thorough manifestation. He was, therefore, a perfect Exemplar for humanity. In connection with the Mosaic dispensation, prophet after prophet makes his appearance, but each one serves as a model in a particular line. But the Holy Prophet Muḥammad, all by himself, combines in his person, in a much higher degree, the collective virtues of all the Israelite prophets - the manliness of Moses, the tender heartedness of Aaron, the generalship of Joshua, the patience of Job, the daring of David, the grandeur of Solomon, the simplicity of John and the humility of Jesus. The first link of the Israelite chain of prophets, Moses, was the embodiment of power and glory and the last, Jesus, that of humility and meekness, but the Holy Prophet gave expression to both of these phases in his own person. Thus every spiritual luminary sent forth but one ray, a beam of light in one particular direction, but the Prophet Muḥammad was the centre from which went forth rays of light in every direction, and this is the fourth characteristic.

Greatness in all directions

Fifthly, while the achievements of every great man are limited to a definite sphere, those of the Prophet cover the whole field of human conditions. If, for instance, greatness consists in the reformation of a degraded people, who can have a greater claim to greatness than the one who uplifted a nation, sunk low as the Arabs were, and made them the torch-bearers of civilization and learning? If greatness lies in unifying the discordant elements of society into a harmonious whole, who can have a better title to the distinction than the one who welded together a people like the Arabs, rent into warring tribes with blood-feuds extending over generations? Like the sand of their desert, the Arabs lay scattered when the Prophet appeared, and he cemented them into a solid whole, endowed with the strength of withstanding the attacks of the most powerful empires of the age. If greatness consists in establishing the kingdom of God on earth, even then the Prophet stands unrivalled. He wiped idolatry and polytheism off the face of Arabia and illumined it with Divine light. If it lies in displaying high morals, who can be a match for one admitted by friend and foe as al-Amīn, the Trustworthy? If in conquest is to be found the greatness of a man, surely history cannot point to the like of the Prophet, who rose from a helpless orphan to a mighty conqueror and king, who founded a great empire that has withstood all these thirteen centuries the united world-attempts at its destruction. If the living driving-force that a leader commands is the criterion of greatness, the Prophet's name even to-day exerts a magic charm over four hundred million souls spread all over the world, whom it binds together in a strong cord of fraternity, irrespective of caste, colour or clime.

Not a product of environment

The sixth distinguishing feature of the Prophet lies in the fact that he was not the product of his environment. As a matter of course, it is the prevailing state of society that gives birth to its own great man. For instance, whenever there is a general yearning among a people after metaphysical truth, a philosopher is bound to arise. If there is a passion for conquest, the birth of a conqueror is inevitable. Likewise moral teachers, poets, sculptors, eminent men in various branches of human activity, spring up from the very atmosphere of the society in which there is a general demand for the particular accomplishment. Such leaders of men only embody in themselves the very spirit that permeates the age. In other words, they arise, in the ordinary course of evolution. But the Holy Prophet stood for what was in diametrical opposition to the then state of Arab society. He had to carry on his mission in the very teeth of prevailing notions. Idolatry and polytheism were the order of the day; but even as early as the age of sixteen, the Prophet had an abhorrence of idols. Superstition was keeping out the light of reason, and society was consequently enshrouded in thick layers of ignorance. Could such an atmosphere give birth to a philosophic mind such as the Holy Prophet had? All over Arabia, individuals took pride in revolting against their tribes while the latter in their turn abhorred the idea of a central authority. Under such circumstances, the appearance of one who upholds the principle of harmony and unity could not be expected in the ordinary course of events. Drinking, gambling, adultery were common pastimes. Infanticide was also in vogue among them, and women were treated as chattels. Such conditions could not of themselves create a moral tower and an emancipator of women. The fact is that the same Divine hand that prepares a pure gem in the darkest depths of the deep had created and fostered this Light under its direct influence, to penetrate such thick clouds of all round corruption and illumine every spot on the earth.

Universal peace

The last and the greatest distinction the Prophet enjoys is the fact that he laid the foundation of universal peace. He taught not only how one individual could live at peace with another, but also how different families and tribes of the human race could live in peace and harmony with each other, and to crown all - what nobody in the world had even attempted - how peace could be brought about among the contending religions of the world. Greatest of mankind as he admittedly was, he yet looked upon himself just as an ordinary member of mankind in general: "Surely I am a man like yourselves."[1] Man and woman, master and servant, king and subject all have their mutual rights. This equality of man with man not only formed a topic for lip-sermons but was scrupulously carried out in the every-day life. In the daily prayers, five times a day, the king and the peasant stand shoulder to shoulder before their common Lord on High. A slave must enjoy the same civic rights as a man of high birth, to demonstrate which, Zaid, a liberated slave of the Prophet, was put in authority over the proud Quraish. As regards tribal and national equality, he taught that the variety of tribes and nationalities was not meant to give one any preference over another. They were simply a means of identification. Nationality, it was taught, was no criterion of greatness: "Surely the most honourable among you with Allāh is the one who is the most virtuous."[2] But above all he brought about a reconciliation between the conflicting religions of the world by laying it down as a fundamental principle of faith for a Muslim to believe in all the Prophets of the world, to whichever people they were sent, as much as in himself. He taught, and never before him had the truth found expression through any Prophet, that there is not a nation on the face of the earth but has had a Divine messenger of its own. Profession of faith in all the religious reformers, raised from time to time, is in fact the only principle, that can form a common meeting ground for the various religious systems of the world. Again, he taught his followers to refrain from speaking ill of even the obviously false deities of others: "Do not abuse those whom they take up as gods besides Allāh."[3] This is another practical step towards creating a spirit of inter-religious goodwill and amity. And a yet more definite method settling all religious differences was thus pointed out: "Come to an equitable proposition between us and you."[4] In other words, taking what is common to all the religions as a basis, we should proceed to raise a superstructure thereon. Thus we would be able to build up a Common Religion.

1 The Qur'ān, 18 : 110.; 2 Ibid., 49 : 13.; 3 Ibid., 6 : 108.;
4 Ibid., 3 : 64.

In brief, the Prophet spared no pains, to establish, on the one hand, the Unity and Glory of the Lord, and on the other, the Universal Brotherhood of Man under the Universal Providence of One God. May Allāh shower His choicest blessings on him!

CHAPTER XII

THE PROPHET'S MARRIAGES

"O Prophet, say to thy wives: If you desire this world's life and its adornment, I will give you a provision and allow you to depart a goodly departing" - 33 : 28.

Khadījah

The Holy Prophet's first marriage came about at the age of twenty-five with Khadījah, who was then a widow of forty. Excepting his son Ibrāhīm, all the Prophet's children were born of Khadījah. She passed away more than three years before the Hijrah. At the time of her death, the Holy Prophet was fifty years old. Thus, the two lived together for no less than twenty-five years. Though it was a common practice in Arabia to have a number of wives, yet till the good old age of fifty, the Holy Prophet, peace and blessings of Allāh be upon him, had only Khadījah as his wife.

'Ā'ishah

Khadījah's loss weighed heavily upon the Holy Prophet. Seeing this, one of his women companions suggested that he should marry 'Ā'ishah, Abū Bakr's daughter, and then approached Abū Bakr on his behalf. The girl was one possessing exceptional qualities, and both Abū Bakr and the Holy Prophet saw in her the great woman of the future who was best suited to perform the duties of the wife of a teacher whose words and deeds had to be preserved for the guidance of mankind. But there were two difficulties in the way. The first was that 'Ā'ishah was already betrothed to Jubair and so Abū Bakr could not agree until the matter was settled with Jubair. But Jubair himself wanted now to get out of the engagement as the gulf between Muslims and non-Muslims had by now widened to such a degree that the match was undesirable. The other difficulty was that 'Ā'ishah had not yet attained majority. This was solved by the postponement of the consummation of marriage till 'Ā'ishah reached the age of majority. And thus the marriage ceremony that was gone through amounted virtually to a betrothal. It was on the ninth of Shawwāl in the tenth year of the Call.

'Ā'ishah's age

The popular misconception as to 'Ā'ishah's age may be removed here. That she had not attained majority is clear enough, but that she was not as young as six years of age is also true. In the first place, it is clear that she had reached an age when betrothal could have taken place in the ordinary course and must therefore have been approaching the age of majority. Again, Iṣābah, speaking of the Holy Prophet's daughter Fāṭimah, says that she was about five years older than 'Ā'ishah. It is a well-established fact that Fāṭimah was born when the Ka'bah was being rebuilt, i.e., five years before the Call. 'Ā'ishah was therefore born in the year of the Call or a little before it, and she could not have been less than ten years at the time of her marriage with the Holy Prophet in the tenth year of the Call. This conclusion is borne out by the testimony of 'Ā'ishah herself who is reported to have related that when the chapter entitled, "The Moon" (the 54th chapter) was revealed, she was a girl playing about and that she remembered certain verses then revealed. Now the fifty-fourth chapter could not have been revealed later than the fifth year of the Call, and therefore the report which states her to have been six years old in the tenth year of the Call when her marriage ceremony was gone through cannot be correct, because this would show her to have been born about the time of the revelation of the 54th chapter. All these considerations show her to have been not less than ten years old at the time of her marriage. And as the period between her marriage and its consummation was not less than five years, because the consummation took place in the second year of the Flight, it follows that she could not have been less than fifteen at that time. The popular account that she was six years at marriage and nine years at the time of consummation is decidedly not correct because it supposes the period between the marriage and its consummation to be only three years, and this is historically wrong.

Saudah

As stated above, 'Ā'ishah being very young at the time of her marriage, and the consummation having been postponed for some years, the Holy Prophet married Saudah, a widow of advanced age, in the same year, i.e., the tenth year of the Call. She had emigrated, along with her husband, to Abyssinia. On their return, her husband died on the way, leaving her in a terrible state of destitution. Small as the Muslim brotherhood then was, where could she look for a respectable shelter? So she offered her hand to the Holy Prophet, who accepted it.

Ḥafṣah, Zainab, Umm Salamah

Ḥafṣah, the daughter of 'Umar, was left a widow at the battle of Badr, her husband, Khunais, having been slain in action. 'Umar approached Abū Bakr and then 'Uthmān to take his daughter in marriage. This shows the dearth of marriageable males among the Muslims at the time. Both of them excused themselves, perhaps for the reason that Ḥafṣah had a somewhat harsh temper. At last the Holy Prophet took her in marriage in the year 3 A.H. The same year 'Abd Allāh ibn Jaḥsh having fallen on the field of Uḥud, his widow Zainab was also taken in marriage by the Holy Prophet. A year later, on the death of Abū Salamah, to his widow Umm Salamah was also extended the shelter of the Holy Prophet's household.

Zainab, Zaid's divorced wife

Zainab was the daughter of the Prophet's aunt Umaimah, daughter of 'Abd al-Muṭṭalib. The Prophet proposed to her brother that she should be given in marriage to Zaid, his own liberated slave. Both brother and sister were averse to this, for Zaid was only a freed man and as such could not, according to the pre-Islamic notions of respectability, enter into a matrimonial alliance with a woman of high birth such as Zainab was. They desired the Holy Prophet himself to marry her, but yielded under pressure from the Holy Prophet who was anxious to abolish false distinctions of birth and class. The union, however, was not a happy one. Differences arose and relations were strained to the breaking point. When all attempts at reconciliation had failed, there was only one alternative left - divorce. Thus as a last resort they were separated. She was thereafter taken into marriage by the Holy Prophet himself, that being the wish of Zainab and her relations; and now that the marriage arranged by him had proved unsuccessful, he was morally bound to meet their desire. This marriage came about in the year 5 A.H.

Juwairiyah

The same year, at the battle of Banī Muṣṭaliq, a large number of prisoners, male as well as female, fell into the Muslims' hands. Among them was one Juwairiyah, the daughter of an Arab chief, Ḥārith. Coming to the Holy Prophet to ransom his daughter, he embraced Islam along with his two sons. Juwairiyah's husband had already died, so Ḥārith consented to the marriage with the Holy Prophet. As a consequence of this marriage, the prisoners of Banī Muṣṭaliq, about a hundred families, were all released by the Muslims. The tribe which was so honoured by the Holy Prophet's relationship, they said, should not remain in captivity.

Umm Ḥabībah

Among the emigrants to Abyssinia was also the daughter of Abū Sufyān, Umm Ḥabībah. Her husband, 'Ubaid Allāh, turned Christian there. On his death, while Umm Ḥabībah was yet in Abyssinia, the Holy Prophet married her. She came to Madīnah in 7 A.H.

Ṣafiyyah, Mary and Maimūnah

At the battle of Khaibar in 7 A.H., Ṣafiyyah, the daughter of a Jewish chief, was one of the prisoners taken. Her husband had already fallen in action. The Jews had been a ceaseless source of trouble to the Muslims. The Holy Prophet thought a matrimonial alliance with them might once and for all put a stop to their mischief. Thus Ṣafiyyah joined the Holy Prophet's wives. In this very year Mary, the Copt, who was sent as a present to the Holy Prophet by Muqauqis, also joined the Holy Prophet's household. She gave birth to a son, named Ibrāhīm. The same year another widow, Maimūnah, offered her hand to the Holy Prophet, and it was accepted.

Polygamy is met with among the righteous

Why the Holy Prophet contracted so many marriage relations is a question which disturbs many a mind. And there are some who do not hesitate to call him a profligate simply because he resorted to polygamy. The man who brought about the most thorough transformation of a nation within twenty years; who, alone and unaided, swept away vice and immorality from a whole country, where the most strenuous efforts of powerful missionary nations had hopelessly failed; who by his personal example purified the lives of vast numbers of humanity - could such a man himself be in the grip of sin? An impure man could not consistently preach virtue; how could he take others by the hand and free them from bondage of sin and inspire his very soldiers and generals with sentiments of virtue? Whatsoever may be the views on polygamy of a world itself sunk deep in immoral practices, there is not the least doubt that plurality of wives is met with in the lives of many great religious personages who by a consensus of opinion led lives of transcendent purity. Abraham who is held in reverence by more than half the world up to this day had more wives than one. Similar was the case with Jacob, Moses and David among the Israelites, and with some of the famous and revered sages of Hindūs. The example of Jesus is quite out of question as according to the Gospels he did not marry. Yet it is true that these great sages were not led away by sensual desires to a polygamous life. Purity in all respects was the outstanding characteristic of their lives, and this fact alone is sufficient to condemn the attempt to defame them on the basis of their resorting to polygamy. What was their object in doing so, it is difficult to say at the present day, as their histories are generally enveloped in darkness, but as the life of the Holy Prophet Muḥammad, peace and blessings of Allāh be upon him, can be read in the full light of history, we will take his case in detail.

Four periods of the Prophet's life

The life of the Holy Prophet may be divided into four periods so far as his domestic life is concerned. Up to twenty-five, he led a celibate life, from twenty-five to fifty-four years, he lived in a married state with one wife; from fifty-four to sixty he contracted several marriages; and lastly from sixty till his death he did not contract any new marriage.

First period

The most important period to determine whether the Holy Prophet was a slave to his passions is the period of celibacy. If he had not been a complete master of his passions, he could not have led, up to the age of twenty-five, the exceptionally chaste and pure life, which won him the title of al-Amīn, in a hot country like Arabia where development must necessarily take place early and passions are generally stronger. His worst enemies could not point to a single blot on his character when challenged later (10 :16). Even according to Muir, all authorities agree "in ascribing to the youth of Mahomet a modesty of deportment and purity of manners rare among the people of Mecca". Now youth is the time when passions run riot, and the man who is able to control his passions in youth, and that in celibacy, cannot possibly be conceived as falling a prey to lust in his old age. Thus the first period of his life, his celibacy up to twenty-five years of age, is conclusive proof that he could never fall a prey to his passions. It should be noted in this connection that in Arab society at the time there was no moral sanction against an immoral life, so it cannot be said that he was kept back from an evil course by the moral force of society. Profligacy was the order of the day; and it was among people who prided on loose sexual relations that the Holy Prophet Muḥammad led a life of transcendent purity, and therefore all the more credit is due to his purity of character.

Second period

Take now the next period, the period of a monogamous married life. When twenty-five years of age, he married a widow, Khadījah, fifteen years his senior, and led a life of utmost devotion with her till she died, when he was fifty years of age. Now polygamy was the rule in Arabia at the time; and the wife had no cause of complaint, nor did she ever grumble, if the husband brought in a second or a third wife. Marriage with Khadījah had enriched him, though polygamy in Arabia was not limited to the rich; the poor as well resorted to it.

The wife being a help-mate in the real sense of the word, because she helped the husband in earning his livelihood as the woman generally does in the labouring classes, the poor had nothing to lose by resorting to polygamy.

The Holy Prophet belonged to the noblest family of the Quraish and if he had chosen to marry another wife it would have been quite easy for him. But he led a monogamous life of the utmost devotion to his wife during all this period. When Khadījah died, he married a very elderly lady named Saudah, whose only recommendation for the honour was that she was the widow of a faithful companion of his who had to fly to Abyssinia from the persecutions of the Quraish. The main part of his life, from twenty-five to fifty-four, was thus an example for his followers that monogamy was the rule in married life.

Third period

Now comes the third period. In the second year of the Flight began the series of battles with the Quraish and the other Arab tribes, which appreciably reduced the number of males, the bread-winners of the family. These battles continued up to the eighth year of the Flight and it was during this time that the Holy Prophet contracted all the marriages which appear objectionable to the modem mind but which neither friend nor foe looked upon with disapprobation at the time. And how could they do so, for they perceived them as acts of compassion and not of indulgence of the passions. Even a Christian writer admits this when he says: "It should be remembered, however, that most of Muḥammad's marriages may be explained, at least, as much by his pity for the forlorn condition of the persons concerned, as by other motives. They were almost all of them widows who were not remarkable either for their beauty or their wealth, but quite the reverse."[1]

1 Bosworth Smith.

And what other motives could there be? Let us look facts straight in the face. The Holy Prophet had now a young and beautiful wife in 'Ā'ishah in his house. None of the other wives whom he married later compared with her either in youth or beauty. Surely then it was not attraction for beauty that led to these marriages. And we have already seen that from youth till old age the Holy Prophet remained a complete master of his passions. The man who could live in celibacy up to twenty-five years, and still have the reputation of a spotless character, who up to the age of fifty-four lived with a single wife, and this notwithstanding the fact that polygamy was more the rule than the exception at the time and that a polygamous connection was not in the least objectionable - such a man could not be said to have changed all of a sudden after fifty-five, when old age generally soothes the passions even of those who cannot control their passions in youth. No other motive than compassion for the ladies who were given this honour can be attached to these marriages. If there had been any less honourable motive, his choice would have fallen on others than widows, and under the Arab custom a man in his position could have had several of youthful virgins.

Circumstances in which the Holy Prophet lived

And what were the circumstances in which he lived at Madīnah during these years? It was not a life of ease and luxury that he was leading at the time; it was a life of hardness, because it was at this very time that he had to carry on a life and death struggle with the enemies of Islam. Huge armies came to crush him and the small band of Muslims at Madīnah. The whole of Arabia was aflame against him. He was not secure for a minute. Battles had to be fought in quick succession. Expeditions had to be arranged and sent. "Prophet of God! we are tired of being in arms day and night," his companions would say to him; and he had to console them by telling them that time would come when a traveller would be able to go from one end of the country to the other without having any arms. Jews and Christians were his enemies along with idolaters. His best friends were falling sometimes in battles and sometimes by treachery. Is it possible for a man to lead a life of ease and luxury under such circumstances? Even if a man had a mind to lead a life of self-indulgence, which the Holy Prophet according to all available evidence had not, this was not the opportune time for it. Under such circumstances of warfare, with enemies within Madīnah and enemies all around it, with the number of the Muslims being insignificantly small in comparison with the enemy, with news of assaults by overwhelming numbers on all sides, even a profligate's life would be changed, to say nothing of a man of admitted purity of character, which no temptation could shake, turning into a profligate.

How he passed his nights

He had a number of lawful wives, but did he spend his nights in enjoyment with them? There is the clearest evidence on record in the Qur'ān (73 : 1-4, 20) as well as the Ḥadīth that he passed half the night, and sometimes even more than that, in praying to God and in reciting the Holy Qur'ān while standing in prayer. He would stand so long that his feet would become swollen. Could such a man be said to be taking wives for self-indulgence when the minutest details of his life as available to us show conclusively that it was a strenuous life farthest away from indulgence of every kind?

Simplicity of his life

Let us now take another point. Was any change really witnessed in the later phase of the Holy Prophet's life when he became the ruler of a state? "In the shepherd of the desert, in the Syrian trader, in the solitary of Mount Hira, in the reformer in the minority of one, in the exile of Madīnah, in the acknowledged conqueror, in the equal of the Persian Chosroes and the Greek Heraclius, we can still trace a substantial unity. I doubt whether any other man, whose external conditions changed so much, ever himself changed less to meet them: the accidents are changed, the essence seems to me to be the same in all" (Bosworth Smith). From the cradle to the grave, the Prophet passed through a diversity of circumstances - a diversity which can hardly be met with in the life of a single man. Orphanhood is the extreme of helplessness, while kingship is the height of power. From being an orphan he climbed to the summit of royal glory, but that did not create the slightest change in his way of living. He lived on exactly the same kind of humble food, wore the same simple dress, and in all particulars led the same life as he led in the state of orphanhood. It is hard to give up the kingly throne and lead the life of a hermit, but it is far harder that one should wield the royal sceptre and at the same time lead a hermit's life, that one should possess power and wealth yet spend it solely to promote the welfare of others, that one should ever have the most alluring attractions before one's eyes yet should never for one moment be captivated by them. When the Holy Prophet actually became the ruler of a state, the furniture of his house was composed of a matting of palm leaves for his bed and an earthen jug for water. Some nights he would go without food. For days no fire would be lit in his house to prepare food, the whole family living only on dates. There was no lack of means to live a life of ease and comfort. The public treasury was at his disposal. The well-to-do among his followers, who did not shrink from sacrificing their lives for his sake, would have been only too glad to provide him with every comfort of life, had he chosen to avail himself of them. But worldly things carried little weight in his estimation. No mundane craving could ever prevail over him, neither in times of indigence nor of plenty. Just as he spurned wealth, power and beauty, which the Quraish offered him when he was yet in a state of utmost helplessness, so did he remain indifferent to them when God granted him all these things out of His grace.

Prophet's wives led a simple life

Not only did he himself live the simplest life of a labourer, but he did not even allow wealth to have any attraction for his wives. Shortly after their immigration into Madīnah, the condition of the Muslims had changed, and they carried on a prosperous trade. The later conquests went further to add to the comforts of life which they enjoyed. Quite a human desire crept into the hearts of the Holy Prophet's wives that, like other Muslim families, they too should avail themselves of their share of comforts. Accordingly they approached the Holy Prophet in a body to prevail upon him to allow them their legitimate share of worldly comforts. Thereupon came the Divine injunction: "O Prophet! say to thy wives, If you desire this world's life and its adornment, come, I will give you a provision and allow you to depart a goodly departing. And if you desire Allāh and His Apostle and the abode of the Hereafter, then surely Allāh has prepared for the doers of good among you a mighty reward" (33 : 28, 29). Thus they were offered alternatives. They could either have worldly finery, or remain in the Holy Prophet's household. Should they decide to have the former, they would have plenty of what they wanted, but would forthwith forfeit the honour of being the Holy Prophet's wives. Can this be the reply of a sensual man? Such a man would have done everything to satisfy the whims of the objects of his affection. Nay, he would himself have desired that his wives should wear the most beautiful dress and live in comfort. No doubt the Holy Prophet cherished great love and regard for his wives. "The best of you," he is reported to have said "is the one who treats his wife best." This illustrates his attitude towards womanhood. He had immense regard for the rights of women and was the champion of their cause. But when his wives came to him with what was apparently quite a legitimate demand to have more of finery and ornaments they were coldly told that if they would have these things, they were not fit to live in the Holy Prophet's household. Does anyone who is the slave of his passions disregard the wishes of his wives in such a matter? This shows beyond the shadow of a doubt how free the Holy Prophet's heart was of all base and sensual thoughts. He was prepared to divorce all his wives rather than yield to what he regarded as unworthy of his wives - an inclination towards worldly things. It shows conclusively that the object of his marriages was anything but self-indulgence.

Protection of women was the underlying idea

Let us consider once more the historical facts which led the Holy Prophet to take a number of wives within the short space of five years from the 3rd year of Hijrah to the 7th, while before that he passed nearly thirty years of his life in a monogamous state. This period coincides exactly with the period during which incessant war was carried on between Muslims and non-Muslims. The circle of Muslim brotherhood was at the time very narrow. The perpetual state of war created disparity between the male and the female elements of society. Husbands having fallen on the field of battle, their widows had to be provided for. But bread and butter is not the only provision needed in such cases, as is supposed by certain short-sighted statesmen. Sex inclination is implanted in human nature, and the statesman who neglects sex requirements leads society to moral corruption, ending ultimately in the ruin of the whole nation. A reformer with whom morals are all in all could not content himself with making provision merely for the eating and drinking of the widows. The Holy Prophet was anxious for their chastity to a far greater extent than their physical needs. It became therefore necessary to allow polygamy. This is the reason that he himself took so many women to be his wives during the period when war was raging. Nearly all of his wives were widows. Where self-indulgence is the motive, the choice does not fall on widows. Lust must needs have virginity for its gratification. And there was no dearth of virgins. It would have been an enviable privilege for any Muslim to be father-in-law of the Holy Prophet. But the object was a far nobler one - the protection of the widows of his friends. In polygamy alone lay the moral safety of the Muslim society situated as it then was.

Political reasons

Again, certain political reasons also led to some of the marriages. This was the case in the marriage with Juwairiyah, a lady belonging to the Banī Muṣṭaliq; and such was also the case in the marriage with Ṣafiyyah, the widow of a Jewish chieftain. The Holy Prophet wanted to conciliate both tribes and that was the only motive in these marriages.

Other considerations

The case of the marriage with Zainab may, however, be specially noted here as calumny has been at work in this case. Zainab was the Holy Prophet's first cousin, being the daughter of his aunt. When she reached the age of majority, she was offered in marriage to the Holy Prophet by her brother. But the Holy Prophet wedded her to Zaid, a slave whom he himself had freed and who was deeply attached to him. The couple could not, however, pull on together and after a time Zaid wanted to divorce her. The Holy Prophet dissuaded him, as plainly stated in the Holy Qur'ān (33 : 36, 37). But ultimately a divorce was thought necessary. The divorced woman is generally looked down upon in popular estimation, and this was a case in which a freed slave divorced a lady of high birth. By taking such a divorced woman as his wife the Holy Prophet wanted to remove the false notion that divorce degraded women. Thus by this act, to which he was morally bound because the lady had been at first offered in marriage to him, he elevated the whole class of divorced women who would otherwise suffer life-long humiliation in society. If he had any desire of self-gratification or if he had any passion for the lady, he would not have refused her when she was offered to him as a virgin. Refusal of her hand in the first instance, and taking her in marriage when being divorced she was lowered in general estimation, shows conclusively that his motive in this marriage was anything but self-gratification.

Fourth period

We now come to the fourth period. With the conquest of Makkah in the year 8 A.H., internal warfare came practically to an end. Disturbances there were, but on the whole peace had been established in the country and normal conditions were restored. And it is from the 8th year of the Flight to the end of his life that we find that the Holy Prophet did not contract any new marriage. What is the evidence of facts then? It is clearly this that the Holy Prophet added to the number of his wives only during the time that he had to live in a state of warfare when the number of males was reduced, so that many women would have been left without protection and without a home if the difficulty had not been solved by permitting a limited polygamy. Before the Holy Prophet had to enter on a defensive warfare, he lived in the company of a single wife, and after war was ended, he contracted no new marriage, and this sets all doubts at rest as to the motives of the Holy Prophet. In all the marriages which he contracted during the war, there was some hidden moral end in view. There arose situations in his life under which he could not, consistent with the moral and religious mission of his life, help taking more wives than one. In that, he only showed compassion to the weaker sex.

Prophet's natural liking was not for polygamy or war

Although living in a country in which polygamy was the rule, the Holy Prophet had no liking for polygamy. He passed the prime of his life, up to 53 years of age, as the husband of a single wife, thus showing that the union of one man and one woman was the rule under normal conditions. But when abnormal conditions arose, he did not, like a sentimentalist, shirk his duty for the sake of an idea. He saw that the chastity of women was at stake if polygamy was not allowed, and for the sake of a higher interest he permitted polygamy as an exception to meet exceptional circumstances. Exactly thus he had to resort to war, though by disposition he was averse to it. Full forty years before the Call, he had been living in a land where the sword was wielded as freely as a stick elsewhere, where fighting and feuds were the order of the day, where men would fly at one another's throats like wild animals, where there was no chance of survival for one who could not use the sword; yet not once during these forty years did he deal a blow at an enemy. The same was the case with him for fourteen years after the Call. That he was peace-loving by nature is shown by the clear injunctions relating to peace in the Holy Qur'ān: "And if they incline to peace, incline thou also to it, and trust in Allāh ... And if they intend to deceive thee, then surely Allāh is sufficient for thee" (8 : 61, 62). His acceptance of the truce of Ḥudaibiyah though its conditions were humiliating to Muslims, who were ready to lay down their lives one and all rather than accept those terms, is also a clear proof of his peace-loving nature. But when duty called him to take the field to save his community, he did not hesitate to take up the sword against an overwhelming majority. He acted as a sagacious general in all fields of battle and behaved like a brave soldier when opportunity demanded. He knew how to ward off an enemy in time before it had gained sufficient strength to deal a severe blow to the Muslims. And once, in the battle of Ḥunain, when his army was in flight owing to the severe onslaught of the enemy's archers, he alone was advancing towards the enemy, till his soldiers rallied round him. By disposition he had no inclination for war, yet circumstances arose which dragged him into the field of battle, and he then displayed the wisdom of a general and the bravery of a soldier. So by disposition he was not inclined to polygamy, living a celibate life of unexampled purity up to twenty-five years and a married life of a monogamous husband up to fifty-four, but when duty called him to take more women under his shelter, he answered the call of duty. It may be added in conclusion that the verse limiting the number of wives to four when a necessity for polygamy arose was in all probability revealed after the Holy Prophet had contracted those marriages, but he was expressly permitted to retain under his shelter all the women whom he had married (33 : 50), and he did not contract any marriages after the revelation of that verse (33 : 52).

CHAPTER XIII

FALSE ALLEGATIONS OF ATROCITIES

"Thus it is by Allāh's mercy that thou art gentle to them. And hadst thou been rough, hard-hearted, they would certainly have dispersed from around thee" - 3 : 159.

Biased criticism

European criticism seems to have lost its sense of justice in dealing with the Prophet. All the rules of that criticism seem to be subject to the one consideration that whatever is unfavourable and damaging to the Prophet's reputation must be accepted as true. As an example of this trend of criticism, I take Mr. Cash's "Expansion of Islām" to which the author has attached an appendix of four pages in which he has collected examples of what he calls "assassinations,'' carried out at the Prophet's instigation and for which he calls the Prophet "cruel, treacherous and relentless" (p. 29). With one exception Mr. Cash has taken his material from Muir and, though a list of original authorities had been added, not the least attempt has been made to consider them critically before condemning a man who is looked upon as a model of virtue and kindness by 400 millions of men. The cases of alleged "assassinations" are five in all and a sixth case is that of Banī Quraiẓah which has already been dealt with in the 9th chapter. The last charge is that of permitting a rape, a charge false on the face of it and unknown even to Muir. A brief discussion of these cases is given below.

How Muslims bore abuses

The first thing that strikes us here is that five out of the six alleged cases of "assassination" and "massacre" relate to Jews. The Jews were "the people of the Book," and ordinarily the dealings of Muslims with the people of the Book were much more lenient than their dealings with Arab idolaters. How was it then that the people of the Book, people whose Prophets are frequently mentioned with the utmost respect in the Holy Qur'ān - how was it that these very people were chosen for assassination and such crimes were not perpetrated against the Arab idolaters who had most relentlessly persecuted the Muslims for thirteen years at Makkah, and had taken up the sword to deal a decisive blow at Madīnah? Sir William Muir and Mr. Cash assert that all these persons were murdered for no offence other than that of composing verses "which annoyed the Mussalmans." Poetry was not a special vocation of the Jews, and verses abusing Islām and the Muslims were produced in much greater abundance by idolatrous Arabs than by Jews. In fact it was the Arab, not the Jew, whose particular vocation was poetry, and satire and abusive poetry were used as weapons to discredit and defame Islām specially by the Arabs. Neither Muir nor Cash has taken the trouble of testing the reliability of the record on whose basis he has dared to condemn the most merciful and truest of men as cruel and treacherous. If the writer had gone to the root of the question, he would have found that the Prophet and the Muslims bore patiently the severest abuses and the annoying verses of all their opponents, whether Jews or idolaters. Indeed, the Holy Qur'ān had plainly enjoined on them that they should bear all abuses patiently, whether they came from idolaters or from Jews and Christians. Here is a verse belonging to a period when the Muslims had already entered on a state of war with their opponents: "And you will certainly hear from those who have been given the Book before you and from the idolaters much abuse. And if you are patient and keep your duty, surely this is an affair of great resolution" (3 : 186). This verse occurs in a chapter which contains an account of the battle of Uḥud, fought in the 3rd year of Hijrah, and could not therefore have been revealed earlier than that year, and this is just the period to which most of the alleged assassinations relate. How was it possible for the Prophet and his followers to go directly against the plain injunction of the Holy Qur'ān? The Holy Prophet could not go against any Quranic injunction, and the Qur'ān says plainly, and says it at a time when war was going on with both the polytheistic Arabs and the Jews, that Muslims shall have to hear such abuse, and they must not only bear the abuse patiently but should even guard against doing similar evil, to say nothing of murdering their abusers. How could the Prophet in the face of such a plain injunction order the murder of those who abused him, and how could the Muslims carry out an order which was directly opposed to the Holy Qur'ān? It was simply impossible, and if Ibn Hishām or Wāqidī says that the Prophet ordered the assassination of his abusers, it is Ibn Hishām or Wāqidī - a frail authority after all - that must be rejected, and not the Qur'ān, which is admittedly the most reliable source of information as to the doings of the Prophet. The Qur'ān had allowed fighting against an aggressive enemy, yet it refused to give sanction to the murder of any who abused the Prophet and Islām; nay, it plainly required such abuse to be borne patiently. It is simply inconceivable that the Prophet should order the murder of people for annoying poems and, at the same time and in the same breath, forbid that abuse should be met with otherwise than by patient endurance.

Interdiction against killing women

Let us now take the cases individually. The first case cited by Mr. Cash is that of Asmā' of the tribe of Aus. She is said to have been a poetess who wrote some verses stating that the Prophet was an upstart who had slain many of their chiefs, referring to the battle of Badr. It is stated that she was brutally murdered for this abuse by a Muslim named 'Umair, and that the Prophet not only approved of this murder but also praised 'Umair for the deed. The authorities quoted are Wāqidī, Ibn Hishām and Ibn Sa'd. That this is not a reliable record is shown not only by what has been stated above - that the Holy Qur'ān never allowed the murder of an abuser - but also by clear directions repeatedly given by the Holy Prophet that no woman was to be killed even though she took part in actual war with the Muslims. No less an authority than Bukhārī has a chapter on the "Murder of Women during War" *(Kitāb al-Jihād)* in which the following report from Ibn 'Umar is recorded: "A woman was found killed in one of the battles fought by the Holy Prophet, so the Holy Prophet forbade the killing of women and children." If the Holy Prophet forbade the killing of women even when they were actually accompanying the enemy forces, how could he approve or applaud the killing of a woman for simply abusing or composing some annoying verses? Even the companions of the Holy Prophet were so well aware of his strict orders against the killing of women that when Abul Huqaiq's wife interposed herself between them and Abul Huqaiq, they had to withhold their raised swords "because they remembered that the Holy Prophet had forbidden the killing of a woman" (*Fatḥ al-Bārī*, ch. Killing of Abul Huqaiq). In the face of this clear testimony, none but a biased mind can accept as reliable a report which relates that the Holy Prophet had ordered and applauded the killing of a woman simply for the offence that she composed annoying verses. This report is undoubtedly a forgery.

The fact is thus established beyond the shadow of a doubt that the Holy Prophet gave a clear interdiction against the murder of women even in wars. In this connection, a saying of the Holy Prophet has been quoted from the most reliable traditionist of Islām, the Imām Bukharī. The heading under which Bukharī quotes this saying is "Murder of Women during Wars," thus showing that the interdiction against the murder of women was to be observed even in wars. Bukharī is not alone in reporting the incident and the interdiction; it is contained in all the books of the Ṣiḥāḥ Sittah (the six reliable collections) with the exception of only one, and therefore its authenticity is beyond dispute. Moreover, their interdiction is accepted as a basic principle by later jurists. Thus according to Mālik and Auzā'ī, the killing of women and children is not allowed under any circumstances whatsoever, and according to Shāfi'ī and Kūfīs, a woman may be killed only when she is a combatant, while according to one authority, even when a woman is a combatant it is not lawful to kill her intentionally unless she is about to kill or attack a man with the intention of killing him. (*'Aun al-Ma'būd,* Commentary *on Abū Dāwūd,* ch. Murder of Women). According to Mālik and Auzā'ī, however, as already stated, a woman should not be killed under any condition, so much so that if a fighting force takes the shelter of women and children or takes shelter in a fort or a boat in which there are also women and children with them, it is not lawful to shoot at or set fire to the fort or the boat *(Fatḥ al-Bārī*, ch. Ahl al-dār-i yabītūn). In the face of these facts it is simply unthinkable that the Prophet should have ordered the assassination of a woman, under *peaceful* conditions, for no other fault than singing certain annoying verses.

Abū Afak

The next incident related by Mr. Cash is that relating to the alleged assassination of Abū Afak, "an aged Jewish proselyte, whose offence was similar to that of Asmā'." We have no hesitation in calling this story as baseless a fabrication as that relating to the murder of Asmā'. Our reason for doing this is that the interdiction against the murder of women also included two other classes, *viz.*, children and old men. It is true that the saying of the Prophet as reported in the *Bukhārī* mentions only women and children, and not aged persons, but there is a ḥadīth in *Abū Dāwūd* (ch. Du'ā al-Mushrikīn) reported by Anas, son of Mālik, according to which the Holy Prophet said: "Do not kill an aged person, nor a child, nor a minor, nor a woman." That the Prophet expressly forbade the killing of old men appears also from the directions given by Abū Bakr, the first Caliph, to Yazīd, son of Abū Sufyān, when he sent him in command of an army to Syria. In the directions given to him the following relates to our subject: "Do not kill children, nor women, nor old men." *(Fatḥ al-Qadīr,* vol v, p. 202.) It is clear that Abū Bakr could give such directions only on the authority of the Holy Prophet. Hence there was an interdiction against the killing of old men as there was against the killing of women. And it is impossible, we repeat, that the Holy Prophet should have given such clear injunctions and then himself ordered the killing of "an *aged* Jewish proselyte," as Abū Afak is said to have been, and for no offence but that he composed some annoying verses.

Only combatants could be killed

In fact, as the *Hidāyah* has put it clearly, a person's life, unless he is a murderer, cannot be taken on any ground other than that he is a combatant: "And they should not kill a woman, nor a child, nor an aged person, nor one who does not take part in a war, nor a blind man, because what makes it lawful to take a man's life, according to us, is his being a combatant, and this is not true in their case" (ch. *Kaifiyyat al-Qitāl).* In fact, this conclusion, which is the basic principal of the Ḥanifite law, is based on the express words of the Holy Prophet himself. As Abū Dāwūd reports on the authority of Rabāḥ, son of Rabī': "We were with the Prophet in a certain battle, and he saw the people gather together in one place. So he sent a man to make an inquiry as to why the people had gathered together. The messenger came back and said, "There is a woman killed." The Holy Prophet said, *She was not fighting.* The reporter says that Khālid was leading at the time. So the Prophet sent a man to Khālid and asked him to tell Khālid that he should not kill a woman nor a hireling". (ch. *Qatl al-Nisā').* By remarking that "she was not fighting", the Holy Prophet made it plain that even in battle only such persons could be killed as actually took part in fighting, and along with women he excepted hirelings, because they were only hired for other work and did not take part in actual fighting. It is on this basis that the Ḥanifite law excepts, along with women, children and old men, all such persons as cannot take part in fighting. And the conclusion is inevitable that according to the Holy Prophet's own injunctions the killing of a person was not lawful unless he took part in fighting, and any report to the effect that a person was killed though he was not a combatant is either untrue or defective, even if it is met with in a reliable collection of traditions. And as for biographies, they cannot be trusted at all in such matters, and the case of Ibn Sunainah's murder must be rejected as untrue. The statement that this murder was due to the Prophet giving a general order for the slaughter of the Jews is sufficient to discredit this report, for not only would such an order be against the clear injunctions of the Qur'ān, but also because if such an order were given it would not have resulted in the murder of a single Jew.

Ka'b ibn Ashraf

We now come to the genuine cases which are mentioned in collections of Hadīth. The first of these is the case of Ka'b ibn Ashraf. We propose to discuss it in detail, for this one case would show how the Holy Prophet has been misrepresented. Ka'b's father belonged to the tribe of Ṭayy, but coming over to Madīnah he became an ally of the Jewish tribe of Banī

Naḍīr and became so influential that he succeeded in marrying the daughter of a Jewish leader. Ka'b thus stood in a very near relationship to both Jews and Arabs. When the Holy Prophet came to Madīnah, the Jews made an agreement with him, by the terms of which Jews and Muslims were to live as one people, both retaining their own faith, and in the case of an attack on Madīnah or an unaggressive war with a third party they bound themselves to help each other. The Prophet was accepted as the final court of appeal in all disputes. When, however, a Makkan army advanced on Madīnah in the 2nd year of Hijrah, the Muslims had to meet them alone, and notwithstanding that they were less than a third of the Makkan army and very inferior in efficiency and arms, they inflicted a crushing defeat on the invading army at Badr. The Muslim victory only added to the Jewish spite against Islām. Ka'b, who was bound by the Madīnah treaty, now used his poetic gift freely to excite hatred of Islām and the Muslims. Not content with this, he proceeded to Makkah and openly joined hands with the enemies of Islām. He urged upon the Quraish the necessity of attacking Madīnah with a strong force at an early date, and swore in the Ka'bah that he would fight against the Muslims when Madīnah was invaded. Not only this; he returned from Makkah with a plan to put an end to the Prophet's life by underhand means. It is only in the true Christian missionary spirit that Muir, in his *Life of Mahomet*, has no place for these acts while he has sufficient room for the minutest details as to how Ka'b was put to death, and he gives vent to his inner feelings when he concludes his description of one of the alleged "assassinations" in the following words:

> "*The progress of Islām begins to stand out in unenviable contrast with that of early Christianity. Converts were gained to the faith of Jesus by witnessing the constancy with which its confessors suffered death, they were gained to Islām by the spectacle of the readiness with which its adherents inflicted death. In the one case conversion imperilled the believer's life; in the other, it was the only means of saving it.*"

And if Muir conceals the facts which show that from an ally Ka'b had turned into a combatant, Cash, notwithstanding his parading the original authorities, is guilty of the same offence. That there was a war between Muslims and non-Muslims at the time of the alleged "assassination," in the third year of the Hijrah, is an undeniable fact. The question is whether Ka'b was among the combatants or the non-combatants. If he actually joined hands with the enemies of Islām and placed himself among those who were fighting with the Muslims, and he was killed by the Muslims, can this be called a case of treachery, cruelty or butchery? That Ka'b had openly joined the combatants and become their ally is borne out by all historical accounts; nay, some of them go so far as to say that he had planned to murder the Holy Prophet treacherously. Here are a few authorities:

> *"He went to the Quraish, weeping over their killed (at Badr) and inciting them to fight with the Prophet."*
> *(Zurqānī, vol ii, p. 10)*

> *(The Prophet said): "He (Ka'b) has openly assumed enmity to us and speaks evil of us and he has gone over to the polytheists (who were at war with Muslims) and has made them gather against us for fighting"* *(Zurqānī, vol. ii, p. 11)*

> *"And according to Kalbī, he united in a league with the Quraish before the curtains of the Ka'bah, to fight against the Muslims."* *(Zurqānī, vol. ii, p. 11)*

> *"And he prepared a feast, and conspired with some Jews that he would invite the Prophet, and when he came they should fall on him all of a sudden."* *(Zurqānī, vol. ii, p. 12)*

Commenting on Bukhārī's report relating to the killing of Ka'b, the author of *Fatḥ al-Bārī* relates the reports which we have quoted above from *Zurqānī*, viz., Ka'b's going to Makkah and inciting the Quraish, entering into a league before the curtains of the Ka'bah to fight against the Muslims, the Holy Prophet's declaration that he had assumed open enmity, and his plan to kill the Prophet by inviting him to a feast. Bukhārī himself speaks of the incidents relating to the killing of Ka'b under headings in which the word *ḥarb* (fighting) occurs, thus showing that he was looked upon as a combatant. Abū Dāwūd speaks of the incident under the heading, "When the enemy is attacked and he is unprepared," showing that Ka'b was dealt with as an enemy at war with Muslims. And the comment on this is that "Ka'b used to incite people to murder the Muslims"; and discussing the legality of what the party sent out for the punishment of Ka'b did, the same commentator adds: "This is not allowed in the case of an enemy after security has been given to him or peace has been made with him ... but it is allowed in the case of one who breaks the covenant and helps others in the murder of Muslims." And Ibn Sa'd tells us that when the Jews complained to the Holy Prophet that their leader was killed, "he reminded them of his deeds and how he urged and incited (the Quraish) to fight against them," and adds that "the Prophet then called upon them to make an agreement with him", and this agreement "was afterwards in the possession of 'Alī." All this evidence is too clear to show that Ka'b was put to death for having broken the agreement with the Prophet and joining his enemies who were at war with him and he was therefore treated as a combatant, while the other Jews who did not go to this length, though they were not less active in speaking evil of the Holy Prophet, still lived at peace with him and all that they were required to do was to sign an agreement that they would not join hands with those who were at war with the Muslims.

The only question that is worth considering is why Ka'b was put to death by certain Muslims attacking him suddenly and unawares. In the first place, it must be clearly understood that responsibility for the manner in which he was put to death cannot lie with the Prophet. That the Prophet considered Ka'b as deserving death is quite true, but there is no proof at all that he gave any directions as to the manner in which that sentence was to be carried out. On the other hand, according to one report, when the Prophet was asked by Muḥammad ibn Maslamah whether he should kill him he assumed silence, while according to another he said: "If you are going to do it, be not in a hurry until you have consulted Sa'd ibn Mu'ādh" (*Zurqānī*, vol. ii, p. 12). At any rate he knew nothing about the details, and it is even doubtful whether the details as given are true, the Holy Prophet had nothing to do with them. And leaving aside the question of the Prophet's responsibility, there was no other method to which resort could be had under the circumstances. The hostile critic takes it for granted that the conditions under which the Muslims lived at Madīnah were very like those under which he lived in the twentieth century. They had to deal with an enemy, and they dealt with him in the only way in which it was possible to proceed under circumstances then existing. Ka'b had chosen to enter into a league with an enemy at war with Muslims, and according to all human and Divine laws he could not but be treated as an enemy at war. And dealing with him as a combatant, the Holy Prophet sent a party against him; it is definitely called a *sariyyah (lit. a portion of an army)* in all biographical works, thus showing that the party was sent to fight with him; but it rested with the leader of the party to choose the best way in which he could deal a blow at the enemy. And Muḥammad ibn Maslamah, the leader, chose a method which was recognised among the Arabs and which in his opinion was the best and most effective way under the circumstances. If the leader of the party had chosen to attack Ka'b openly, there would have been much more bloodshed, and probably the whole Jewish tribe of Banī Naḍīr would have suffered along with Ka'b. Ka'b had broken his agreement with the Prophet, he had revolted against him, he had entered into a league to fight against the Muslims till they were extirpated, and he had secretly planned to take away the Prophet's life. For every one of these offenses he had forfeited his life. A party was sent to execute this decree and his life was taken in a manner which, if it had the fault of being secret, had also the merit of not involving innocent people along with the culprit, which would surely have been the result in the case of an open attack. But the Holy Prophet was not in any way responsible for the method of the execution.

Abul Huqaiq

Having discussed the case of Ka'b at length, the case of Abul Huqaiq (Abū Rāfi') need not detain us long. In fact, Muir had admitted his guilt with a suppressed tongue. Thus under the heading, "Assassination of Abul Huqaiq, a Jewish Chief," he says:

> *"A party of the Banī Nazīr, after their exile, settled down among their brethren at Khaibar. Abul Huckeick, their chief, having taken a prominent part in the confederate force which besieged Medina, was now suspected of encouraging certain Bedouin tribes in their depredations. An expedition was therefore undertaken by Ali against the Jews of Khaibar ... As a surer means of stopping these attacks, Mahomet resolved on ridding himself of their supposed author, the Jewish chief ... The assassination of Abul Huckeick did not relieve Mahomet of his apprehensions from the Jews of Khaibar;*

for Oseir, elected in his room, maintained the same relation with the Ghatafan, and was even reported to be designing fresh movements against Medina."

The Banī Naḍīr, a Jewish tribe, originally lived at Madīnah, and were in alliance with the Holy Prophet, but being suspected of keeping up correspondence with the Quraish, and one of the Arab tribes in alliance with them having murdered some Muslims treacherously, they were asked to renew the alliance, which they refused, and were ultimately banished from Madīnah. They settled at Khaibar, a Jewish stronghold and became a source of immense trouble to Muslims, constantly inciting the tribes around Madīnah to commit depredations on the Muslims. Abul Huqaiq, their head, was also a leader in the "Battle of the Allies" in which the Arabian and Jewish tribes had gathered together to give a crushing blow to Islām. Abul Huqaiq and the Jews had thus come out into the field of battle against the Muslims, and even after the allies had to go back in discomfiture, Abul Huqaiq continued to excite and help the Arab tribes living around Madīnah in their depredations against the Muslims. The Holy Prophet was thus justified in sending an expedition against the Khaibar Jews, but before doing this in the 7th year, he sent a small party to deal with Abul Huqaiq alone in 6 A.H. Undoubtedly the underlying idea was that bloodshed might be avoided, as far as possible, and that if the ring-leader was taken away, the mischief might cease. But even Abul Huqaiq's death did not bring peace to the Muslims, and, accordingly, Khaibar had ultimately to be attacked and conquered. That the party sent against him chose to adopt the method which was successfully adopted against Ka'b, again throws no blame on the Prophet.

Permitting rape is a grievous calumny

Mr. Cash's last charge against the Holy Prophet, i.e., having allowed rape of the women of Banī Muṣṭaliq, is a grievous calumny. And the allegation that "all the Tradition Books" mention it is a bold statement. Not a single collection of Ḥadīth contains testimony establishing the charge - a charge of which even a hostile writer like Muir is unaware. The only thing that is met with in the collections of Ḥadīth is a report from Abū Sa'īd Khudri that some people in the Muslim army intended contracting temporary marriage relations with some women who were prisoners of war and making use of a birth control device, but there is not the least evidence that they ever did it. Abū Sa'īd's report, in fact, relates to the legality of *'azl,* a birth control device, and it does not say at all how the women of Banī Muṣṭaliq were treated. It is a fact that before the advent of Islām, temporary marriage relations were allowed, The Holy Qur'ān put an end to them, but all reform was, and had to be, gradual. The Qur'ān is explicit on marriage with prisoners of war, and the verse quoted below is a clear rebuttal of Mr. Cash's unfounded charge:

> *"And whoever among you cannot afford to marry free believing women, (let him marry) such of your believing maidens as your right hands possess ... so marry them with the permission of their masters, and give them their dowries justly, they being chaste, not fornicating, nor receiving paramours; then if they are guilty of adultery when they are taken in marriage, they shall suffer half the punishment for free married women. This is for him among you who fears falling into evil. And that you abstain is better for you. And Allāh is Forgiving, Merciful" (4 : 25).*

As regards the treatment of the women of Banī Muṣṭaliq in particular, there is the clearest historical evidence in all Ḥadīth books that they were all set free without ransom because one of them, Juwairiyah, was set free and married by the Holy Prophet, peace and blessings of Allāh be upon him.

INDEX

A

C

D

E

F

Z

Books on Islam

World-renowned literature produced by
The Ahmadiyya Anjuman Ishā'at Islam, Lahore **(U.S.A.)**

"Probably no man living has done longer or more valuable service for the cause of Islamic revival than Maulana Muhammad Ali of Lahore. His literary works, with those of the late Khwaja Kamal-ud-Din, have given fame and distinction to the Ahmadiyya Movement" — M. Pickthall, famous British Muslim and translator of Holy Quran.

Books by Maulana Muhammad Ali:

The Holy Qur'ān **ISBN: 0-913321-01-X** Pp. lxxvi + 1256

Arabic text, with English translation, exhaustive commentary, comprehensive Introduction, and large Index. Leading English translation. Has since 1917 influenced millions of people all over the world. Model for all later translations. Thoroughly revised in 1951.

"To deny the excellence of Muhammad Ali's translation, the influence it has exercised, and its proselytising utility, would be to deny the light of the sun" — Maulana Abdul Majid Daryabadi, leader of orthodox Muslim opinion in India.

"The first work published by any Muslim with the thoroughness worthy of Quranic scholarship and achieving the standards of modern publications" — Amir Ali in *The Student's Quran*, London, 1961.

The Religion of Islam **ISBN: 0-913321-32-X** Pp. 617

Comprehensive and monumental work on the sources, principles, and practices of Islam. First published 1936.

". . . an extremely useful work, almost indispensable to the students of Islam" — Dr Sir Muhammad Iqbal, renowned Muslim philosopher.

"Such a book is greatly needed when in many Muslim countries we see persons eager for the revival of Islam, making mistakes through lack of just this knowledge" — 'Islamic Culture', October 1936.

A Manual of Hadith **ISBN: 0-913321-15-X** Pp. 400

Sayings of Holy Prophet Muhammad on practical life of a Muslim, classified by subject. Arabic text, English translation and explanatory notes.

Muhammad The Prophet **ISBN: 0-913321-07-9** Pp. 220

Researched biography of Holy Prophet, sifting authentic details from spurious reports. Corrects many misconceptions regarding Holy Prophet's life.

Early Caliphate ISBN: 0-913321-27-3 pp. 214

History of Islam under first four Caliphs.

"(1) Muhammad The Prophet, (2) The Early Caliphate, by Muhammad Ali together constitute the most complete and satisfactory history of the early Muslims hitherto compiled in English" — 'Islamic Culture', April 1935.

Living Thoughts of Prophet Muhammad ISBN: 0-913321-19-2 Pp. 150

Life of Holy Prophet, and his teachings on various subjects.

The New World Order ISBN: 0-913321-33-8 Pp. 170

Islam's solution to major modern world problems.

Founder of the Ahmadiyya Movement ISBN: 0-913321-61-8 Pp. 100.

Biography of Hazrat Mirza by Maulana Muhammad Ali who worked closely with him for the last eight years of the Founder's life.

Bayan-ul-Quran ISBN: 0-913321-21-4 Pp. 1539

Encyclopedic Urdu translation and commentary of the Holy Qur'an

Muhammad and Christ ISBN: 0-913321-20-6 Pp. 97

The Antichrist Gog and Magog ISBN: 0-913321-04-4 Pp. 72

Introduction to the Study of the Holy Qur'an ISBN: 0-913321-06-0 133

The Muslim Prayer Book ISBN: 0-913321-13-3 Pp. 68

Other major publications:

The Teachings of Islam by Hazrat Mirza Ghulam Ahmad. Pp. 226

Brilliant, much-acclaimed exposition of the Islamic path for the physical, moral and spiritual progress of man, first given as a lecture in 1896.
". . . the best and most attractive presentation of the faith of Muhammad which we have yet come across" — 'Theosophical Book Notes'.

Other English translations as well as original Urdu books of Hazrat Mirza are also available. ISBN: 0-913321-34-6

Testimony of the Holy Quran, By Hazrat Mirza Ghulam Ahmad,
ISBN: 0-913321-43-5 Pp. 103

Muhammad in World Scriptures by Maulana Abdul Haque Vidyarthi. Pp. 1500 in 3 vols.

Unique research by scholar of religious scriptures and languages, showing prophecies about the Holy Prophet Muhammad in all major world scriptures.

Ahmadiyyat in the Service of Islam, by Naseer A. Faruqui, Pp. 149
ISBN: 0-913321-00-1

For prices and delivery of these books and inquiries about other books and free literature, please contact: **A.A.I.I.**
1315 Kingsgate Rd.,
Columbus, Ohio, 43221 U.S.A.